Culture and Customs
of Puerto Rico

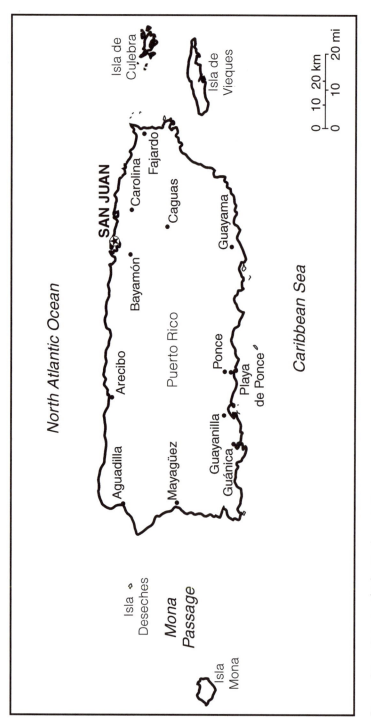

Puerto Rico. Cartography by Bookcomp, Inc.

Culture and Customs of Puerto Rico

JAVIER A. GALVÁN

Culture and Customs of Latin America and the Caribbean
Peter Standish, Series Editor

GREENWOOD PRESS
Westport, Connecticut • London

Library of Congress Cataloging-in-Publication Data

Galván, Javier A., 1965–
    Culture and customs of Puerto Rico / Javier A. Galván.
        p. cm.—(Culture and customs of Latin America and the Caribbean, ISSN 1521–8856)
    Includes bibliographical references and index.
    ISBN 978–0–313–35119–8 (alk. paper)
    1. Puerto Rico—Social life and customs.   2. Puerto Rico—Civilization.   I. Title.
    F1960.G35   2009
    972.95–dc22   2008045343

British Library Cataloguing in Publication Data is available.

Library of Congress Catalog Card Number: 2008045343
ISBN: 978–0–313–35119–8
ISSN: 1521–8856

First published in 2009

Greenwood Press, 88 Post Road West, Westport, CT 06881
An imprint of Greenwood Publishing Group, Inc.
www.greenwood.com

Printed in the United States of America

The paper used in this book complies with the
Permanent Paper Standard issued by the National
Information Standards Organization (Z39.48–1984).

10 9 8 7 6 5 4 3 2 1

Contents

Series Foreword

Culture is a problematic word. In everyday language we tend to use it in at least two senses. On the one hand, we speak of cultured people and places full of culture—uses that imply a knowledge or presence of certain forms of behavior or of artistic expression that are socially prestigious. In this sense, large cities and prosperous people tend to be seen as the most cultured. On the other hand, there is an interpretation of culture that is broader and more anthropological; culture in this broader sense refers to whatever traditions, beliefs, customs, and creative activities characterize a given community—in short, it refers to what makes that community different from others. In this second sense, everyone has culture; indeed, it is impossible to be without culture. The problems associated with the idea of culture have been exacerbated in recent years by two trends: less respectful use of language and a greater blurring of cultural differences. Nowadays, culture often means little more than behavior, attitude, or atmosphere. We hear about the culture of the boardroom, of the football team, of the marketplace; there are books with titles like *The Culture of War* by Richard Gabriel (1990) or *The Culture of Narcissism* by Christopher Lasch (1979). In fact, as Christopher Clausen points out in an article published in the *American Scholar* (Summer 1996), we have got ourselves into trouble by using the term so sloppily.

People who study culture generally assume that culture (in the anthropological sense) is learned, not genetically determined. Another general assumption made in these days of multiculturalism has been that cultural differences should be respected rather than put under pressure to change. But these assumptions, too, have sometimes proved to be problematic. Multiculturalism is a fine ideal, but in practice it is not always easy to reconcile with the beliefs of the very people who advocate it—for example, is female circumcision an issue of human rights or just a different cultural practice?

The blurring of cultural differences is a process that began with the steamship, increased with radio, and is now racing ahead with the Internet. We are becoming globally homogenized. Since the English-speaking world (and the United States in particular) is the dominant force behind this process of homogenization, it behooves us to make efforts to understand the sensibilities of members of other cultures.

This series of books, a contribution toward that greater understanding, deals with the neighbors of the United States, with people who have just as much right to call themselves Americans. What are the historical, institutional, religious, and artistic features that make up the modern culture of such peoples as the Haitians, the Chileans, the Jamaicans, and the Guatemalans? How are their habits and assumptions different from our own? What can we learn from them? As we familiarize ourselves with the ways of other countries, we come to see our own from a new perspective.

Each volume in the series focuses on a single country. With slight variations to accommodate national differences, each begins by outlining the historical, political, ethnic, geographical, and linguistic context, as well as the religious and social customs, and then proceeds to a discussion of a variety of artistic activities, including the media, cinema, literature, and the visual and performing arts. The authors are all intimately acquainted with the countries concerned; some were born or brought up in them, and each has a professional commitment to enhancing the understanding of the culture in question. We are inclined to suppose that our ways of thinking and behaving are normal. And so they are . . . for us. We all need to realize that ours is only one culture among many, and that it is hard to establish by any rational criteria that ours as a whole is any better (or worse) than any other. As individual members of our immediate community, we know that we must learn to respect our differences from one another. Respect for differences between cultures is no less vital. This is particularly true of the United States, a nation of immigrants, but one that sometimes seems to be bent on destroying variety at home and, worse still, on having others follow suit. By learning about other people's cultures, we come to understand and respect them; we earn their respect for us; and, not least, we see ourselves in a new light.

Peter Standish
East Carolina University

Preface

Puerto Rico has never been an independent and sovereign nation. Its official name is the Commonwealth of Puerto Rico (or Estado Libre Asociado de Puerto Rico, in Spanish). Despite the fact that the island has now been part of the United States for over one hundred years, the legal and economic relationship between the two regions is not always crystal clear to most Americans. At first, the island seems to be full of political contradictions and ambiguities. For example, Puerto Ricans (known as *boricuas*) are citizens of the United States, but they cannot vote for the U.S. president when they live on the island. They select a resident commissioner to represent them in the U.S. Congress, but that person is only allowed to voice opinions and is not permitted to vote. *Boricuas* can be drafted into the U.S. military, but they cannot control the foreign policy decisions that sometimes send them to armed conflicts. They are exempt from paying federal taxes as long as they live on the island, but they do qualify for federal social programs like welfare, food stamps, and unemployment payments. However, once they move to any of the fifty states, they have to follow the same tax and fiscal rules, just like any other U.S. citizen. These examples reveal that many features are not simply black and white in Puerto Rico; there is a large gray area in which most of the population functions quite well. In fact, during my visits to the island, many of my questions were usually answered by "it depends." It will become apparent throughout this book that this disclaimer applies to so many aspects of daily life on the island.

Tourists visiting the capital city of San Juan are attracted by gorgeous beaches, colonial architecture, and cultural festivals. Most of them, however, spend only two to three days there before boarding a cruise ship. Taking advantage of its natural beauty and location, Puerto Rico has developed its tourism industry into the most active economy in the Caribbean, including the largest airline and cruise hubs in the region. To further capitalize on their ideal tropical location, the official tourism agency (the Puerto Rico Tourism Company) has recently adopted the slogan "Explore Beyond the Shore." The aim is to get tourists to venture beyond San Juan and discover the unexpected beauty of El Yunque Tropical Forest, the surfing paradise of Rincón, the world's largest radio telescope in the Arecibo Observatory, the carnivals of Loíza Aldea, the mysterious waters of the Bioluminescent Bay, and the impressive art museum in Ponce. Another recent benefit is that since the island is part of the United States, travelers between Puerto Rico and the mainland are not required to show U.S. passports, hence increasing the number of visitors. One of the goals of this book is to go beyond the glossy photographs displayed in travel brochures and incorporate the cultural experiences of average Puerto Rican people. The book is also not limited to covering only the historical icons, famous artists, and talented athletes. For example, it covers not only the plastic arts worthy of museum exhibitions but also the intrinsic value of folkloric arts and crafts.

Another crucial objective of this book is to analyze the contrast between the apparent wealth displayed on the island and the dismal economic statistics emerging from sociological studies. It seems that both opulence and poverty coexist as two parallel realities. At first sight, San Juan shows incredible signs of prosperity, with an abundance of five-star hotels, golf resorts, and luxury car dealerships. Puerto Rico has what is considered to be one of the best economies in the Caribbean, and many immigrants from the region arrive in San Juan looking for jobs. The Puerto Rican tourism industry is certainly a well-oiled machine; however, this is a business that relies heavily on low wages to make it profitable. So, not everything is what it seems; it all depends on an array of social conditions. This is precisely when signs of economic disparities begin to emerge. For example, it is paradoxical that Puerto Rico offers five-star hotels at which the cost of one night's stay is more than what low-wage earners on the island earn in an entire month, even when constantly working overtime. Various resorts hire chefs who create amazing (and expensive) lobster feasts, while many poor people get their seafood from street vendors who sell *bacalaíto frito* (fried codfish), which is a very tasty snack. Statistics show that over half the island's population receives food stamps, the unemployment rate is 13 percent (more than double the average of the U.S. mainland), and almost 55 percent of the population lives below the poverty line. A point of comparison makes it even worse: the per capita income of Puerto Rico in 2006 was only $22,058, which is less than half of Mississippi's, the poorest state in the Union. However, the problem is compounded because the cost of living on a tropical island is greater than living in Mississippi. While not justified, these social inequalities are economic indicators that help to partially explain the recent sharp increase in violent crime, drug use, and poverty rates. Unfortunately, these circumstances also push Puerto Rican college-educated professionals to leave the island in search of better opportunities.

This book is focused on the twentieth and twenty-first centuries; however, history has left a tangible imprint on Puerto Rico that is still part of everyday life. There are four historical markers that have shaped the island's culture, economics, and politics. First, the arrival of Christopher Columbus on November 19, 1493, sparked a transatlantic demographic movement without precedent in history. Even today, the Puerto Rican culture is best described as a blend of Taíno heritage, Spanish customs, African rhythms, and the recent Americanization influence. Second, the Spanish-American War of 1898 forced Spain to transfer Puerto Rico to the control of the United States, and ever since, the expectations these regions have had of each other have gone through a series of political and cultural adjustments. Third, Puerto Ricans received U.S. citizenship in 1917, which sparked a diaspora toward the northeastern part of the United States beginning in the 1930s. For the past seven decades, roughly three generations of Puerto Ricans have lived shuttling back and forth between the island and the U.S. mainland. Actually, the 2005 Census reports that there are almost 4 million people living on the island, and there are slightly over 4 million *boricuas* living in the United States. Fourth and last, Puerto Rico was allowed to create its own constitution in 1952 and organize its infrastructure for self-government without direct political appointments from the U.S. mainland. These events have contributed to making the Puerto Rican culture what it is today; their influence is visible in all aspects of daily life such as music, language, law, literature, religion, architecture, festivals, food, and the arts.

Puerto Ricans are still trying to define themselves. However, it is hard to develop a national identity when the island has never existed as a country. They see themselves as U.S. citizens, but they are also fiercely proud of their cultural heritage. Writers like Manuel Alonso Pacheco and Alejandro Tapia y Rivera immortalized the image of the *jíbaro* (mountain farmer) in Puerto Rican national literature. Later, poets like Julia de Burgos exposed the intense mixture of cultural identity and political protest that have been characteristic of the twentieth century. In addition, painters like Francisco Manuel Oller Cestero and Ramón Frade have also tried to portray with images what it means to be Puerto Rican. It is a search that continues to evolve in different arenas. However, it certainly helps that the Puerto Rican government actually does have authority over a few specific political and cultural affairs. For example,

Puerto Ricans elect their own government leaders, strongly rally behind the island's Olympic teams, support their own Miss Universe contestants, and proudly sing their patriotic anthem, "La borinqueña." The song "En mi viejo San Juan" (In My Old San Juan) also serves as a melancholic reminder for those *boricuas* living abroad. Even when most Puerto Ricans cannot agree on the political future of the island, they strongly defend some of their cultural pillars such as music and language. As a matter of fact, Puerto Rico has declared both Spanish and English as official languages, but Puerto Ricans see Spanish as a definite marker of cultural pride and English as a tool necessary for success.

From a cultural perspective, one of the greatest accomplishments of the twentieth century was for the local government to establish the Instituto de Cultura Puertorriqueña in 1955. It has been entrusted to conserve, enrich, and promote the cultural values of the Puerto Rican people. That is no easy task since its functions are extremely complex. It is responsible for promoting musical events, organizing plastic arts exhibitions, managing the Puerto Rican General Archive, overseeing most historical and art museums, coordinating efforts to restore historical architectural areas, publishing scholastic journals, organizing conferences that highlight popular arts, promoting the national program of dance and theater, and marketing several international film festivals. It is clear that supporting (and financing) cultural activities is a crucial priority for the Puerto Rican government. It is not enough to promote culture only as a tourist activity; it must also nurture the creative talents of the entire population. It is through these shared experiences that Puerto Ricans are able to define who they are.

There is a tremendous amount of creative talent in Puerto Rico. The tireless energy of writers, dancers, painters, actors, journalists, musicians, poets, and filmmakers has certainly contributed to the cultural enrichment of the island. Puerto Ricans have also participated in the creation of entirely new musical genres, literary movements, and the production of public art. However, Puerto Rico has also retained centuries-old traditions of popular art such as making carved religious saints, delicate *mundillo* lace, and colorful masks for special festivals.

Music has a long heritage in Puerto Rico. Its rhythms and instruments are a reflection of its history and creative energy, which permeate all aspects of life. Salsa is still the main musical genre preferred by most Puerto Ricans, and most are intensely proud of their dancing abilities. Other genres, such as boleros, classical, and mambo, are also popular—some more than others. However, *reggaeton* is the latest musical creation developed in the streets of San Juan and exported to the Spanish-speaking world. In 2005, the song "La gasolina" by singer Daddy Yankee launched this new genre into the mainstream. It became a huge sensation in dance clubs throughout Latin America, Europe, and the United States. In addition, the world has also recently discovered other famous contemporary *boricua* singers such as Ricky Martin, Cheyenne, Ivy Queen, Luis Fonsi, and Marc Anthony, especially since some of these artists also sing in English.

The topic of politics eventually finds its way into most conversations in Puerto Rico. It consistently dominates the main pages of most newspapers on the island. Actually, pointing out the shortcomings of political leaders is almost a national sport on the island. However, Puerto Ricans have been discussing the same political issue for over one hundred years: the nature of their relationship with the United States. This topic has taken a sense of urgency in the past two decades. Puerto Rico has had three special votes (plebiscites) to define their political status, and they have attempted to exercise three apparent options at their disposal: (1) independence, (2) requesting to become the fifty-first state of the federal union, or (3) retaining their current commonwealth status. The results of the three plebiscites in 1967, 1993, and 1998 did not produce a clear winner since none of the three choices obtained even a simple majority of the vote. They did, however, reveal a *boricua* population closely united from a cultural perspective but deeply divided regarding their political future. Puerto Ricans are keenly aware that by becoming independent, they would lose the U.S. citizenship that currently allows them to work and study on the mainland, and they would also stop receiving unemployment and welfare checks. While they see the benefits of becoming the fifty-first state, they are absolutely clear that the idea of losing Spanish as an official language is a nonnegotiable item. Moreover, a large number of *boricuas* continue to resist being assimilated into American mainstream society. So the choice that has prevailed is to retain the status quo. There are also recent critics, especially Nuyoricans from the mainland, who have expressed concern over reasons why the local government is even having these special votes. Contemporary writers like Esmeralda Santiago are correct when they state that these votes are nonbinding resolutions; they represent, at best, a simple recommendation to the U.S. Congress. Other political pundits also speculate that these special votes actually distract the local population from the fact that the government is not dealing with the real problems on the island such as the huge increase in violent crime, the high rates of unemployment, and the chronic poverty levels, which keep escalating.

While different political parties push a different agenda when they get to power in Puerto Rico, the majority of the population is now rather cynical when they express opinions about their leaders, especially when so many cases of corruption continue to make headlines on the island. As recently as March 2008, the governor of Puerto Rico, Aníbal Acevedo Vilá, was arraigned by the U.S. federal government and the Federal Bureau of Investigation when he was accused of nineteen separate charges of corruption, financial fraud, and abuse of power. Despite these accusations, he firmly announced his intentions to remain active in politics beyond the end of his term in late 2008.

This book is organized into two major sections. Roughly, the first half of the book (Chapters 1–4) covers material on how people live such as concerning religion, food, political ideology, and social customs. The position of Puerto Rico in the Caribbean also makes it imperative to include sections on geography and history. The political status of the island deserves a separate chapter that explains the legal and constitutional details of the island's relationship with the United States; I have attempted to explain in a straightforward manner an issue that is not simple at all. The second half of the book (Chapters 5–9) is based on the tangible cultural items that are produced by Puerto Ricans, including literature, paintings, architecture, sculpture, film, theater, and both print and broadcast media. The latter part of the book is essentially a view of the artistic and innovative energy that blends historical tradition with the need for new forms of expression. It is precisely this collection of shared cultural values that defines the national identity of Puerto Ricans today.

Acknowledgments

The writing process is inherently a lonely experience. Fortunately, I am also surrounded by caring and loving people who complete my life. This book is dedicated to two special people in my heart. My wife, Maya, has offered remarkable support for all my personal and academic endeavors, including writing this book and traveling with me to do research and further explore the amazing cultural mosaic of Puerto Rico. My son Marco was just a baby during the process of writing this manuscript. By the time I was almost done, he was old enough to travel with me to enjoy and discover the natural beauty of the island and the warmth of its people. He certainly allowed me to see layers of cultural activities that I had not recognized before. To both Maya and Marco, I owe a tremendous amount of gratitude and love.

There is only one name in the front of this book, but it is actually a collaborative effort of many people. My assistant, Norma Cepeda, provided valuable help with library research. The editorial staff at Greenwood was extremely helpful to see this project to the end, especially my acquisitions editor, Kaitlin Ciarmiello. Her dedication and professionalism are certainly an inspiration. My project and production managers, Matthew Byrd and Peggy M. Rote, offered valuable suggestions when copyediting the manuscript. I also need to acknowledge many average *boricuas* who were willing to sit on a park bench with me and share their views and experiences. Any errors of fact or omission that still remain in this book are entirely my responsibility.

Chronology

1000   Estimated arrival of the Taíno Arawak Indians. They name the island Borinquén, which means the "Land of Great Lords."

1493   Christopher Columbus lands on the island of Borinquén during his second voyage, claims it for the Spanish Crown, and renames it San Juan Bautista (St. John the Baptist).

1508   Juan Ponce de León establishes Caparra as the first Spanish settlement in Puerto Rico, which is right across the bay from the current city of San Juan.

1511   The Taíno Arawak indigenous population rebels against the Spanish for the first time.

1513   Spain introduces the use of African slaves to the island.

1515   Sugarcane is imported from Santo Domingo and first planted in Puerto Rico, increasing the need for African slave labor.

1521   San Juan is founded and becomes the capital city of Puerto Rico. The first Spanish governor assigned to the island is Juan Ponce de León.

1589   Construction of El Morro Fortress is completed.

1599   The British attack Puerto Rico but fail to control it.

1600   Most Taíno Indians have been killed or have died due to poor working conditions and diseases.

1625   Dutch forces attack San Juan and burn it to the ground.

1797   The English make another unsuccessful attempt to attack and control San Juan.

1806   The first newspaper, *La Gaceta de Puerto Rico,* is published in San Juan.

1849   Manuel Alonso y Pacheco writes *El jíbaro* (The Mountain Farmer), the first novel published in Puerto Rico.

1858   The telegraph is introduced to the island. Samuel F. B. Morse installs the first line at Arroyo, a town on the southern coast where his daughter lives.

1868   Manuel Rojas organizes a revolutionary movement in the town of Lares and declares Puerto Rico a republic; however, the movement is quickly dismantled by the Spanish military, and Rojas is sent into exile. The event becomes known as the Grito de Lares, or the "Shout of Lares."

1873   The Spanish Crown abolishes slavery in Puerto Rico.

1891   The first railroad is built.

1895   The Puerto Rican flag is approved.

1897   Spain allows Puerto Rico to take control of specific tasks of self-government. In May 1898, Spain provides the island with complete autonomy.

1898   The U.S. Congress issues a formal declaration of war between Spain and the United States. President William McKinley requests to intervene in Cuba to stop the war between Cuban revolutionaries and Spain (April 25).

        Spain and the United States sign the Treaty of Paris on December 10. As a result, Spain loses and transfers all its remaining territories to the United States, including Puerto Rico, Guam, Cuba, the Virgin Islands, and the Philippines.

1899   The U.S. Congress places high tariffs and taxes on Puerto Rican exports to protect the sugar and tobacco industries on the mainland.

1900   The U.S. Congress approves the Foraker Act, which provides the infrastructure to create a civilian government in Puerto Rico, but one controlled by the United States. The island can now select a resident commissioner, its leader in the House of Representatives, but that candidate cannot vote in Washington.

1901   Federico Degetau becomes the first Puerto Rican resident commissioner in Washington to represent the island in the House of Representatives.

1903   The University of Puerto Rico is founded.

1912   The Partido Independentista becomes the first party on the island to officially push for independence from the United States.

        Rafael Colorado D'Assoy directs *Un drama en Puerto Rico,* the first film produced in Puerto Rico.

1917   On March 2, President Woodrow Wilson signs the Jones Act, which grants U.S. citizenship to all Puerto Ricans.

1922   The U.S. Supreme Court declares that Puerto Rico is a territory, rather than part of the union.

        The island opens its first radio station, WKAQ el Mundo, in San Juan.

1930   The Great Depression in the United States also affects the island. Puerto Ricans start migrating in large numbers in search of better opportunities. They begin to settle in the northeastern part of the mainland, in states such as New York and New Jersey.

1932   Women obtain the right to vote, but only if they can read and write.

1933   Cockfighting is legalized in Puerto Rico. Despite public and international protests, cockfighting is still authorized today as a recreational activity.

        Noel Estrada, a Puerto Rican serving in a military mission abroad, writes "En mi viejo San Juan." It is a song that evokes sadness and nostalgia for Puerto Ricans living abroad. It quickly becomes perhaps the most recognizable song about Puerto Rico.

1936   Women receive complete suffrage, without restrictions.

1937   On March 21, a student march in southern Puerto Rico goes terribly wrong: the students are peacefully protesting the economic conditions of the island when the calm and civil protest is shattered by gunfire, leaving nineteen people dead (seventeen students and two police officers). The event becomes known as the Ponce Massacre.

1941   The U.S. military establishes new bases on two small islands belonging to Puerto Rico: Culebra and Vieques.

1943   Puerto Rico creates the Committee for the Design of Public Works. It includes architects like Miguel Ferrer, Osvaldo Toro, and Henry Klumb, all of whom have a strong influence on the modernist architectural style of Puerto Rico during the 1950s and 1960s.

1946   U.S. President Harry Truman designates Jesús T. Piñero as governor of Puerto Rico, and he becomes the first native-born Puerto Rican to govern the island.

1947   The U.S. Congress amends the Jones Act to allow Puerto Ricans to vote for their own governor.

1948   Luis Muñoz Marín becomes the first elected governor of Puerto Rico. He serves until 1965.

        For the first time, Puerto Rico participates in the Olympic Games as an independent "nation."

Operation Bootstrap is introduced with the aim of bringing industrialization to the island. It is intended to help raise the standard of living for the people of Puerto Rico.

1951   The U.S. Congress passes Public Law 600, which allows Puerto Ricans to establish a government with its own local constitution.

1952   The United States proclaims Puerto Rico as a commonwealth, or *estado libre asociado* in Spanish. A new constitution makes the island a self-governing territory but still under the control of the United States.

Puerto Rico adopts its official patriotic anthem, "La Borinqueña."

1954   The first commercial television station, Telemundo, begins broadcasting regular programming. It is the first TV station in Puerto Rico and the fifth in the world.

1955   The Puerto Rican government establishes the Institute of Puerto Rican Culture.

1957   Political parties start receiving financial aid for their operations as long as they obtain at least 5 percent of the vote in general elections.

1959   The island's government founds the Music Conservatory of Puerto Rico.

1964   The Fania Record Company organizes the musical group Fania All Stars in New York City, including Tito Puente, Héctor Lavoe, Willie Colón, Celia Cruz, and Rubén Blades. These artists are the pioneers of salsa music.

1967   On July 23, the island holds its first plebiscite (special public vote) to determine the political status of Puerto Rico. The results for the three choices are as follows: commonwealth (60%), statehood (39%), and independence (1%). So the island retains its status quo, and no major political changes are instituted.

1969   Musician José Feliciano wins a Grammy Award.

1970   Marisol Malaret becomes the first woman representing Puerto Rico to win the title of Miss Universe. The United States is the only country that has won more Miss Universe titles than Puerto Rico.

1972   Roberto Clemente becomes the first Hispanic to get three thousand hits in the game of baseball, and he also becomes the first Puerto Rican to be included in the Baseball Hall of Fame.

1973   The Nuyorican Poets Café is established in New York City.

1976   Section 936 of the U.S. Tax Code is instituted. This provision allows American companies to earn profits on the island without paying federal taxes. The result is unprecedented growth in the textile and pharmaceutical industries.

Over one hundred thousand Puerto Ricans obtain jobs in the new employment venues on the island.

1977   A new set of lyrics is accepted for the anthem "La borinqueña." The previous words, written originally in 1952, were considered to be too subversive.

1989   President George Bush Sr. appoints Antonia Novello (a Puerto Rican) as surgeon general of the United States. She is the first woman and the first Hispanic to hold the position.

1991   Puerto Rico declares Spanish the only official language of Puerto Rico, a position that would be revised two years later.

1992   The five hundredth anniversary of Christopher Columbus's arrival in the Americas serves as an impetus for massive renovation projects of Spanish colonial architecture in Old San Juan and the city of Ponce.

1993   Puerto Rico revises its position and declares both Spanish and English as official languages of the island. Currently all public education is done in Spanish, and children are required to study English as a second language all the way through elementary school.

        The second plebiscite takes place for the general population to vote on the political status of the island: 48.6 percent vote to remain a commonwealth of the United States, 46.3 percent support statehood, and 4.4 percent choose independence.

1996   President Bill Clinton signs the bill sent by Congress to overturn Section 936 of the Tax Code, which pushes many U.S. firms to close their facilities, creating high levels of unemployment on the island.

        The mayor of San Juan, Sila Marí Calderón, starts an urban art project, which commissions $3 million worth of public art sculptures to be placed throughout San Juan.

1998   Puerto Rico holds the third nonbinding referendum to gauge the political future of the island. The five choices are (1) to remain a U.S. commonwealth, (2) to become a U.S. state, (3) to declare independence from the United States, (4) to enter a "free association" status, and (5) none of the above; the last choice obtains over 50 percent of the vote. The result reflects the wide division that exists among Puerto Ricans on this issue, but politicians and social leaders question if people actually understood their choices. Puerto Rico remains a commonwealth.

1999   A bomb is mistakenly dropped, killing one civilian in Vieques and prompting civil protests demanding a complete stop to live-ammunition military exercises and the departure of the U.S. military from its bases in Puerto Rico.

2000   Sila Marí Calderón is elected as the first female governor of Puerto Rico.

2001   The Music Conservatory of Puerto Rico launches Despertar Musical, a comprehensive educational program for preschool and elementary school students to promote music education and cultural awareness.

2002   Governor Sila Marí Calderón announces the Puerto Rico Public Art Project. It uses $15 million to fund over one hundred pieces of public art to be displayed throughout the island.

2003   After multiple protests, President George W. Bush orders a stop to the bombing of Vieques as military target practice. The cleanup process is predicted to take over twenty years at a high financial and environmental cost.

2005   The legislature of Puerto Rico, for the first time in its history, passes a resolution demanding that the U.S. government analyze the case of Puerto Rico and provide a more permanent solution to its political status. President George W. Bush forms a White House task force on Puerto Rico to review the constitutional merits of such a request.

2006   Extreme budget deficits affect the island. Most social services, such as schools and government offices, shut down for over two weeks, affecting tens of thousands of students and public employees.

2007   From January onward, all Americans are required to use a passport when traveling to most Caribbean islands, which hinders tourism. However, since Puerto Rico is a U.S. territory, the official tourism company implements the slogan "No Passport Required," creating a local advantage for tourism in the area.

        On December 21, the White House task force on Puerto Rico submits a report stating that Puerto Rico will continue to be a territory under the plenary powers and jurisdiction of the U.S. Congress.

2008   Massive teacher strikes cripple the public education system in January and February.

        In March, the governor of Puerto Rico, Aníbal Acevedo Vilá, is formally charged by U.S. federal prosecutors on nineteen counts of corruption. This is the first time a governor is accused in federal courts and investigated by the Federal Bureau of Investigation—one of a series of modern-day political scandals on the island.

1

The Context: Geography, History, and People

THE SMALL CARIBBEAN island now called Puerto Rico has had different names, which reflect its rich history and cultural heritage. The Taíno Arawak Indians originally called their island Borinquén, which means the "Land of Great Lords." When Christopher Columbus arrived in 1493, he renamed the island San Juan Bautista, and he also established a small settlement by the port, which he called Puerto Rico (Rich Port). After Juan Ponce de León and other Spanish settlers arrived on the island in 1508, the names were reversed: the main town and harbor became known as San Juan, and the entire island was called Puerto Rico. The Spanish ruled this territory continuously for over four hundred years, until the Spanish-American War of 1898. The United States won the military conflict, and it took possession of Puerto Rico in the same year. This location is the only territory of the United States where Christopher Columbus ever landed during his transatlantic voyages. The current official name of the island is the Commonwealth of Puerto Rico, or Estado Libre Asociado de Puerto Rico in Spanish. Puerto Ricans nowadays often refer to themselves as *boricuas*, a word of endearment used in memory of the original name of the island.

GEOGRAPHY

Puerto Rico is a rectangular island located in the Caribbean Sea. It is viewed as a tropical paradise that attracts visitors to its lush rainforest, astonishing beaches, and rich cultural activities. Its unofficial, endearing name is

La Isla del Encanto, or the "Enchanted Island." It measures about one hundred miles in length and thirty-five miles across, with an area of 3,500 square miles (9,100 square kilometers). It is part of the Greater Antilles, which also include Jamaica, Cuba, and the island of Hispaniola, which is itself divided between the Dominican Republic and Haiti. This cluster of islands is also sometimes called the West Indies. To the east of Puerto Rico, a chain of smaller islands, including St. Lucia, Martinique, the Virgin Islands, Aruba, and Tobago, make up the Lesser Antilles.

Puerto Rico itself also has several satellite islands such as Vieques, Culebra, Caja de Muertos, and Mona Island. The largest of them is Vieques. Most of the island's fifty square miles and its small mountain range were used by the U.S. Navy for military training, and it has been the location of large protests by Puerto Ricans since the early 1990s. After an intense decade of peaceful protests and civil disobedience, President George W. Bush finally ordered the Vieques training facility to be closed in 2003. A long period of cleaning up military debris of heavy metal and chemicals is expected to follow for the next ten to fifteen years. Culebra Island is actually an archipelago, surrounded by twenty small coral islets. Mona Island has an area of only twenty square miles (fifty square kilometers). Most of its territory has been designated as a sanctuary to protect wildlife, and it is managed by the U.S. National Park Service. The island of Caja de Muertos (Dead Man's Coffin) is located off the southern coast of Puerto Rico. It is mostly a protected sanctuary for endangered flora and fauna. During the summer months, most of its beaches are closed because the U.S. Fish and Wildlife Service protects the nesting grounds of green sea turtles that the island harbors.

Tropical rain feeds over forty main rivers and large streams that run from the central mountains toward the foothills and, eventually, the ocean. The amount of rainfall is almost even throughout the entire year, but it is heaviest from early May to late August. The Central Mountain Range runs from east to west along the center of the island. Most of the rivers originate in the mountains and foothills and travel to the northern and western sides of the island. The longest river in Puerto Rico is the Río Grande de Loiza, and it flows north toward the Atlantic Ocean. This is the only navigable river on the island. Other large rivers are the Río Culebrinas, Río Grande de Arecibo, Río de La Plata, and Río Grande de Añasco. The Río Camuy has a special feature in the northwest part of the island. It has created the impressive Camuy Caves, and it is considered to be one of the world's largest underground rivers. None of these rivers, however, is navigable by large ships. All these waterways provide much-needed irrigation to the agricultural areas in the western part of the island, where sugarcane and tropical fruits are grown for commercial purposes. Tobacco and coffee are also grown in the foothills along the southern and western parts of the island. In addition, these rivers are used to generate electricity in hydroelectric plants at several strategic locations. Despite the large number of rivers and streams, there are very few natural lakes in Puerto Rico. The government has created about twenty artificial lakes to collect rainwater and use it more effectively for irrigation purposes. These lakes have also been stocked with fish to offer recreational opportunities to both foreign tourists and the local population.

Two geographical features are unique to Puerto Rico and do not exist in any other part of the United States. First, the El Yunque Tropical Forest (Forest of Clouds) covers twenty-eight thousand acres of land, and it has a peak that is 3,533 feet (1,077 meters) tall. This area was originally set aside by the Spanish Crown in 1876 to be protected as a natural wonder. It is located only twenty-five miles (forty kilometers) east of the capital city of San Juan, and its official name is the Caribbean National Forest. Its rainfall is extremely heavy, reaching almost two hundred inches a year. This great amount of rain creates hundreds of streams that flow along the mountains, making a large number of waterfalls. This water supports a complex and dense vegetation system that includes large ferns and tall hardwood trees. El Yunque is the only tropical forest in the United States, and it is managed by the U.S. Forest Service. Second, the Bioluminescent Bay is located in the southern part of the island near the town of La Parguera. It offers a unique experience that is better revealed at nighttime, especially during cloudy weather or when there is no moon. In this location, there are billions of marine microorganisms that cause the water to glow phosphorescently when the water is touch or disturbed. There are another two locations in eastern Puerto Rico with fluorescent waters: Mosquito Bay, in Vieques, and Las Cabezas, near the town of Fajardo.

The three largest cities of Puerto Rico are San Juan in the north, Ponce in the south, and Mayagüez on the western coast. In an island that is about one hundred miles long and thirty-five miles wide, these cities are actually only about two hours away from each other. The original capital of the island was Caparra, founded in 1508, which is located just across the bay from San Juan. However, San Juan has been the capital city ever since it was founded in 1521 by the Spaniards. It is the second oldest European settlement in the Americas, after Santo Domingo, which was founded in 1496. The historical Old San Juan has been conserved and renovated to highlight its original colonial architectural style.

The largest concentration of Puerto Ricans now lives in San Juan or its suburbs. In 2005, the city's population was over 1.5 million people (almost one-third of the island's citizens). The main motivation for moving to San Juan is to seek a job. Today, the capital city is the economic, artistic, educational, and industrial center of the island. Moreover, tourism is heavily concentrated in

Renovated colonial homes in Old San Juan. Photo courtesy of the author.

San Juan because most flights arrive in the city from abroad. In addition, cruise ships dock and depart in large numbers from the San Juan shores. In fact, the official tourism agency of Puerto Rico, the Puerto Rico Tourism Company, has adopted the motto "Explore Beyond the Shore" to encourage travelers to venture inland and beyond the capital city of San Juan.

Ponce is the second largest city in Puerto Rico. It was named after the Spanish explorer Juan Ponce de León, and it was founded in 1630, when Spanish settlers built a small cathedral there and named it after the Virgin of Guadalupe, who was already considered to be Mexico's patron saint. The city is known as La Perla del Sur (Pearl of the South). This area was used originally to raise cattle and horses with the purpose of supporting the Spanish colonial expeditions into New Spain (now Mexico) and the coasts of South America. With little oversight from the Spanish government settled in the north of the island, this area became prosperous via illegal trade with foreign vessels. In the 1830s, Ponce became wealthy based on the sugar and tobacco industries. The Spanish built a central area of colonial architecture and grandiose houses that are still preserved today. However, most signs of prosperity changed in the early 1900s. When the United States took over Puerto Rico in 1898, most of the progress accomplished in the south came to a halt as

Museo de la Masacre de Ponce. Photo courtesy of the author.

the financial investment concentrated in the northern part of the island. The local population protested and advocated independence from the United States. On March 21, 1937, a large number of students participated in a civil march that somehow went terribly wrong. The students started singing "La Borinqueña," which is the patriotic anthem, and suddenly, massive gunfire exploded over the calm, civil protest. In total, over two hundred people were injured, and nineteen people died, including seventeen students and two police officers. An investigation of the events revealed that there were no guns among any of the marchers, and that most of the students had been shot in the back. This event became known as the Ponce Massacre, and the city was essentially isolated from the rest of the island. Even though a formal investigation was carried out, and the police officers were found at fault, not a single person was taken to court to be held accountable for the tragic event. A museum now stands at the very corner where the massacre took place.

Ponce's economy came to a sudden stop, and it took decades to recover. Things started to turn around in the 1960s, when many industries and manufacturing plants became located around the city, focusing on canning, sugar exports, and iron production. Between 1995 and 2005, in a conscious effort to attract more tourism, the government spent almost five hundred million dollars to renovate its colonial historic buildings and highlight its cultural traditions. The local tourism office actively promotes its highly rated art museum and its national dance festivals. As a result, tourism has generated tremendous optimism in the southern part of the island. The local airport has already begun to attract nonstop international flights from the United States. Nevertheless, despite the apparent economic progress in Ponce, the surrounding area still shows evidence of poverty in small towns that display abandoned former factories rusting away in the Caribbean sun. This dichotomy reflects the common division in Puerto Rico, where affluence and poverty seem to coexist simultaneously.

Mayagüez is the third largest city in Puerto Rico, with a population of about 110,000 people. Located on the western coast, its industry focuses on fishing and packing. It provides about 50 percent of the tuna eaten in the United States. In addition, it has attracted many pharmaceutical companies, which originally received tax benefits for settling on the island. These two industries offer this port city a wealth of employment opportunities for many Puerto Ricans. The same progress, however, gives the city an industrial atmosphere, crowded with factories, freeways, and shipping facilities. This western part of the island is also the departure point of the supersized ferry that sails between Puerto Rico and the Dominican Republic.

Finally, Puerto Rico's geographical position in the Caribbean has both advantages and perils. The government quickly recognized that its privileged location would attract tourists searching for warm weather and a tropical setting. Puerto Rico has developed the largest cruise ship terminal in the area and a wide network of connecting flights to the region. These two features generate both economic revenue for the local government and employment opportunities for Puerto Ricans. On the other hand, it is precisely its geographical position that places Puerto Rico in the path of potential hurricanes on a yearly basis. These are a constant threat. In fact, the word *hurricane* is derived from the indigenous word *juracán*, which the Taínos used to name their god of evil winds. The official hurricane season on the island starts on June 1 and continues until November 30. From a historical perspective, it was these winds that originally brought the indigenous population to the island and permitted the eventual arrival of the Europeans.

HISTORY

The first indigenous group to occupy Puerto Rico was the Ciboney, who had arrived from Florida via Cuba. They were mostly hunters and gatherers and did not necessarily build permanent settlements. The second group to arrive was the Ignery Indians, who migrated to Puerto Rico from the coasts of Venezuela around A.D. 200. There is little concrete knowledge about the Ignery's social structure, but anthropological information reveals that they produced colorful pottery with intricate designs. Perhaps the most well known group to arrive on the island was the Taíno Arawak Indians, who arrived in A.D. 1000. They called the new territory Borinquén. The Taínos were knowledgeable about sailing techniques and traveled the oceans to trade with their Central American and South American neighbors. They were also a sedentary group skilled in farming and were active in growing tobacco, cassava, cotton, and sweet potatoes. Archeological evidence shows that they produced rudimentary musical instruments carved out of wood, such as drums and maracas. The Taínos were a peaceful group who did not necessarily engage in warfare, but they were constantly threatened by the more aggressive Caribs living on the nearby islands of the Lesser Antilles. In 1493, however, a more powerful foreigner landed on the coasts of their Borinquén: Christopher Columbus arrived on November 19, 1493, claimed the island for the Spanish Crown, and baptized it San Juan Bautista (St. John the Baptist).

This territory remained virtually abandoned by the Spaniards until Juan Ponce de León arrived in 1508 with orders to create permanent settlements not only on San Juan Bautista (now Puerto Rico) but on the nearby islands as well. At his arrival, it is estimated that between thirty thousand and forty thousand Taínos lived on the island. In an effort to obtain a labor force, the Spaniards rapidly enslaved the indigenous population to work in the local mines. However, the Taíno Indians were not used to this level of work and started to die rather quickly from exhaustion, rebellion, overwork, and disease. Consequently, by the middle of the sixteenth century, most Taínos were already dead. As a result, the Spaniards began importing African slaves in 1513 to satisfy the growing demand for agricultural and mining labor. However, the initial discovery of gold was quickly exhausted by the 1530s, and other mining ventures proved disappointing. Next, the Spanish introduced sugarcane to Puerto Rico in 1515, and this crop rapidly increased the need for an even larger number of slaves to work on the profitable sugar plantations. By this time, roughly half the island's population of three thousand people were actually African slaves. To satisfy its labor needs, Spain was actively engaged in the transatlantic slave trade for over three hundred years. The practice of slavery would not be abolished in Puerto Rico until 1873.

During the early 1500s, the Spaniards concentrated their efforts on the capital city of San Juan in the north. Meanwhile, a sizable illegal trade developed in the southern part of the island. Dutch, French, and English sailors traded and sold goods near the city of Ponce despite the fact that Spanish laws did not allow Puerto Rico to trade with foreign carriers, or even with other colonies. This lack of control and supervision only emboldened the ambitions of pirates

Fortified city walls built around San Juan. Photo courtesy of the author.

and other foreign empires. As a result, the Spanish strengthened their defense of the island, and they started to build forts to protect San Juan. By the 1530s, Puerto Rico had become a strategic location in the Western Hemisphere but also a territory under potential attack by other enemies. The current tourist attractions of El Morro Fortress, La Fortaleza, El Boquerón, and the long wall along the coast of San Juan all tangibly point to the lengths the Spaniards went to retain control of Puerto Rico during the Spanish colonial period. For example, La Fortaleza was built as the heavily fortified house for the governor of Puerto Rico, and it is the oldest executive mansion in the United States and the Western Hemisphere. It has been the site of Puerto Rico's government for more than four hundred years. More than 170 governors have used it as the official government site, and it is still in use today.

Spain ruled Puerto Rico uninterruptedly as a colony for over four hundred years (from 1493 until 1898). During that period, it survived both indigenous rebellions and foreign attacks. The British invaded Puerto Rico twice in the 1590s. Sir Francis Drake brought four thousand men to attack San Juan, but the cannon fire from the forts prevented his ships from landing. Another Englishman, George Clifford, actually captured the island in 1598 and held control of Puerto Rico for almost five months. However, an epidemic among his British soldiers forced them to abandon the island. In the process, his men took most valuable items and burned multiple buildings and important locations around San Juan. The Dutch also attacked the island in 1620 and controlled it for a month before burning the entire city of San Juan to the ground. The English made another attempt to take control of Puerto Rico in 1797, but it was not successful either. All these attempts to seize Puerto Rico failed mostly due to Spanish military efforts and the spread of epidemics that quickly struck the new British and Dutch settlers.

Puerto Ricans today are often asked why they migrate to New York City (and not other cities in the United States) in such high numbers. Their response is quite often a joke based on historical truth. It turns out that in one of those Dutch attacks in the 1700s, the pirates stole even the church bells from the cathedral located in San Juan. They took them north and sold them in a Dutch colony called New Amsterdam; that city by the Hudson River is now called New York. So when Puerto Ricans respond to the question of migrating to New York City, they simply say, "We came to get our bells back."

By the 1850s, it was apparent that Spain's control of its American colonies was disappearing. All the viceroyalties of Mexico, New Granada, Peru, and Río de La Plata had already obtained independence in the 1820s. The only remaining colonies were Cuba and Puerto Rico. During the 1820s to 1850s, Puerto Rico remained loyal to Spain, especially since the limited trade between Spain and the Americas provided the island with economic prosperity. However, things began to change in the 1860s. Puerto Rico started developing a type of nationalism based on government repression when the local landowners of large sugar plantations refused to free their slaves. At this time, Ramón Emeterio Betances made a strong claim for independence from Spain and the abolition of slavery. His claim for self-rule was quickly defeated and silenced. His initial efforts were not successful mostly because he failed to galvanize enough support for his ideals. He was exiled from the island, but his fight continued when he formed the Puerto Rican Revolutionary Committee. In 1868, the Grito de Lares (Shout of Lares) consisted of a few hundred men, who captured the town of Lares and declared the Republic of Puerto Rico as an independent nation. The movement was quickly squashed by the Spaniards. Since Spain no longer had to protect the entire American continent, it increased its military efforts in Cuba and Puerto Rico. In an attempt to mitigate local resentment and the growing number of protests, Spain eventually abolished slavery in 1873. However, the nationalistic movement had grown stronger and the demands for independence continued to increase. In 1897, the Spanish Crown made substantial concessions, and it allowed Puerto Rico to control many aspects of local authority. Finally, in May 1898, an autonomous government led by Luis Muñoz Rivera took over Puerto Rico. However, this autonomy lasted only a few weeks due to the start of the Spanish-American War against the United States.

The war between Spain and the United States came to the Puerto Rican shores in 1898. On July 25, 1898, the USS *Massachusetts* arrived with 3,300 soldiers and took over the southern part of Puerto Rico near Ponce. Under the command of General Nelson Miles, the U.S. military landed in Guánica Bay, after they actively bombed the capital city of San Juan. The Spanish-American War, however, did not have much to do with Puerto Rico, but rather with American interests in Cuba and its intention to expel Spain from the Caribbean. After brief battles in Cuba and Puerto Rico, the United States defeated the moribund Spanish Empire. Both Spain and the United States sent a commission to meet in Paris on October 1, 1898, to discuss an agreement that would include a declaration of surrender on behalf of Spain. Two weeks later, all Spanish troops left Puerto Rico and returned to Spain.

The Treaty of Paris was actually signed on December 10, 1898, and Spain transferred Puerto Rico to the control of the United States. The Puerto Rican leaders were somewhat confused about the results because they were never invited to or included in the discussions about a treaty that would have serious consequences for the future of their island and its population. The treaty also included the transfer of Cuba, Guam, and the Philippines. Initially, Puerto Ricans accepted the Americans because they saw in them the potential to bring freedom and eventual prosperity to the island. However, it quickly became clear that Puerto Rico would just revert to being a colony once again. The island had spent only two months as a semiautonomous entity. The arrival of the twentieth century would bring difficult choices for Puerto Rico.

The United States also struggled with the idea of how to manage Puerto Rico as a new colony inhabited by almost a million people. It encountered a vibrant culture with a social structure already established, but also a high rate of poverty. At this time, most people worked in farming, but only 2 percent of the population owned all the arable land. In addition, the island population was mostly Roman Catholic and Spanish speaking.

The initial transition to U.S. control took a military direction. The first appointed governor was a military officer. General Brook became the first U.S. governor of Puerto Rico since he was the leader of the U.S. military forces there. The first order of business was to impose English as the official language. Then, the U.S. dollar was established as the only accepted currency. All local forms of government were dissolved. The entire spectrum of economic activity came under the control of the military governor, and all existing presses for books and newspapers were ordered to close business operations. The powerful lobbies of the sugar and tobacco industries on the mainland influenced the U.S. Congress to place a high tariff on Puerto Rican products to make them less attractive for Americans to purchase. As a result, most of the island's agricultural products, such as sugar, coffee, and tobacco, lost potential buyers and created an even higher level of unemployment on the island. To make matters worse, a strong hurricane hit the island in 1899, killing almost 3,300 people. It is also worth noting that at the time, Puerto Ricans did not have citizenship anywhere in the world: Puerto Rico was not an independent nation, Spain was forced to give up the island, and the United States did not yet know what to do with it. As a result, Puerto Ricans actually turned out to have even less control of their territory than they had under the ephemeral autonomy they had obtained from Spain. The islanders started to protest and express concern over the direction of the political status of Puerto Rico. It quickly became clear that military rule was not the best method to use to control a newly acquired colony.

The first concession by the United States came two years after taking possession of the island in the form of the Foraker Act of 1900. It allowed Puerto Rico to set up a local government, but the United States would still appoint the local governor; this time, however, the emphasis would be on a *civilian* head of government. The United States appointed Charles H. Allen as the first civil governor to Puerto Rico, whose focus was on investing heavily in the economy and the social infrastructure of the island. The United States built multiple roads, schools, and port facilities (see Chapter 9 for a discussion on the architectural styles used for these projects). Export taxes were lowered to make Puerto Rican products more competitive for American consumers. A wave of tangible improvements and job opportunities were created for most of the local population. The economy was certainly improving within a year of Allen's arrival. Luis Muñoz Rivera continued to ask for greater autonomy for Puerto Rico. This time, however, he was making his case to the U.S. Congress, instead of to the Spanish Cortes.

During the 1910s, Puerto Rico obtained more political benefits, rights, and responsibilities. For example, it was allowed to send a resident commissioner to the U.S. Congress, even though that person could not actually vote like the rest of the serving congresspeople. The representative would essentially be an observer and provide Puerto Rico with a voice in government. In 1916, Muñoz Rivera was elected as resident commissioner to the U.S. Congress, and he convinced the U.S. government to grant Puerto Rico an increased role in self-government. In fact, on March 2, 1917, President Woodrow Wilson signed the Jones Act, which granted all Puerto Ricans U.S. citizenship. It also created a new legislature to be elected locally, rather than appointed from the mainland. The United States, however, retained control over fiscal and economic issues as well as immigration, mail services, and the overall defense of the island.

These concessions would appear to be benevolent in nature, but the timing has to be analyzed within a greater context. The sudden benefit of American citizenship granted to Puerto Ricans came with civil responsibilities. This is the period during which the United States was embroiled in World War I, and German military vessels were exploring the Caribbean waters. Now Puerto Ricans, as brand-new U.S. citizens, could also be drafted into military service and sent to war. In fact, more than eighteen thousand Puerto Rican soldiers served in the U.S. Army during World War I.

The Great Depression of the United States affected Puerto Rico as well. Actually, the 1930s was a disastrous decade for the island. The effects of two major hurricanes left the agricultural industry in shambles. The failed economy triggered massive unemployment, and large numbers of families sank below the poverty line once again. Under these difficult conditions, many Puerto Ricans questioned the wisdom of being part of the United States, and the independence movement articulated its demands in a more forceful tone, sometimes even using terrorism tactics. During this period, large numbers of Puerto Ricans started migrating to the mainland of the United States, especially to New York City and New Jersey. They also started to enlist in the different branches of the armed forces to escape poverty and unemployment on the island.

Noel Estrada, a musician and composer, was one of the Puerto Ricans who joined the U.S. Army at the beginning of World War II; it was the first time that he had been away from the island, and he missed it terribly. In 1933, he wrote the song "En mi viejo San Juan," which became internationally famous. It is a bolero song with lyrics that evoke sadness and nostalgia for Puerto Ricans who are away from their homeland. Since almost half of Puerto Ricans live abroad, this song quickly obtained the status of the second national anthem of Puerto Rico, after "La borinqueña." The city of San Juan adopted it as its official song.

The decade of the 1940s was a decisive turning point in Puerto Rican–American relations. In 1942, Spanish was restored as an additional official language along with English. This is a factor that proved crucial for maintaining the Puerto Rican culture. In 1948, the United States ceded control of the entire educational system to a commissioner of education who is elected at the regional level and not appointed by the mainland. Currently all public education is done in Spanish, and students are required to take English as a second language from elementary school onward. In 1946, President Harry Truman appointed the first Puerto Rican–born governor to the island. His name was Jesús T. Piñero. One year later, the U.S. Congress approved the Craford Bill, which allowed Puerto Ricans to vote and elect their own governor. The new executive position would also have power to appoint its own cabinet, rather than have any intervention from the United States. Luis Muñoz Marín (the son of Luis Muñoz Rivera) became the first elected governor of Puerto Rico in 1948 under the Popular Democratic Party. He instituted a profound economic reform that provided the island's citizens with financial prosperity, job creation, and tangible social improvements. For example, Operation Bootstrap was a group of federal- and local-government-sponsored programs aimed at diversifying the economic base of the island. It reduced the overreliance on agriculture and added an industrial perspective that Puerto Rico was lacking. These programs offered American companies tax advantages if they relocated to the island and set up manufacturing plants that would hire the local Puerto Rican workforce. The main industries that settled on the island were manufacturers of electronics and pharmaceuticals. This program was a great success and provided Puerto Rico with a progressive point of view.

The 1950s solidified the political status of Puerto Rico and its relationship with the United States. In 1952, President Truman signed a congressional resolution (the Constitution Act) that provided Puerto Rico with the political status of a commonwealth associated with the United States, or Estado Libre Asociado in Spanish. Despite the different terminology, the specifics of the agreement were clear: this legislation allowed Puerto Rico to draft its own constitution. Puerto Ricans living on the island became U.S. citizens, but they were exempt from paying federal taxes. They also qualified for Social Security benefits and other programs such as federal welfare. The island was expected to use the U.S. dollar as its official currency and to continue to use the U.S. Post Office for all its postage needs. The issue of suffrage was also clearly defined: Puerto Ricans living on the island could vote for their own leaders, but they did not have the right to vote in U.S. presidential elections. As a result, Puerto Rico does not carry any presidential electoral delegates in the U.S. electoral college system. On the other hand, Puerto Rico was allowed to wave the flag of its choice. This was an important factor for Puerto Rican pride because, between 1898 and 1952, it was a felony to display the Puerto Rican flag. Only the U.S. flag was allowed during that period. Puerto Rico could also now create a patriotic anthem like most modern nations. The name of the official anthem is "La borinqueña." This song has a history of resistance and came to fruition only in stages. The musical composition dates back to 1903. It was adopted as an official anthem in 1952, but the lyrics were considered to be too radical and subversive. Therefore, a new set of lyrics was written and finally accepted in 1977. Puerto Ricans are fond of saying that everything that evokes cultural pride also takes time.

The year 1976 proved to be crucial for Puerto Rico from an economic perspective. Section 936 of the Federal Tax Code provided tax exemptions to companies and corporations from the U.S. mainland that invested in Puerto Rico. These companies were allowed to maintain 25 percent of their financial gains without paying any taxes at all. The requirement was that they had to pay 10 percent into a special fund in the National Development Bank. These incentives sparked the move of electronics, petrochemical, and pharmaceutical enterprises to the island. By the late 1980s, these three industries employed almost 280,000 workers—almost 30 percent of all jobs available on the island. Eventually, these tax benefits had to come to an end, and President Bill Clinton terminated the program in 1996. This action reduced the number of companies moving to the island, and some even left after the federal incentives were no longer available. Nevertheless, this program allowed Puerto Rico to develop one of the most stable economies in the Caribbean. As an example, most pharmaceutical companies have remained in place, and their products still account for almost 60 percent of Puerto Rico's total exports. Actually, in 2008, pharmaceutical companies like Pfizer and Wyeth reported tremendous growth and profits, but mostly overseas, where the dollar is weak and makes U.S. products cheaper (Johnson 2008).

PEOPLE

Since Puerto Rico has nearly 4 million people living on the island, it is considered to be one of the most densely populated islands in the world. Migration patterns have also created large Puerto Rican communities abroad, mostly concentrated in the northeastern part of the United States. According to the U.S. Census of 2005, there are now almost another 4 million Puerto Ricans living abroad. On the island itself, most people are concentrated in the bigger cities of San Juan, Ponce, and Mayagüez. Overall, the island's population is very young since almost 50 percent of Puerto Ricans are under twenty-one years old. It is precisely the young people who have also migrated from agricultural areas in the south to the metropolitan centers in search of better education and employment opportunities.

Puerto Rico has a population with a rich racial and ethnic mix that reflects its complex history and the different migration movements to the island. As a consequence, the majority of Puerto Ricans have a light brown-colored skin. They are often referred to as *trigueños*. Originally, the Taíno Arawak Indians were the original settlers. The arrival of the Spaniards in the early 1500s, however, quickly decimated the indigenous population. They were either killed or died from diseases and overwork. The few remaining Indians intermarried with the Spaniards. Now, there are no full-blooded indigenous people left in Puerto Rico. People who have indigenous facial features are often called *indios,* even though it is not necessarily politically correct to do so. The large numbers of Spaniards who settled on the island during the 1500s were of white background. Currently people who have fair skin are simply called *blancos* (whites). The disappearance of the Taínos from the Puerto Rican landscape in the early sixteenth century created a demand for an additional labor force. As a result, Spain started importing African slaves beginning in 1513, especially to work in small gold mines and, eventually, on the sugar and tobacco plantations.

The African heritage in Puerto Rico is palpable not only in the black population but also in the strong influence it has had on different aspects of the island's culture such as music, food, art, and religious icons. It is important to highlight that the word *negro* in Puerto Rico is not only used to refer to people of African background but is actually a term of endearment that is used for people of all races. The word *mulatto* is also often heard in Puerto Rico, and it refers to the people who have a mixed racial heritage of half black and half white. Currently the area of Loíza Aldea (about twenty-five miles southeast of San Juan) has one of the largest concentrations of blacks on the island. The African heritage here is very visible, and it has been preserved mostly because the people have not intermarried with other racial groups to the degree that has occurred in other areas of the island. This area is an agricultural municipality and somewhat poor. However, the Loíza *fiesta patronal* is perhaps the best-attended cultural event in the entire island. It is the festival dedicated to the patron saint of the town: St. James the Moor Slayer. He became the saint selected by the Yoruba slaves in Loíza after the Spanish Roman Catholics forced the slaves to convert to Christianity. At that time, slaves were forbidden to worship their Yoruba African *orishas,* or gods. The image of St. James as a powerful warrior reminded the slaves of their powerful god Changó. By adopting this patron, the slaves pretended to worship St. James, but they were really paying homage to Changó, right in front of the Spaniards. This festival now lasts nine days, from the end of July to early August. It is a colorful event with drummers, singers, bright costumes, the traditional *plena* music, and masks carved out of coconut husks with devil-type designs.

During the 1900s, multiple waves of people came to the island and contributed to a further ethnic, social, and cultural mix. American businesspeople brought organizational ideas that helped to develop a middle class. Chinese immigrants helped to build roads. During the 1960s, poor immigrants arrived mostly illegally from the closely neighboring island nation of the Dominican Republic. After the Cuban Revolution of 1959, a wave of professional Cubans left the island and settled in Puerto Rico. During the 1970s and 1980s, migrants from Chile, Brazil, and Argentina came in an effort to escape the repressive dictatorships in their countries. All these recent arrivals have been quickly assimilated into Puerto Rican society but have also contributed to enriching the cultural experience on the island.

The main ethnic groups (Indians, African slaves, Europeans, Americans, and Chinese) all mixed to create the population that currently composes

Puerto Rico. This mélange of people has contributed to a unique culture in the Caribbean that is European, Latin American, North American, and African all at the same time. In a greater context, the term *Puerto Rico* can be viewed as defining more a culture than a physical location. As a consequence, Puerto Ricans do not really define themselves with a specific ethnic background, mostly because they are a mixture of historical influences that has galvanized a collective cultural identity. Even the *boricuas* who migrated to the United States do not use a hyphenated version of their heritage such as *Puerto Rican–American*. They simply and proudly use the term *Puerto Rican*. The 2000 Census data reveal an interesting pattern regarding the Puerto Ricans living on the island. The results indicate that an increasing number of Puerto Ricans define themselves as white, even when they are not of white background. These data will certainly need further analysis from a demographic and cultural perspective to understand the social motivation behind such results.

The topic of race relations is a debate that follows a different paradigm in Puerto Rico. It cannot be analyzed in the simple black versus white dichotomy that is typical of the U.S. mainland. That would be a simplistic view. Most people in Puerto Rico claim that there is no racial discrimination on the island. Their point of view is that they are being judged by American standards that define race as a dividing issue and not as a group of Puerto Ricans who collectively try to maintain a cohesive culture with a plurality of races included in it. Another way to look at it is that cultural identification as Puerto Rican takes priority over belonging to a specific race. In contrast, in the United States, racial identification is one of the most important factors to determine cultural affiliation. So when Puerto Ricans are inevitably asked, What are you? they usually answer Puerto Rican, and do not give as an answer a certain skin color such as black, white, or any other combination. This does not mean that they are not aware of race. Another factor that offers a contrast between Puerto Rico and the U.S. mainland is the social distribution of different races. In the United States, most racial minorities have a history of living in segregated areas. However, this has never been the case in Puerto Rico. *Boricuas* are more accustomed to seeing a society of biracial couples and children at all levels of society. This simply reflects the notion that Puerto Rican cultural identification supersedes their racial perspective of the world and themselves.

The official point of view in Puerto Rico is that there is no racial discrimination on the island. However, in reality, social and economic status is often related to skin color. A simple driving trip into the shantytowns near San Juan (like La Perla) or the island's interior areas quickly reveals a few simple observations. It is not difficult to notice that the poorest people happen to be mostly black, and the most affluent neighborhoods are populated almost exclusively by whites. Low-income Puerto Ricans often argue that there may be economic discrimination at play. For example, it is noticeable that blacks and mulattoes seem to be more prevalent in lower-paying jobs, such as in restaurants and the behind-the-scenes operations of hotels. Whites and *trigueños* are more visible in management positions and television programming. Whites are usually placed in the front operations of the tourism industry such as resorts and cruise terminals. This dichotomy appears to be the legacy of the Spanish colonial system that is still pervasive throughout Latin America. The selection of employees to work dealing directly with the public are often required to have what is known as *buena presentación,* or "good appearance." This practice could never be legally tolerated or advertised as a job requirement, but it is often a subtle factor that determines who gets hired for specific customer-friendly positions.

The plurality of races, unified by their love for the Spanish language, is actually what makes Puerto Rico such a rich cultural mosaic with a complex heritage. This cultural pride has permeated every aspect of Puerto Rican life, including religion, language, sports, cuisine, literature, music, and cinema.

The best way to get to know Puerto Rico is to communicate with the people. Initially, sometimes, Puerto Ricans are a little reluctant to open up to strangers. History has taught them that outsiders usually want something from them. However, once they know people a little better, they frequently open up to create bonds that sometimes develop into lifelong relationships. Most *boricuas* enjoy the simple pleasures that the island offers such as beautiful beaches, a rich musical heritage, and a passion for life. Eventually, most conversations with Puerto Ricans would touch on at least one of the following themes: music, food, baseball, or the political status of the island. Most of them usually have a passionate opinion on these topics. The discussion of politics has a long tradition in Puerto Rico. However, *boricuas* often find that the relationship that exists between their island and the United States remains somewhat hazy for most Americans on the mainland. This topic certainly deserves a more detailed discussion.

REFERENCES

Aliotta, Jerome J. *The Puerto Ricans.* Peoples of North America Series. New York: Chelsea House, 1991.

Davis, Lucille. *Puerto Rico.* New York: Grolier, 2000.

Delano, Jack. *Puerto Rico Mío: Four Decades of Change.* Washington, DC: Smithsonian Institution Press, 1990.

Fradin, Dennis Brindell. *Puerto Rico.* Danbury, CT: Children's Press, 1995.

George, Linda, and Charles George. *Luis Muñoz Marín.* Danbury, CT: Children's Press, 1999.

Harlan, Judith. *Puerto Rico: Deciding Its Future.* New York: Twenty-first Century Books, 1996.

Jiménez de Wagenheim, Olga. *Puerto Rico's Revolt for Independence: El Grito de Lares.* Boulder, CO: Westview Press, 1985.

Johnson, Linda A. "Weak Dollar, Foreign Sales Boost Drug Makers." *San Juan Star,* July 24, 2008.

Johnston, Joyce. *Puerto Rico.* Minneapolis, MN: Lerner, 1994.

Lee, Edward R. "Talking Color with Spanish-Speaking Caribbean Brethren." *Blackfax* 11, no. 48 (2007): 27–30.

Levy, Patricia. *Puerto Rico—Cultures of the World.* 2nd ed. Tarrytown, NY: Marshall Cavendish International, 2005.

Loveman, Mara, and Jerónimo Muñiz. "How Puerto Ricans Became White: An Analysis of Racial Statistics in the 1910 and 1920 Censuses." Paper presented at the Center for Demography and Ecology at the University of Wisconsin–Madison, February 2006.

Morales Carrión, Arturo. *Puerto Rico: A Political and Cultural History.* New York: W. W. Norton, 1983.

Muckley, Robert I., and Adela Martínez-Santiago. *Stories from Puerto Rico/Historias de Puerto Rico.* Side by Side Bilingual Books Series. Lincolnwood, IL: Passport Books, 1999.

Murillo, Mario. *Islands of Resistance: Puerto Rico, Vieques and U.S. Policy.* New York: Seven Stories Press, 2001.

Rezvani, David A. "The Basis of Puerto Rico's Constitutional Status: Colony, Compact, or Federacy?" *Political Science Quarterly* 122, no. 1 (2007): 115–140.

Rivera-Batiz, Francisco. "Color in the Tropics: Race and Economic Outcomes in the Island of Puerto Rico." Paper presented at the conference Puerto Ricans on the Island and in the Mainland United States, New York, May 21, 2004.

Rivero, Yeidi M. *Tuning Out Blackness: Race and Nation in the History of Puerto Rican Television.* Durham, NC: Duke University Press, 2005.

Rodríguez, Clara E. "Puerto Ricans: Black and White." In *Boricuas: Influential Puerto Rican Writings—An Anthology,* ed. Roberto Santiago, 81–90. New York: Random House, 1995.

Santiago, Roberto, ed. *Boricuas: Influential Puerto Rican Writings—An Anthology.* New York: Random House, 1995.

Thompson, Kathleen. *Puerto Rico.* Austin, TX: Raintree/Steck Vaughn, 1996.

Web Site

Office of the Governor of Puerto Rico, http://fortaleza.govpr.org/. A bilingual Web site with information on the island's highest government official.

2

The Political Status of Puerto Rico

PUERTO RICANS HAVE been passionately discussing the same political topic for over one hundred years. It all began when the United States took possession of Puerto Rico in 1898 as a result of the Spanish-American War. The single issue that has dominated heated conversations ever since is the political status of the island. More specifically, the focus of the discussion is the legal relationship that Puerto Rico should have with the United States. The lack of agreement among Puerto Ricans on this topic generates a plethora of opinions that take sides along three basic alternatives: (1) becoming an independent nation, (2) requesting to become the fifty-first state of the United States, and (3) maintaining the island's current status as a commonwealth associated with the United States.

Most people do not really understand the intricate details of the political status of Puerto Rico in a global perspective. It is a territory of the United States, but it also has more latitude to manage its local affairs than other U.S. territories such as American Samoa, Guam, or the U.S. Virgin Islands. Traditionally, a commonwealth is a group of nations that collaborate for mutual benefit. In the case of Puerto Rico, history has contributed to the island's forming a different relationship with the United States. It is of crucial importance to discuss two key aspects of the commonwealth arrangement: (1) the territory clause in the U.S. Constitution and (2) the specific details of U.S. citizenship granted to Puerto Ricans in 1917.

The legal and political relationship between Puerto Rico and the United States is under the jurisdiction of the U.S. Constitution. More specifically, the territory clause (Article IV, section 3, clause 2) gives the U.S. Congress power to "liberate" Puerto Rico and provide it with independence, much like the way it was provided to the Philippines in 1945. Another portion of the U.S. Constitution called the admission clause (Article IV, section 3, clause 1) provides a way to allow territories to become a state, similar to the way Alaska was admitted in 1958 and Hawaii in 1959. So the legal authority to provide Puerto Rico with either independence or statehood is based on complete congressional discretion. The legal relationship is further complicated by the fact that Puerto Rico was granted the benefit of creating its own constitution on July 25, 1952. The latest discussion on the territory clause took place in federal court. The Court of Appeals for the Eleventh Circuit declared in 1993 that just because the U.S. Congress allowed Puerto Rico some self-governance benefits does not mean that the island became a sovereign nation. Furthermore, the U.S. Congress can unilaterally repeal the Puerto Rican Constitution and determine the future of the island.

On March 2, 1917, President Woodrow Wilson signed the Jones Act, granting U.S. citizenship to all Puerto Ricans, but not based on the U.S. Constitution: they enjoy the freedom to live, work, and study in any part of the United States without legal restrictions. However, the apparent controversy on the island is that their legal status is not permanent, but at the pleasure of the U.S. Congress, which can change, amend, or terminate that benefit to future Puerto Rican children born on the island. The U.S. Congress reviewed the issue in 1940 and 1952 but made no changes to the legislation. The distinction comes from the fact that there are different types of U.S. citizenship. In the case of Puerto Rico, the Jones Act provided its people with *statutory,* and not *constitutional,* citizenship. The latter is conferred on people born in any of the fifty states. However, statutory citizenship allows the U.S. Congress to treat Puerto Ricans as a separate and different category of U.S. citizen. This citizenship benefit can be revoked if Congress decides to do so. It should be highlighted that a congressional decision would not revoke the citizenship of people who already have it, but would apply to people born in Puerto Rico after the legal decision was made. The momentum continues in Puerto Rico to discuss and search for a more permanent future for the island.

INDEPENDENCE, STATEHOOD, OR COMMONWEALTH?

Discussions of political status have intensified since the 1960s, especially in times of economic downturns. Puerto Rican voters participated in three referendums (special votes) in 1967, 1993, and 1998, which have not produced a change in status. It is worth mentioning that the average voter turnout for these events is an impressive 90 percent. Obviously, Puerto Ricans are passionate about politics, and they want to be active participants in determining the future of their island. Nevertheless, the population remains deeply divided on the choices, though the argument is no longer just political, but economic and cultural as well.

Independence

Puerto Rico has never achieved its national independence. It was a Spanish colony for over four hundred years, and it has been controlled by the United States since 1898. Therefore it is not surprising that there is somewhat of a nostalgic feeling surrounding the idea of independence. There have been sporadic claims for independence from the United States, but the most dramatic and desperate effort took place on November 1, 1950. Two members of the Nationalist Party of Puerto Rico, Oscar Collazo and Griseldo Torresola, attempted to assassinate President Harry Truman but failed at their efforts. Their plan was to kill President Truman at Blair House (across the street from the White House), where he lived during the extensive renovation of the White House that took place from 1948 to 1952. The motive of these two nationalists was a strong resentment that U.S. corporations were benefiting from investing in Puerto Rico, while local business ownership was limited and economic improvements were being denied to the population of the island. They truly believed that their bold move would bring attention to their cause and consequently advance the chances of Puerto Rico becoming independent. The members of the nationalistic agenda were quickly labeled as a terrorist group with communist ideals that did not represent the majority of Puerto Ricans. The governor of Puerto Rico at the time, Luis Muñoz Marín, publicly denounced the attempted crime and clearly stated that a revolutionary road was not the way to improve conditions in Puerto Rico. Instead, he advocated a diplomatic approach with a focus on negotiation as the best way to obtain more regional control for Puerto Rican political and economic affairs.

However, most Puerto Ricans realize by now that their island has become economically dependent on the U.S. government. The relationship with the United States has attracted large amounts of foreign investment and tourism dollars. In addition, it would be very expensive to survive as an independent nation since independence would incur expenses for which the mainland government currently provides, such as a comprehensive diplomatic core, a customs and immigration force, federal tax incentives for corporations moving to the island, a military budget, a coast guard with drug enforcement capabilities, and the funding of expensive social programs. One such program aimed at helping low-income households is the Nutritional Assistance Program (NAP), a federal program funded by the U.S. Department of Agriculture that provides monthly payments to be spent on nutritional needs, especially for infants. These food vouchers are known locally simply as *cupones*. The plan is based on the U.S. Food Stamp Program, but it is not part of it since it was designed to address the specific needs of the Puerto Rican population. The last quarterly informational bulletin produced by Resident Commissioner Luis G. Fortuño in July 2008 reported that the Agriculture Law of 2008 extended the food voucher program until 2012, offering benefits to 460,000 Puerto Rican families at a total cost of 1.6 billion dollars (Fortuño 2008). If the island became independent, its residents would lose this valuable benefit. Moreover, Puerto Ricans would lose their U.S. citizenship and their right to live and work legally in any state of the federal union. As a result of economic dependence on these crucial benefits, the independence choice has never attracted wide support among voters.

Statehood

The option of becoming the fifty-first state has both advantages and perils. Becoming the fifty-first federal state within the United States would provide Puerto Ricans with the right to vote in federal elections and to have actual voting representation in the U.S. Congress and the Senate. Local representatives would be able to advocate directly for the needs of the island's population. Proponents of the statehood option also hope that poor Puerto Ricans would qualify for higher payments within the federal welfare system. The amount they currently receive is much lower than the standards set for any of the fifty states. On the other hand, Americans living on the mainland worry about allowing another state to join the union that would bring a high level of poverty. In fact, Puerto Rico would replace Mississippi as the poorest state in the union.

The advantages and disadvantages of the statehood option are often discussed on the basis of political, economic, and cultural arguments. By becoming a state, Puerto Ricans would reaffirm a permanent U.S. citizen status. Currently U.S. citizenship is often viewed as a temporary benefit that the U.S. Congress has the power to change, review, restrict, or completely terminate. Some of the disadvantages are discussed along economic lines. For example, Puerto Ricans would have to pay federal taxes, something from which they are currently exempt. Considering that local taxes are already extremely high, an added deduction would be a hard hit to economically disadvantaged families. The other disadvantages are proposed in cultural terms. Puerto Ricans are concerned that their vibrant culture would be diluted and eventually disappear as future generations are incorporated into American traditions and lifestyles. One cultural trait that is not negotiable with Puerto Ricans is the threat of losing Spanish as their main language since they would be required to accept English as the only official language of the new state. However, cultural pride is sometimes put aside when young professionals encounter limited job opportunities and a depressed economy. College-educated Puerto Ricans continue to leave the island in large numbers in search of a better life.

Continuing the Commonwealth Status

The choice of remaining as a commonwealth (Estado Libre Asociado) has received wide political support since the first plebiscite in 1967, proposed by Luis Muñoz Marín, the first elected governor of Puerto Rico. That year, 68 percent of the voting population supported the commonwealth option. Even today, a large number of Puerto Ricans believed that it is better to be economically tied to the U.S. government, while simultaneously being culturally unique and different. The current arrangement provides almost complete control at the regional level of government, while maintaining an acceptable level of nationalistic pride. It is expected that this option has, and will continue to have, both strong critics and passionate advocates. At the beginning of the twenty-first century, the majority of Puerto Ricans still prefer the choice of remaining as a commonwealth and have practically discarded the possibility of independence. This option provides Puerto Rico with a relative level of local autonomy, while benefiting from the political and economic connection to the United States.

THE RESULTS OF TWO PLEBISCITES

The 1993 plebiscite did not produce any changes in the current status of Puerto Rico as a commonwealth of the United States. Actually, 48.6 percent voted in favor of retaining the commonwealth status; 46.3 percent favored statehood; and only 4.4 percent approved of independence. This was a narrow defeat to the political party advocating that Puerto Rico become the fifty-first state of the union. So, the issue was bound to resurface a few years later.

Another referendum in 1998 offered a choice that was not available to Puerto Ricans in the 1993 vote. This time, the voting ballots included five options, not just the usual three: (1) complete independence, (2) statehood, (3) the existing commonwealth arrangement, (4) a commonwealth with enhanced benefits, and (5) none of the above. Surprisingly, 73 percent of Puerto Ricans voted for the last option of "none of the above." The message sent to local politicians was that the general population did not like how the different options were written on the ballot. Another important result was that only 2 percent of the votes advocated independence, an indicator that this option is almost dead.

Despite the optimism that average Puerto Ricans invest into the political process, these votes and referendums are nonbinding resolutions. Their results are similar to simply sending a suggestion to the U.S. government. In reality, just because Puerto Ricans declare one option, it does not necessarily mean it has to be approved by the United States. For example, if the majority of Puerto Ricans voted for independence, it does not automatically follow that the U.S. Congress is going to allow Puerto Rico to go free. Therefore it has been suggested that these periodic referendums only offer the illusion of political empowerment, and that they actually provide a distraction from dealing with more pressing problems on the island. For example, by campaigning for these special votes, local politicians do not address the issue of the escalating unemployment rate of roughly 12 percent (more than double the number on the U.S. mainland) or the increasing rates of violent crime. The drawback to all this effort is that even if Puerto Ricans select to pursue the independence road, they will still want to negotiate certain ties and benefits with the U.S. government. At this point, it is not clear what those connections would be.

POLITICAL PARTIES

The main political parties of Puerto Rico have formed by developing a platform that supports one of the three viable options for the political status of Puerto Rico. The three principal parties have sophisticated ideologies and political machinery to express their point of view in favor of either independence, statehood, or an enhanced version of a commonwealth. According to Puerto Rican law, any political party that gets 5 percent of the votes qualifies for financial assistance from the local government.

The Independence Party proposes complete independence and the development of a foreign nation. They have never won an election for governor. The Popular Democratic Party (PDP) participated in the development of the current commonwealth status arrangement and continues to support the status quo, and perhaps a few enhancements to the commonwealth agreement. The New Progressive Party (NPP) actively supports the position that Puerto Rico should become the fifty-first state in the U.S. federal union. The two parties (PDP and NPP) have alternated administering the government of the island since 1952. They have both elected governors from their respective parties.

EXISTING GOVERNMENT STRUCTURE

For over four hundred years, the governor of Puerto Rico was always appointed by outside forces: either the Spanish Crown or the president of the United States. On March 3, 1952, Puerto Ricans approved their own constitution. Now they have control over the electoral process to select their own leaders to the executive, legislative, and judicial branches.

Governors are elected to four-year terms, and there is no limit to how many times a governor can be reelected. The candidate must be a U.S. citizen, thirty-five years of age or older, and reside on the island for a minimum of five consecutive years. There is no vice governor or lieutenant governor. In case of resignation, death, or impeachment, the secretary of state becomes the governor. When in doubt, the line of succession is as follows: governor, secretary of state, attorney general, and the secretary of the treasury. Since 1952, Puerto Rico has had eight governors, including Sila Marí Calderón (PDP), who was the first woman to hold that post. The latest governor is Aníbal Acevedo Vilá, from the PDP, elected in 2004. The official house of the head of government in Puerto Rico is La Fortaleza, a fortified house that is the oldest executive mansion in the United States and the Western Hemisphere. It has been the house of the governor of Puerto Rico for over four hundred years.

The representatives elected to the other branches of government also serve four-year terms. The legislative branch has a bicameral structure and is divided between the Senate and the House of Representatives. The requirements for government office are that a candidate must be bilingual in English and Spanish and be at least thirty years old. In the judicial branch, justices to the different courts are appointed by the governor of Puerto Rico with advice from a Senate committee. Attorneys of the local bar association must be fluent in Spanish to represent their clients in municipal and superior courts, which use Spanish as the standard language of operation. However, attorneys dealing with federal-level courts must be fluent in English because they are subjected to U.S. jurisdiction, and the cases are always presented in English. The judges can serve in their posts until they are seventy years old. Puerto Ricans also vote for a resident commissioner (a representative to the U.S. Congress but without voting power), who is also elected for a four-year term.

POTENTIAL NEW OPTIONS

For the first time in the history of Puerto Rico, the island's legislature unanimously approved resolutions in early 2005 demanding that the U.S. government deal with the political status of the island in a more definitive manner. Puerto Rico wanted to move beyond the colonial-like status that seems to be temporary in nature and search for a solution that offers its population a permanent option of either statehood or independence. The proposal was signed and supported by both the Puerto Rican governor at the time, Aníbal Acevedo Vilá, and the resident commissioner, Luis Fortuño. This request sparked a renewed interest in the issue by the U.S. Congress. In addition, President George W. Bush requested that a White House task force discuss the topic in 2005. The goal was to explore whether the commonwealth status is still a viable choice for Puerto Rico. The U.S. secretary of state

Condoleezza Rice also included a diplomatic analysis that appeared within the White House report. Even the United Nations has previously intervened to review the potential right of Puerto Rico to be a self-governing nation and to discuss its status in international forums. Nevertheless, the White House task force for Puerto Rico produced a report in 2005 that essentially did not change much of the current situation. It made it clear that Puerto Rico is still an unincorporated federal territory and that it is subject to the plenary powers of the U.S. Congress. It also specified that Congress can overturn at any time the self-government benefit that Puerto Ricans currently enjoy. Moreover, it could also terminate the right to U.S. citizenship from which Puerto Ricans have benefited since 1917. The reaction by the governor of Puerto Rico was to find legislators in the U.S. Congress to challenge the results of the 2005 report.

In 2007, there were two new bills proposed in the U.S. Congress to clarify the status of Puerto Rico, again. Politicians in Washington spent over a year developing this new legislation. It is intended to present the population of the island with a simple ballot that lacks the complicated options of previous plebiscites. Representative José Serrano (a Democrat from New York) and Resident Commissioner Fortuño jointly proposed bill HR900, better known as the Puerto Rico Democracy Act, in February 2007. The bill would allow Puerto Ricans to vote in a two-step referendum without any confusing rhetoric. First, by the end of 2009, Puerto Ricans would answer only one straightforward question: if they want to change their relationship with the United States. It would be presented as a simple yes-or-no question to avoid any potential confusion. If people vote not to change the current status, then the proposal will be repeated every eight years. However, if the majority votes in favor of changing the status, they will be required to engage in a second vote and make a simple choice: statehood or independence. Serrano's position advocated for Puerto Rico to be incorporated as the fifty-first state of the U.S. federal union.

On the other hand, Representative Nydia Velázquez (another Democrat from New York) introduced into Congress the Puerto Rico Self-Determination Act. Her proposal argues that a set of representatives from the island should be in charge of writing the new referendum and should include four choices: (1) independence, (2) statehood, (3) the current commonwealth, and (4) a new commonwealth with enhanced benefits. The benefits requested under the enhanced commonwealth include rights to engage in foreign treaties and veto power over federal laws. While politicians on the island have promoted this enhanced version, it is not a realistic option. These benefits could never be approved because currently none of the fifty states has those rights under the U.S. Constitution. In effect, this option is simply a misleading position aimed at the emotional issue of nationalism with the hope that it will translate into more local votes. Representative Velázquez has expressed support for the current commonwealth option. Despite all the discussion on the topic, on December 21, 2007, the task force on Puerto Rico organized by the White House to study the matter at hand responded to both bills with the same answer previously articulated: Puerto Rico continues to be a territory of the United States under the plenary powers and jurisdiction of the U.S. Congress.

Despite the well-intentioned activities of these two U.S. congressional representatives from the mainland (both of Puerto Rican heritage), most Puerto Rican politicians from the island actually oppose both bills. A crucial factor is that they would provide for the first time voting rights to the Puerto Ricans living on the mainland. The diaspora of Puerto Ricans started in the 1930s and has continued ever since, mostly focusing on the northeastern part of the United States. However, a remarkable new statistic has recently emerged: the 2005 Census estimates revealed that the population of *boricuas* was larger on the U.S. mainland (3,780,000) than on the island itself (3,670,000). The number of Puerto Ricans on the mainland increased dramatically in the 1990s and spread out beyond the confines of the Northeast. It is precisely the stateside Puerto Ricans who have been recently elected to the U.S. Congress and advocate a more definitive position on the political status of the island, especially since the resident commissioner of Puerto Rico does not have a vote in Congress. The uncertainty of the island's political parties lies on the fact that the stateside Puerto Ricans have not been polled in decades, so nobody really knows how they are likely to vote. Several politicians living in Puerto Rico quickly expressed their strong opposition to the idea that stateside *boricuas* vote via absentee ballots. They clearly state that only residents living on the island should be entitled to vote in matters that determine the political future of their homeland. In their opinion, Puerto Ricans who abandoned the island in search of a better life should not decide the future of the very land they left behind; rather, the future of Puerto Rico should only be decided by residents of the island and not by well-intentioned Puerto Ricans living in New York City, Los Angeles, or Miami. The general fear is that, once again, the future of the island may ultimately be decided by outsiders, even if they are of Puerto Rican heritage.

REFERENCES

Aliotta, Jerome J. *The Puerto Ricans.* Peoples of North America Series. New York: Chelsea House, 1991.
———. *The Puerto Rican Americans.* Broomall, PA: Chelsea House, 1995.

Bea, Keith. *Political Status of Puerto Rico: Background, Options, and Issues in the 109th Congress.* Washington, DC: Congressional Research, 2008.

Bernier-Grand, Carmen T. *Poet and Politician of Puerto Rico: Don Luis Muñoz Marín.* New York: Orchard Books, 1995.

———. *In the Shade of the Níspero Tree.* New York: Orchard Books, 1999.

Dávila, Jesús. "U.S. Hardens Position on Puerto Rico." *El Diario Prensa: Nuestros países,* December 22, 2007.

Delano, Jack. *Puerto Rico Mío: Four Decades of Change.* Washington, DC: Smithsonian Institution Press, 1990.

Falcón, Angelo. "The Diaspora Factor: Stateside Boricuas and the Future of Puerto Rico." *NACLA Report on the Americas* 40, no. 6 (2007): 28–31.

Fortuño, Luis. "People of Puerto Rico to Determine Their Own Status." *Puerto Rico Herald,* July 14, 2005.

———. "Repleta de Beneficios la Ley Agrícola." *Boletín de la Oficina del Comisionado Residente* 3, no. 3 (2008): 3A.

González, David. "Heroes, Poets and Even a Dog, but No Puerto Ricans." *New York Times,* June 1, 2004.

Harlan, Judith. *Puerto Rico: Deciding Its Future.* New York: Twenty-first Century Books, 1996.

Johnston, Joyce. *Puerto Rico.* Minneapolis, MN: Lerner, 1994.

Makavet, Pedro A. *America's Colony: The Political and Cultural Conflict between the United States and Puerto Rico.* New York: New York University Press, 2004.

Muckley, Robert I., and Adela Martínez-Santiago. *Stories from Puerto Rico/Historias de Puerto Rico.* Side by Side Bilingual Books Series. Lincolnwood, IL: Passport Books, 1999.

Murillo, Mario. *Islands of Resistance: Puerto Rico, Vieques and U.S. Policy.* New York: Seven Stories Press, 2001.

Needham, Vicki. "Puerto Rico Status Bill Heading to Floor." *Congress Daily AM,* October 24, 2007.

Ramírez de Ferrer, Miriam. "Only Residents of Puerto Rico Should Be Entitled to Vote in the 1998 Plebiscite." *Puerto Rico Herald,* July 31, 1997.

Rehrmann, Alexis. "A Better Life Here, Yes, but Not without Worries." *New York Times,* January 10, 2008.

Rezvani, David A. "The Basis of Puerto Rico's Constitutional Status: Colony, Compact, or Federacy?" *Political Science Quarterly* 122, no. 1 (2007): 115–140.

Santiago, Esmeralda. "Island of Lost Causes." In *Boricuas: Influential Puerto Rican Writings—An Anthology,* ed. Roberto Santiago, 22–24. New York: Random House, 1995.

Suter, Keith. "Puerto Rico: Beyond the 'West Side Story.'" *Contemporary Review* 289, no. 1687 (2007): 442–448.

Thompson, Kathleen. *Puerto Rico.* Austin, TX: Raintree/Steck Vaughn, 1996.

Vazquez, Carlos M. "Puerto Ricans Have Shown They're Happy with Status Quo." *Puerto Rico Herald,* July 13, 2005.

3

Religion

FOR CENTURIES, HUMANS have searched for something greater than themselves, and religion usually brings comfort and spirituality to its followers. The current religious practices of Puerto Rico are the result of centuries of change and influence by outside groups. The modern culture of the island reveals a mix of races, languages, musical influences, and religions. Prior to the arrival of the Europeans, the Taínos had a polytheistic belief system that took into account the elements of nature. Water was a basic element to worship since it represented the essence of life. The Spanish Crown ushered in the colonial period in 1493, and soon Roman Catholicism became the predominant feature of daily life. The Roman Catholic faith left a strong imprint in Puerto Rico that is still visible today in colorful festivals, joyous celebrations, and social customs. After the early 1500s, African slaves were brought to the island, and they brought their own religious practices and blended them with the Roman Catholic faith imposed on them by the Spaniards. The result was the Afro-Caribbean religion of Santeria, with a strong following in Cuba and Puerto Rico. Then, when the United States took over the island in 1898, it opened the gates for a group of influential Christian Protestant religions. Pentecostal and Presbyterian groups also aimed to nurture the social needs of the communities with which they worked. They opened schools, hospitals, and universities. Today, like most of its Latin American neighbors, Puerto Rico is predominately Roman Catholic, even though the Protestant religions are converting people at increasing rates. Legally, the Constitution of the Commonwealth of Puerto Rico, adopted in 1952, explicitly protects religious freedom for all its residents. Taking this background into account, it is important to analyze the positions that religious institutions take on specific—and sometimes controversial—social issues such as the death penalty, birth control, premarital sex, and the definition of marriage.

THE NUMBER GAME

Puerto Rico has nearly 4 million people. Since there are many reports available, there is no consensus on how many Puerto Ricans belong to each religion. However, a general trend shows that approximately 80 percent of the population is Roman Catholic, even if they are not highly active in religious attendance at church services. Another 15 percent belong to the Christian Protestant religions: Pentecostals, Methodists, Presbyterians, Mormons, Jehovah's Witnesses, and others. Roughly 2 percent of the population are nonreligious. The remaining 3 percent constitute the people belonging to religions in smaller numbers such as Islam and Judaism. The numbers alone are not always crystal clear, especially taking into account that many parishioners of mainstream religions also practice local hybrid religions like Santeria and spiritualism. For example, most followers of Santeria are also professed Roman Catholics. The saint images they worship are Roman Catholic, but they are intended to represent African Yoruba gods, or *orishas*. A large number of Puerto Ricans also follow *espiritismo* (spiritualism), a semimagical belief in the occult forces and communication with the deceased. However, the number of *espiritistas* is not always easily counted because most people do not openly declare this practice, and most of them also consider themselves Christian. Furthermore, there is a sizable group who follow so-called popular spiritualism, which has infused elements of Christianity, particularly Roman Catholicism, Taíno heritage, and African imagery. To better understand the religious experience in Puerto Rico, it must be viewed in a larger context that includes history, politics, economics, health, art, and general social customs.

THE TAÍNO INFLUENCE

The Taíno indigenous population is now extinct, but their influence is very much alive in Puerto Rico. Archeological evidence reveals that they venerated multiple deities. Not all Gods were necessarily benevolent in nature; some had to be worshipped and feared at the same time. The Taíno polytheistic beliefs were divided between major and minor gods. For example, Atabei was the earth mother and the goddess of water, and hence of life and fertility. Some women in Puerto Rico still take her into account when praying for the safe birth of a child. Yucahú was the supreme creator and also the main guide for spiritual life. Juracán was the god of strong winds, and his name is the origin of the word *hurricane*. He was certainly a deity to be both admired and feared.

Living on an island, the metaphor of sacred waters was crucial in the Taíno religion. The image and symbolism of water were central tenets of their beliefs—it was the source of all life. Daily nourishment depended on the rivers providing fish and water for crops. In addition, Taínos used shells from the ocean to make musical instruments for religious rituals. Perhaps the most basic premise was that rain was essential for both agriculture and drinking. However, they prayed to a set of twin gods to maintain the right balance between rain and fair weather. Too little of one would not produce enough rain, and too much of the other would end up in a hurricane.

In 2007, the U.S. Army Corps of Engineers was working on building a dam in the southern part of the island when they stumbled into an archeological discovery. This dig has been called the largest and best preserved archeological site in the Caribbean. Anthropologists already working on the ancient petroglyphs expect that they will provide tangible evidence of Taíno sacred rituals and everyday lifestyles. This discovery reveals that there is much more to be known about the Taíno civilization.

ROMAN CATHOLICISM

Today, the Roman Catholic Church is still the most dominant religion in Puerto Rico. Historically, it has been the most accepted faith on the island. It was introduced by the Spaniards over five hundred years ago, and it has lasted long after the Spanish departed in 1898. Actually, the island was the site of first administrative dioceses in the Americas. Nowadays, the Roman Catholic religion, at the regional level, has morphed to include traditions of indigenous roots, African influence, and even spiritualism. Roman Catholicism is completely infused into the social fabric of most communities. It is a central part of social events like weddings and *quinceañeras*. Even today, long after the Spaniards left, every town celebrates its *fiestas patronales* (small-town patron saint holidays), which are carnival-like events that include music, food, dance, and crafts. One noticeable difference is that Puerto Ricans have a tendency to pray to their saints at home much more than their Latin American neighbors do. These saint figures provide comfort and a sense of spiritual protection. As a result, church attendance is also less frequent than in other Roman Catholic countries.

One of the most common samples of religious arts and crafts available in Puerto Rico is the carved saint statue. These colorful decorations are about twelve inches tall and carved out of a single piece of wood. The most popular

The Cathedral of San Juan. Photo courtesy of the author.

pieces are the Virgin Mary and the Three Wise Men, or *Los Tres Reyes Magos*. These saints are made especially in Ponce and Loíza Aldea but are widely available throughout the island. This tradition blends both Roman Catholic and indigenous beliefs by using them both as objects of religious value and also as protectors against evil spirits.

Religious art flourished during the Spanish colonial period (1493–1898), but this was a field usually dominated by Spaniards. The first local artist to emerge in Puerto Rico was the self-taught painter José Campeche (1751–1809). He painted a great many landscapes, but his focus was on religious images, especially the life of Jesus. He eventually became one of the most recognized artists in his genre throughout the Americas. His works are proudly displayed at the Museo de Arte e Historia in San Juan and at the Museo de Arte de Ponce.

Social Activism

Since the 1980s, Roman Catholicism has experienced a decline in church attendance in Puerto Rico. It is estimated that fewer than 50 percent of

The cemetery in Old San Juan is one of the oldest cemeteries on the island and is located next to the ocean. Photo courtesy of the author.

members actually attend religious services. A common reason provided is that Roman Catholics do not see a social connection between Church theology and practical social applications. The leaders of the Church are keenly aware of this problem and are actively discussing potential solutions. For example, they participate in more social celebrations, and they also provide shelter and food for needy people. However, one of the responses by the Church came in an unlikely format in the late 1990s. The Roman Catholic leaders became visibly involved in the protests against the United States, demanding the withdrawal of military troops from Vieques, a satellite island of Puerto Rico used for live-ammunition military exercises. This was an unexpected move since the Roman Catholic Church has usually positioned itself against social changes. Due to their support of the Vieques protests, Roman Catholics were praising Church leaders, and they appeared to be denouncing local politicians for their lack of specific concern over this topic. At the time, most political leaders were involved in never ending social scandals that consistently appeared in the media.

The catalyst event for the Roman Catholic clerics was a bomb dropped on April 18, 1999, that landed on Puerto Rican civilians, killing at least one person (David Sanes) and injuring others. As part of civil disobedience, *boricuas* started to occupy the beaches that the U.S. Navy had been using for military practices since 1941 and demanded a complete stop to these military exercises with live ammunition. However, this was not the first time that civilians had been killed. Several Protestant churches had been urging the federal government to stop this practice for decades. The difference in 1999 was that the Roman Catholic Church chose to mobilize people and take an active role in politics, a move usually discouraged by the Vatican. This is one social issue over which both Roman Catholic and Protestant church leaders unified for the benefit of the local population. Their social activism seemed to pay off. President Bill Clinton stopped the military exercises to start an investigation of possible alternative locations for the exercises and alternative variations of military training exercises. Eventually, President George W. Bush signed the final withdrawal of the U.S. forces from Vieques in 2003, putting an end to this controversy. While the Roman Catholic Church seems to have found a cause to connect with the population at the social level, it is not yet clear if its emerging role in politics will translate into increasing attendance of its religious services. In fact, Puerto Rico was the host of the Fifth General Conference of Catholic Bishops of Latin America and the Caribbean in 2007, and it discussed the great need to rekindle the faith of its parishioners. The Roman Catholic Church in Puerto Rico is certainly looking to the future to find significant ways to reenergize the spiritual needs of its followers.

Losing Interest in Religion

The Roman Catholic Church of Puerto Rico has noticed a declining interest in its services in the past thirty years. An increasing number of parishioners are converting to many of the Protestant churches actively recruiting new members on the island. However, a recent trend is that many *boricuas* are choosing to follow no religion at all. This decision does not necessarily imply that they are leaning toward atheism. Studies reveal that they actually continue to believe in God but that they are rejecting organized religion. Roman Catholics leaving the church often cite that they are searching for something more than simply religious rules and guidance; they actually want religious leaders who take an active role in their social services and are aware of current cultural needs and realities.

PROTESTANT RELIGIONS

When the United States took control of Puerto Rico in 1898, Protestant religions started to arrive and quickly thrived. Several Protestant denominations actually agreed to divide the island by geography to facilitate the work of their missionaries and to avoid duplicating and competing efforts. The Pentecostal church increased its membership tremendously, especially among the poor and rural areas. Several Protestant religions also started to offer crucial

An Evangelical church in Ponce. Photo courtesy of the author.

social services. For example, the Presbyterians founded schools and hospitals. The Adventists opened universities. Other institutions also included Evangelical seminaries and a council of churches. These Protestant groups now include Pentecostals, Episcopalians, Adventists, Presbyterians, Jehovah's Witnesses, Lutherans, Baptists, Mormons, and nondenominational groups. In the past three decades, these religions have grown tremendously, mostly by persuasively converting Roman Catholics to the new faiths. Currently there are over 1,400 Evangelical churches registered on the island. Today, Puerto Rico is well known as the most Protestant country among its Latin American neighbors, especially due to its historical relationship with the United States.

The arrival of the United States in 1898 also instituted the separation of church and state, in accordance with the U.S. Constitution. This separation was an attractive option for Puerto Ricans, especially since they were aware that such a union had not been very beneficial for the general population under old Spanish rule. For example, the Roman Catholic Church was not very supportive of independence efforts in Puerto Rico.

SANTERIA

African slaves imported to Puerto Rico came with their own religious beliefs and spirituality, which helped them survive the horrors of slavery. Since they were forcefully converted to Christianity, they assigned Roman Catholic images to their own Yoruba gods from Nigeria and thus were able to worship their own *orishas* (gods) right in front of the Europeans. For example, Obatala was made equivalent to Jesus, and Obubua, the goddess of the underworld, was paired with the Virgin Mary. Another popular saint is Santa Barbara, who is the parallel representation of Changó, one of the main Yoruba gods. In the New World, the combination of these two belief systems together with indigenous traditions gave birth to Afro-American religions like Candomblé in Brazil and Santeria in both Cuba and Puerto Rico. While Cubans are very open about their Santeria beliefs, Puerto Ricans remain somewhat cautious and secretive about declaring their membership in the religion. It is worth noting that since Santeria beliefs are usually transmitted orally, and the religion does not have a sacred religious book to follow, its growth has been more limited than the spread of Islam or Christianity. In addition, Santeria does not have an equivalent of the devil since Yoruba beliefs do not function according to a binary distinction between good and evil; it all depends on the context and the circumstances.

Santeria was always prohibited during the Spanish colonial period, but the beliefs and rituals have persevered until modern times. Spain actively tried to discredit the religion. In fact, the name Santeria itself was an insult used to mock followers who venerated saint images and ignored God. The Spanish never understood that these saint images were actual equivalents to the slaves' own Yoruba gods. Nowadays, Santeria is sometimes called a cult on the basis of vague notions about its offerings and traditions. Its rituals with drummers and dancers are sometimes also misunderstood. In reality, Santeria does not have a central leader who is worshipped, which is a basic tenant of a cult. The *santero* priests can be either men or women and are known as Babalawo (Father Who Knows the Secrets) or Lyanifa (Mother of Destiny), and the religion is certainly open to new members.

Santeria actually has many similarities to the Roman Catholic religion, including the use of candles, a mass or religious service, holy water, and saint images. Both Santeria and Roman Catholicism use a day to celebrate and remember the dead, falling either on November 1 or November 2. All ceremonies in Santeria begin with a section for remembering the people's ancestors. With so many similarities, it is not strange that most Puerto Ricans who practice Santeria are also self-professed Roman Catholics. However, the Roman Catholic Church does not accept Santeria as a religion. Nevertheless, a large number of *boricuas* seem to follow both religions on their own terms. A good example of how these two religions are intertwined into the Puerto Rican lifestyle is when a person requests the blessing of a new home. The family would often invite a Roman Catholic priest to come to a house and bless their new home. The priest usually would offer a prayer asking for family harmony, peace, and tranquility in the house. Then, just in case, they also invite a *santero* priest to perform a *riego* (water spraying), which is a cleansing of the house using special plants and herbs boiled in water, which is then sprinkled throughout the house with the intent to expel evil spirits. One of the main differences between the two religions is that Santeria aims to obtain balance while here on earth, while Roman Catholicism's goal is to find peace in the afterlife.

One of the most controversial rituals of Santeria (or Regla de Ocha) is animal sacrifices. Offerings to the *orishas*, or gods, are not uncommon in religions around the world. According to Santeria, a priest can organize an offering of flowers, candles, or even food to protect people from evil spirits. The offering of animal blood is only done in cases where the *santero* feels that the gods demand it of him or her. The *santero* would know the wishes of the *orishas* through the reading of seashells, cigars, or a glass of water. The use of an animal sacrifice and its blood would only occur in cases in which the *santeros* ask their gods for answers to big problems or to protect a person when his or her life is in danger. The animals most commonly slaughtered are chickens. The animal's blood is offered to the gods, and the people then eat the chicken, so nothing is wasted. The practice of animal sacrifice has been challenged in the U.S. courts. Animal rights activists claim that the practice amounts to animal cruelty. *Santeros* have explained that they are trained to kill animals in a humane way and that chickens are routinely killed in slaughterhouses every day for daily consumption. In the end, the U.S. Supreme Court ruled in 1993 that banning animal sacrifices in Santeria would represent an unconstitutional infringement of the freedom of religion, so the practice continues, even in the United States.

Botánicas are specialized stores that provide supplies for followers of Santeria to assist them in their offerings and traditions. They sell candles, prayer books, saint images, plants for the cleansing of homes, incense to expel bad spirits, and even books on magic. People go to *botánicas* to purchase items suggested by the *santero* priests. Quite often, the owners of these stores are also *santeros*, and they can assist customers with their spiritual needs.

SPIRITUALISM, OR *ESPIRITISMO*

While over 80 percent of Puerto Ricans define themselves as Roman Catholic, there is a general claim that the true religion of Puerto Rico is spiritualism, or *espiritismo*. Its followers claim that its roots can be traced back to Taíno beliefs that the spirits of the dead are lingering around this earth, and it is possible to communicate with them. They also believe in reincarnation. This religion has often been dismissed as nothing more than primitive, with a magical belief in supernatural phenomena. The tenet that communication with the deceased is possible has created skepticism in the religious community, which often views *espiritismo* as irrelevant, using pejorative terms. However, its advocates and believers claim that it has properties applicable to body healing, eating habits, and alternative medicine using herbal and medicinal plants. This practice is not a recent phenomenon; it has been around since the colonial period. The Spanish Roman Catholic Church clearly opposed it in the late 1800s and forbade it in Puerto Rico. Since the 1950s, spiritualism has actually flourished throughout the island. *Espiritistas* follow very similar values to Christianity, and thus most of them also consider themselves Christian. However, they do not gather in a church building to pray and worship. They just have reunions, where a mediator helps to guide the communication with the spirits. Nowadays, there are two related yet separate branches of *espiritismo* that are followed by different social classes in Puerto Rico.

Scientific spiritualism is practiced mostly by the elite and intellectuals in Puerto Rico. Its origins are based on the writings of Allen Kardec (1804–1869), a French mathematician whose real name was Leon Hypolite Denizarth Rivail. Since the beginning, scientific spiritualism has been concerned with social reform. It quickly developed into a sociopolitical approach to challenge the Spanish Crown in Puerto Rico. It questioned the social approach to poverty, caring for the elderly, traditional medicine, and even established religions. It proposed the need for a more educated population to be able to change society. Since the early 1900s, Puerto Rican *espiritistas* became active in literacy campaigns, founded hospitals, and have expressed their position against the death penalty. To promulgate these views, the magazine *El iris de paz* has been published on the island since 1899. Despite social efforts to obtain mainstream acceptance, the Roman Catholic Church views spiritualism as backward and primitive.

Spiritualism quickly recognized that the highest number of people who actually practice the religion are women. It promoted an agenda of modernization in which women would be agents of change, not only within their own families but also at the larger level of society. For example, these beliefs had a great influence on the feminist movement on the island and served as an ideological foundation to develop empowerment programs for women. They tackled controversial issues like the damage that prostitution was doing to women and society in general. Thus this religion became a mixture of theology and political activism.

The so-called hybrid spiritualism, or *espiritismo popular*, is followed mostly by the working class. It has been infused with Roman Catholicism, African practices, and indigenous beliefs as well. Unlike scientific spiritualism, it includes veneration of Roman Catholic saints and African *orishas*. The lower classes were not attracted to spiritualism because of its theological and philosophical views, but because it offered an alternative healing system to traditional medicine. They use plants and herbs with known medicinal qualities to treat illnesses. This therapeutic system was based on the knowledge of indigenous and African traditions.

ISLAM AND JUDAISM

Puerto Rico also experienced a small migration of Jews and Arabs to the island. Together, they constitute roughly 2 percent of the population. Both groups have built religious centers but have remained concentrated in specific areas of the island. Overall, these two groups are integrated into the island's culture, and there is little mention of anti-Semitism or anti-Arab feelings. They both attempt to follow their traditions, even when they have to adapt them to their own customs. For example, Puerto Rico does not have kosher restaurants, but the island offers a wealth of vegetarian and seafood dishes that Jews can enjoy.

Jewish Congregations

During the Spanish colonial period (1493–1898), Jews generally avoided Puerto Rico because the policies of the Spanish Inquisition did not view them in a favorable light. In fact, Queen Isabel of Spain ordered Jews to be expelled from Spain in 1492. The Jewish migration began after the United States took over Puerto Rico in 1898. Jews originally came representing American companies, but they were then followed by Jewish groups from Eastern Europe after World War II. Nowadays, there are two well-established Jewish congregations in San Juan. In addition, the cities of Santurce and Miramar are home to small synagogues to serve the Jewish population living there.

The ambivalence and opposition that Jews face do not come from the Puerto Rican population in San Juan, but from within the Jewish community itself. The two main Jewish congregations are the Shaare Tzedek Temple and the Beth Shalom Temple. The two main factors that hinder cooperation between them are language and patrilineal versus matrilineal traditions. The Shaare Tzedek congregation is a conservative synagogue. They only follow a matrilineal tradition, in which Jewish children are accepted if they have Jewish mothers, even if they have Christian fathers. They also hold their religious services in Hebrew and Spanish.

Temple Beth Shalom created a reform movement in 1967. They accept children who are of Jewish fathers and Christian mothers, but only if they are raised in the Jewish religion. In contrast to the previous congregation, they hold their religious services and events only in Hebrew and English. The reformed congregation is changing their language practices a little due to the fact that they are accepting more people who have recently converted and only speak Spanish.

Islam

The Islamic religion has a small but growing number of followers in Puerto Rico. The main religious centers for Muslims are located in Río Piedras, Ponce, Arecibo, Aguadilla, and Vega Baja, where mosques have been built to address the needs of the Muslim population. Following the sacred book of the Koran, Puerto Rican Muslims practice the traditional five pillars of the Islamic faith: (1) to recognize Allah as the only God, (2) to pray daily five times a day, (3) to fast during the month of Ramadan, (4) to practice charity, and (5) to make a pilgrimage to Mecca at least once in one's life.

An important cultural center, called Herencia Andalusí, is located in Aguadilla. Its aim is to study and promote cultural relations between the Muslim and Christian populations in Puerto Rico. The center serves as a research center for Islamic and Koranic studies. The American Muslim Association

Islamic center in Ponce. Photo courtesy of the author.

of North America considers Puerto Rico an important location for potential growth, and it has an administrative office in the city of Cayey.

RELIGION AND SOCIAL ISSUES

Religious institutions in Puerto Rico have traditionally held a conservative position on social issues. They usually oppose birth control, abortion, cohabitating couples, premarital sex, and the death penalty. In the case of the Roman Catholic Church, it has even been reluctant to get involved in the social agenda of the population.

Fertility, Birth Control, Abortion, and Sterilization

Puerto Rico first attempted to introduce contraceptive options in the 1920s by creating the Birth Control League. The Roman Catholic Church quickly mounted a strong opposition, and eventually, all the clinics that provided contraceptive information were closed for good in the 1930s. Things are certainly different nowadays. Numerous sociological studies show that more than 75 percent of sexually active women in Puerto Rico use some form of contraceptive. The pill is the most common form of contraception, and the use of condoms is less popular. Despite the strong opposition by the Roman Catholic Church, religious beliefs are apparently not a deterrent for the use of birth control. Recent studies reveal that Roman Catholics and non–Roman Catholics alike use contraceptives at roughly the same rate.

When the United States took over Puerto Rico in 1898, there were fewer than 1 million inhabitants. By the 1940s, the population had already doubled to almost 2 million. The increasing population growth worried the U.S. government. Consequently, during the 1940s and 1950s, Puerto Rico embarked on a program of population control. The local government worked with planning and financing from the U.S. government to enhance family planning services. The method most commonly used was the sterilization of women, especially among the poor population. During that time, most women who delivered babies via cesarean section also selected to be sterilized. During those decades, Puerto Rico reached the highest level of sterilization in the world, when almost 35 percent of the female population was subjected to such operations. This is an excessively high rate. In comparison, India and Pakistan also have public sterilization programs, but their rates are estimated to be 5 percent and 3 percent, respectively. Hospitals and clinics felt the social and financial pressure and decided to discontinue these programs by the 1960s.

Despite the objections of the Roman Catholic Church, abortion is legal in Puerto Rico, just like it is on the U.S. mainland. In the Caribbean, Cuba is the only other country that allows abortions to be performed. According to government figures, almost eighty thousand abortions are performed yearly in Puerto Rico. Here, again, religion is not a determining factor since both Roman Catholics and non–Roman Catholics obtain these services at almost the same rate. Results from health studies show that single women have more abortions than their married counterparts.

Marriage and Proposition 99

One of the most heated debates in Puerto Rico since the beginning of 2008 deals with a potential definition of marriage. Resolution 99 aims to amend the Puerto Rican Constitution to define marriage specifically between a man and a woman, even when gay marriage is not allowed on the island. This amendment is passionately supported by religious organizations in Puerto Rico and vigorously opposed by civil rights groups. Coalitions of pastors, ministers, and priests are seeking the support of legislators to vote in favor of the amendment. Gay rights activists are calling it a clear case of discrimination. The opposition also argues not only against the intrusion of the government into private life but also against the potentially harmful social consequences that could emanate from Resolution 99. For example, according to government statistics, 53 percent of couples in Puerto Rico currently live together without being married. The approval of Proposition 99 would make their unions illegal and disqualify companions and their children from getting medical insurance from their employers, and even from receiving a pension. Whatever the political results are, this divisive issue will remain an active topic of discussion for years.

The Death Penalty: Capital Punishment

Puerto Rico has one of the highest crime rates in the United States. It has the second highest level of violent crime, only after the District of Columbia. As of the year 2000, Puerto Rico experiences fourteen murders for every one hundred thousand citizens. Despite these alarming statistics, there is extremely high opposition to the death penalty on the island. Currently the Constitution of Puerto Rico explicitly prohibits capital punishment. However, the island has no jurisdiction over federal laws. Traditionally, local and federal legal systems have coexisted mostly in harmony since 1952, when the Puerto Rican Constitution was approved. Almost all of the legislators, the governor, and the Roman Catholic Church of Puerto Rico are also opposed to the death penalty. However, two recent cases in 2003 have created an outcry in Puerto Rico when federal prosecutors asked for the death penalty for the accused.

These recent court cases have also prompted several sociological and demographic studies regarding the attitudes that Puerto Ricans have toward capital punishment. Most researchers found that opposition to the death penalty was common across both educational and economic levels. One consistent reason for such opposition was religious conviction. Both the Roman Catholic Church and Protestant religions have preached this position to their followers for decades. Actually, the more that people attended church, the more likely they were to be against the death penalty. The explanation usually was that killing is simply wrong, whether it is done as a crime or on behalf of the government.

Another factor significant in determining support or opposition to capital punishment was language. The death penalty can only be requested in federal cases, which are held in English. Yet only a small number of *boricuas* are completely bilingual. Moreover, sociological studies have discovered that fluency in English actually increases the level of support for the death penalty. A potential problem is that the jury selected for a federal case must be bilingual, thus excluding the potential jurors who only speak Spanish. So an accused person is already facing a jury that is slightly in favor of the death penalty in the first place. Hence the clear question of fairness in capital punishment trials has emerged on the island. This is a discussion that will carry on as long as these cases continue to appear in federal court. It is very likely that religious organizations will express their support for the Puerto Rican Constitution and continue to lobby against the death penalty on the island.

REFERENCES

Brandon, George. *Santería from Africa to the New World: The Dead Sell Memories.* Bloomington: Indiana University Press, 1993.

Camara-Fuentes, Luis Raúl, José Javier, Colón-Morera, and Héctor M. Martínez-Ramírez. "The Death Penalty in Puerto Rico." *Centro Journal* 18, no. 2 (2006): 146–165.

"Church in Puerto Rico Looks to Future." *America* 196, no. 21 (2007): 6.

Ezratty, Harry A. *500 Years in the Jewish Caribbean: The Spanish and Portuguese Jews in the West Indies.* Baltimore: Omni Arts, 2002.

Harold, John M., Charles F. Westoff, Charles W. Warren, and Judith Seltzer. "Catholicism and Fertility in Puerto Rico." *American Journal of Public Health* 79, no. 9 (1989): 1258–1262.

Hernández Hiraldo, Samiri. *Black Puerto Rican Identity and Religious Experience.* Gainesville: University Press of Florida, 2006.

Herzig Shannon, Nancy. *El Iris de Paz: El espiritismo y la mujer en Puerto Rico.* Río Piedras, Puerto Rico: Huracán, 2001.

Jacobs, David, and Jason Carmichael. "The Political Sociology of the Death Penalty." *American Sociological Review* 67, no. 1 (2002): 109–131.

Kornblum, Janet. "More Hispanics Losing Their Religion." *Puerto Rico Herald,* January 4, 2003.

Silva Gotay, Samuel. *Catolicismo y política en Puerto Rico bajo España y Estados Unidos: Siglos XIX y XX.* Río Piedras: University of Puerto Rico Press, 2005.

———. *Protestantismo y política en Puerto Rico.* San Juan: University of Puerto Rico Press, 1997.

Stevens Arroyo, Anthony M. "Catholicism's Emerging Role in Puerto Rico." *America* 182, no. 13 (2000): 8–11.

———. "Taking Religion Seriously: New Perspectives on Religion in Puerto Rico." *Centro Journal* 18, no. 11 (2006): 214–223.

4

Social Customs and Lifestyle

PUERTO RICANS CERTAINLY know how to enjoy life. Despite being a crowded island with almost 4 million people (71% urban and 29% rural), leisure opportunities are plentiful, including lush tropical forests, astonishing beaches, musical performances, and open-air markets. Puerto Ricans possess a natural ability to engage in lively discussions with both friends and new acquaintances. Eventually, most conversations touch on a few predictably passionate topics: food, music, family, and of course, baseball. *Boricuas* are keenly aware of their history because it is still evolving, and their heritage is colorfully portrayed in their arts, festivals, and celebrations.

SPORTS

The four main sporting activities in Puerto Rico are baseball, boxing, surfing, and cockfighting. Like their Caribbean neighbors, Puerto Ricans love baseball, and not necessarily soccer like the rest of Latin America. In addition, Puerto Rico coordinates its own Olympic delegation, and it participates as an independent nation in international competitions. However, Puerto Rican athletes have the option of competing in the Olympic Games representing either Puerto Rico or the United States. The 1948 Olympics held in London, England, were crucial for Puerto Rico since it was the very first time the island competed on its own, even though its delegation only had three athletes.

Baseball

The most passionate sport on the island is definitely baseball. The U.S. Marine Corps brought the sport with them in the beginning of the 1900s. Other Caribbean neighbors also profess baseball to be their national sport, and they have their own winter leagues in Puerto Rico, Panama, and the Dominican Republic. Puerto Rico plays in the Caribbean League from October to March. The island has its own professional baseball league, which has been organized since the early 1920s. There are about six teams in this league, and the champion represents the island in the Caribbean World Series. In addition, teams from the U.S. Major Leagues hold their spring training camps in the tropical setting of Puerto Rico. It is also fairly common to see Major League scouts come to the island hoping to discover new talent.

Puerto Ricans are widely recognized for their athletic ability, and several Puerto Rican professional baseball players are included on the rosters of teams in the U.S. Major Leagues. Perhaps the most accomplished player was Roberto Clemente Walker (1934–1972). He started out with the Santurce Crabbers in Puerto Rico, then he signed with the Brooklyn Dodgers, but he played most of his career with the Pittsburgh Pirates. He played in two World Series, received the Golden Gloves award twelve times, was selected as the most valuable player (MVP) of the National League in 1966, and was chosen as the MVP for the World Series in 1971. In early 1972, his accomplishments led to his induction into the Baseball Hall of Fame. Then, just a few months later, a tragedy occurred. On New Year's Eve 1972, he died in a plane crash while taking food and relief supplies to Managua to help with the devastation of a powerful earthquake. The plane's engines caught fire, and it went down near Isla Verde in the vicinity of San Juan. Clemente's body was never found. He served as an inspiration to other outstanding ball players, including Luis Olmo, of the Brooklyn Dodgers; Hiram Bithon, of the Chicago Cubs; and Orland Cepeda, of both the San Francisco Giants and the Saint Louis Cardinals.

Boxing

Boxing was also introduced to the island by the U.S. military stationed in Puerto Rico. It was part of the soldiers' military training. The boxing competitions held among the U.S. soldiers were open for the public to see. The first official boxing match took place on January 15, 1899. Since then, Puerto Rico has seen many boxers succeed at local events and rise to competitive levels, where they have won international championships. The first Puerto Rican champion in the National Boxing Association was Sixto Escobar (1913–1979). In more recent times, Félix "Tito" Trinidad won multiple world championships in different weight categories: the welterweight in 1993 and the middleweight in both 2000 and 2004. Another outstanding *boricua* welterweight champion is Miguel Cotto. However, he lost his title in July 2008 to his Mexican opponent Antonio Margarito in Las Vegas. This match made boxing enthusiasts develop nationalistic feelings on both sides since Puerto Rico and Mexico have had a boxing rivalry that dates back several decades.

Surfing

Puerto Rico held the World Surfing Championship at Rincón in 1968. Ever since then, surfers have been coming to the western and northwestern parts of the island to enjoy one of the highest-ranking locations for surfing on the American continent. While Puerto Rico has 311 miles (500 kilometers) of coastline, the big, crashing waves are in the western section, where the Atlantic Ocean meets the Caribbean Sea, near the town of Rincón. Also, the rough waves on the northern coast near Isabela can be as high as twelve feet (four meters) and are usually only attempted by surfers with a great deal of experience. The extreme action of waves here is in part created by the Puerto Rico Trench off the northern coast, which is the deepest location in the Atlantic Ocean, at 27,880 feet. As an offshoot of surfing, Puerto Rico also held the Ray-Ban Windsurfing World Cup in 1989. This sport is best practiced in windy but more protected areas such as the southern part of the island near the Bay of La Parguera.

Cockfighting

Cockfights have already been prohibited in most countries around the world, but they continue to be extremely popular in Puerto Rico. Governor Acevedo Vilá signed a bill in August 2007 declaring cockfighting a sport under the jurisdiction of the Departamento de Recreación y Deportes and a "cultural right" for Puerto Ricans. This statement was intended to refute recent attempts by animal activists to ban cockfighting on the island, especially because it is also a very lucrative industry for Puerto Rico. Since it is legal to gamble on this so-called sport, it is highly regulated by the government. This bloody event requires the use of two specially trained *gallos de pelea* (fighting cocks), who wear spurs attached to their legs and attack each other until one of them dies or refuses to fight. The breeding of these animals can sometimes be a full-time occupation as it requires a lot of dedication, patience, and skill. This leisure activity was declared illegal by the United States in 1898, but it continued to thrive in clandestine locations. It was legalized again in the 1930s. At these events, the people place bets on a potentially winning rooster, and the losing cock usually ends up dead or in a moribund state. Individuals make bets with other cockfighting aficionados without official written records.

These bets follow the honor system, and surprisingly, this approach works. In contrast to most Latin American countries, where this activity is usually only attended by men, Puerto Rico's *galleras* (cockfighting rings) have an atmosphere that is more socially accepted. They are almost like casinos with full amenities, where women are also welcome. The Coliseo Gallístico de Puerto Rico in San Juan is the largest *gallera* on the island. It includes at least two bars, a cafeteria, extensive parking, and other facilities to take care of its aficionados.

In January 2008, the government was forced to cancel hundreds of cockfights, a decision that had a serious financial impact on the island. The reason was that there was a virus in the Dominican Republic that resulted in the banning of all bird imports, including the fighting roosters. This event revealed how lucrative the sport is in Puerto Rico. According to the Department of Agriculture, there are over two hundred thousand roosters raised and trained for the purpose of cockfighting, and they generate an agricultural budget of over 20 million dollars a year. The island has 105 licensed cockfighting rings, and collectively, they offer over 220,000 fights a year. The government estimates that the overall annual events generate revenue well over 100 million dollars, including ticket sales, food concessions, alcoholic beverages, and organized bets. Cockfighting is so popular that entrance fees alone amount to over 12 million dollars a year. People buy more tickets to cockfighting events than they do to baseball games, and baseball is supposed to be the national sport.

Sports and Politics

Sometimes, sports and politics do get tangled into complicated international situations. For example, during the cold war, the United States boycotted the Olympics in Russia. At the time, the United States also pressured Puerto Rico not to attend the event. The president of the Puerto Rican international committee, Germán Rieckehoff, expressed a strong position by stating that sports should not be mixed with politics. As a result, he was denied funding for the Puerto Rican Olympic team. The hopes and dreams of the Puerto Rican athletes were squashed. Despite economic hardships, Rieckehoff managed to send one athlete to the Moscow Olympics. Alberto Mercado competed in boxing, and he was the only citizen of the United States who participated in the 1980 Olympic Games. Two years later, in 1982, the Puerto Rican government again restricted economic support for the national team to participate in the Central American and Caribbean Games to be held in Cuba. Since the United States does not have diplomatic relations with Cuba, the *boricua* team was dissuaded from attending the games because they were taking place in a communist country. Once again, Rieckehoff came up with the strategy of asking people directly to provide donations for the event. This time, he was able to send the entire team to these international games. He always maintained his position that politics should not dictate participation in sporting events.

GAMBLING

Gambling is legal in Puerto Rico, but only in locations regulated by the government. The minimum age for gambling is eighteen years, and one must be eighteen years old to enter casinos, *galleras*, and any other specific gambling houses. There are five specific options for legalized gambling on the island: casinos, cockfights, horse races, lottery tickets, and the lotto. Some of the winnings in these activities are tax exempt, and others are taxed locally at extremely high rates. Casinos are only allowed in the tourist resort areas. They offer gambling in slot machines as well as blackjack, roulette, and craps. Usually, casinos have elegant decorations, but since they tend to be in tourist hotels near the beach, their ambiance tends to be informal and casual. Cockfighting aficionados can post bets on individual roosters by using the official betting office in the *galleras*. If customers win, their gains are taxable. However, most bets in cockfights are done among individuals attending the events and are therefore almost impossible to trace. People can also bet on horse races taking place at the Camarero Race Track near San Juan. Customers do not have to be present since bets are accepted at the betting agencies located throughout the island. Customers with the winning bets do not have to pay taxes in Puerto Rico. There are two types of lottery on the island. First, the lotto consists of choosing the correct six numbers out of forty-two possible number sequences. The weekly grand prize is guaranteed to be at least 1 million dollars. Winners of a grand prize can get their money spread over twenty years or request a lump-sum payment. Either way, taxes of almost 40 percent are common on these monetary awards. The other type of lottery consists of buying individual tickets from authorized agents. The weekly draw announces its winning results in the daily newspapers, and the grand prize is only expected to be roughly 750 dollars. Since the awards are lower, the winners are exempt from paying Puerto Rican taxes. These gambling possibilities are an attraction for both tourists and the local population.

NIGHTLIFE

The entertainment does not stop when the sun goes down. Puerto Rico has endless possibilities in the way of formal venues, where tickets are required to be purchased; dancing clubs, where a cover charge is required; and bars and cafés, where live entertainment is virtually free. San Juan offers many choices for experiences in opera, ballet, and classical music. In San Juan, the Luis A. Ferré Performing Arts Center, locally known as Bellas Artes, has three theaters, and it routinely brings local and international stars to its popular stages. The Puerto Rico Symphony Orchestra is well known throughout the Caribbean for its outstanding musicians and performs a season of concerts from September to May. Multiple locations in bars and restaurants offer live music performances to entertain their clientele. The government-regulated casinos offer elegant gambling options in the resort areas, but they are not limited to the registered guests at the hotel. Everyone is welcome.

The areas surrounding university neighborhoods often have a kind of bohemian lifestyle that is attractive to nonstudents as well. The entertainment options often include new local musical bands trying out their material in the local cafés and bookstores. A good example is the academic neighborhood of Río Piedras, a suburb in the southern part of San Juan. This is the site of the expansive campus of the Universidad de Puerto Rico. The student population here actively supports the entertainment available in bars and restaurants in the surrounding streets. Quite often, they offer very energetic performances of music and dance that are easily accessible to anyone supporting those establishments. While these areas attract up-and-coming talent, they are usually not visited by too many tourists, as tourists tend to stay close to the resort areas.

Ponce has its own southern charm, and the small city is known as the cultural capital of Puerto Rico. Being a smaller city, the local people have a reputation for being friendlier than those on the crowded streets of San Juan. At night, there are at least two casinos that offer gambling possibilities. Several nightclubs offer the latest in dancing options both in Puerto Rican music as well as more modern techno music. However, there are simpler alternatives. The city also has a rich cultural program, with the Banda Municipal de Ponce offering free outdoor concerts on weekends.

MISS UNIVERSE COMPETITIONS

Puerto Ricans take beauty pageants seriously. The government actively supports this competition even when it incurs a considerable cost to pay for the participation franchise fee, to promote the event, and to prepare the contestants properly. The participating women must be not only beautiful but also intelligent, well mannered, and cultured. Candidates are judged not only on swimsuit and evening gown competitions but also on providing thoughtful and articulate answers to predetermined questions that are global in nature. The pageant started in 1952, and it is currently owned by the Trump Organization in New York. The only four countries that have competed continuously since the beginning of the pageant are Germany, France, Canada, and the United States.

Puerto Rico competes in the Miss Universe events as an independent nation, and it is extremely successful. Out of all the countries in the world, only the United States has won more Miss Universe competitions than Puerto Rico. As of 2008, Venezuela shares second place with Puerto Rico. While the United States has dominated this international competition, the rivalry between Puerto Rico and Venezuela is often discussed in the gossip magazines and popular culture of Latin America. In chronological order, the five Miss Universe previous title holders from Puerto Rico are Marisol Malaret Contreras (1970), Deborah Carthy Deu (1985), Dayanara Torres (1993), Denise Quiñones (2001), and Zuleyka Jerris Rivera Mendoza (2006). That makes at least one winner every decade. In addition, Puerto Rico has hosted the Miss Universe pageant three times, in the cities of Dorado (1972), Bayamón (2001), and San Juan (2002). These events bring considerable attention to the island, which is converted into tourism dollars and jobs for the local economy.

WOMEN

The success of Puerto Rican women is not limited to beauty pageants. Popular media currently make accessible information on outstanding *boricua* actresses, writers, athletes, scientists, musicians, businesswomen, and politicians. However, several Puerto Rican women had the courage and determination to be pioneers in many fields that opened the doors for future generations of women, and Hispanics in general. One famous Puerto Rican entertainer is Rita Moreno, one of a handful of performers who have earned all the awards available in the field. She has won a Tony, an Oscar, a Grammy, and an Emmy. She still continues to act and perform in television shows, movies, and Broadway plays.

A little known fact is that Puerto Rican women have a long tradition of serving in the U.S. military forces. Dr. Dolores Piñero, born in San Juan, was the first female doctor to serve in the U.S. Army in 1918. She was initially rejected, but she was approved to enlist at the beginning of World War I. She was initially assigned to work in a military hospital in San Juan as an anesthesiologist. Then she was put in charge of opening a new hospital in Ponce that would focus on influenza patients. Ever since then, a long list of women have enlisted to serve in different branches of the U.S. military. Recently, they have also participated in both Operations Desert Storm and Desert Shield in the Middle East. As of early 2008, at least four Puerto Rican women had been killed in battlefields in Iraq and Afghanistan. Their names have been engraved onto the Monument of Remembrance dedicated to local soldiers who have died in service. This monument is proudly located in front of the capitol building in San Juan.

Puerto Rican women have certainly excelled in politics as well. For example, Felisa Rincón de Gautier served as the first female mayor of San Juan for twenty-two years (1946–1968). She was the first female mayor of a capital city decades before any other city in the Western Hemisphere would do something similar. She also created a series of preschool educational centers in Puerto Rico called Las Escuelas Maternales. The curriculum of these schools was such a success that it eventually became the foundation of the Head Start program in the United States. As of 2008, San Juan has had only two female mayors. The second was Sila Marí Calderón. She was also the first woman ever elected as governor of Puerto Rico, in 2000. She had previously also held other government positions, including secretary of state (which has the responsibilities of a lieutenant governor) and chief of staff. During her tenure as governor, she advocated and negotiated a withdrawal of U.S. military troops from Puerto Rico. Another outstanding politician emerging from the field of medicine, Antonia Novello had a successful medical practice in pediatrics, when she was recruited to serve in one of the highest positions in the U.S. government. President George H. W. Bush appointed her to the post of surgeon general of the United States in 1990. She was the first Hispanic woman ever to hold such a post, which she held for thirteen years, until 2003. During her time in this federal position, she was a strong advocate for the health needs of children, promoting immunization campaigns and holding a strong position against underaged drinking. On leaving the office of surgeon general, she served as a representative for health and nutrition for the United Nations Children's Fund.

There are, of course, thousands of Puerto Rican women who are not famous but are extremely hardworking. Since the 1980s, a growing number of women no longer stay home to raise children. Women have joined the workforce with full momentum, and many more have also obtained university training. This trend has changed the environment and dynamics of Puerto Rican families. The high cost of living has also made it commonplace to have both parents working as joint heads of household. The situation is increasingly more difficult for single mothers.

Women in Puerto Rico have fought hard for their rights, including equality in the workplace, suffrage, and the right to choose what to do with their bodies. Since the 1960s, the government has advocated the use of different contraceptive methods because it is keenly aware that large families affect the quality of life. Several health clinics throughout the island distribute free condoms and educate teenagers on the consequences of their sexual acts. These policies, of course, face constant criticism from conservative groups and the Roman Catholic Church. In addition, abortion is also legal in Puerto Rico. The only other place in the Caribbean that allows it is Cuba.

Despite the giant social steps taken, the struggles for women in Puerto Rico are not over. Just like in other countries, businesses are still mostly dominated by male executives, most politicians are still men, and there is an overall feeling of machismo professed by many Puerto Rican men.

FAMILY LIFE, MARRIAGE, AND RITES OF PASSAGE

Respect for family members is one of the pillars of Puerto Rican culture. Families have strong bonds that include extended family members such as uncles, aunts, godparents, and grandparents. Raising children is often done with a strong support network in which nuclear and extended family members participate in reinforcing a strong pride in cultural traditions. For example, one crucial aspect of *boricua* culture is its pride in the Spanish language. The extended family is critical in exposing children to the richness and beauty of Puerto Rico's native tongue. The goal is to transfer the language to the next generation. Puerto Ricans have seen what happens to children whose families migrate to the United States for extended periods of time: they gradually lose their use of Spanish. Puerto Ricans are strong advocates of bilingualism, but not at the expense of losing Spanish.

Currently family size is often linked to the parents' level of education and income projections. While middle-class families with professional parents have a tendency to have only two or three children, it is more common for low-income families to have five or six children. Another factor determining smaller families is the large number of women currently working full-time, especially in the cities.

One social event that always brings extended family together is a wedding. While traditional weddings are extensive family affairs, many young Puerto Rican couples are now opting for smaller and more private weddings. In addition, a growing number of tourists travel to Puerto Rico to celebrate their weddings and stay there for the honeymoon. The legal age for marriage in Puerto Rico is eighteen years, but it is possible to get married younger with parental consent (fourteen to seventeen for girls, and sixteen to seventeen for boys). The exception is that an underaged girl who is certifiably pregnant may get married without parental consent or approval. In all instances, blood tests are mandatory, and they must be certified by a doctor licensed to practice medicine in Puerto Rico. Weddings usually generate tremendous enthusiasm, but official government statistics show that almost 50 percent of marriages in Puerto Rico end up in divorce. This standard is comparable to the U.S. rate but is high in relation to other Latin American countries, and it is even higher for those with predominantly Roman Catholic populations.

The ethnic fusion that has occurred in Puerto Rico promotes a social atmosphere of tolerance and mutual respect, including the acceptance of a sizable gay population. There is, of course, a segment of society that reflects the conservative macho attitudes often prevalent in Latin American countries. In the midst of these two groups, in January 2008, Puerto Rico prepared to hold a referendum to ban same-sex marriage. Resolution 99, as it was commonly known, would in fact create an amendment to the Puerto Rican Constitution to define marriage as only allowable between a man and a woman. Civil rights groups argued that the proposal is discriminatory against the gay population. Moreover, this amendment, as originally proposed, meant that the law would not recognize civil unions and domestic partnerships or assign marital status to unmarried couples. These collateral consequences would affect a significant number of the population since, according to the 2000 Census, 53 percent of Puerto Rican couples live together without being married. Despite the opposition of civil rights organizations, the governor of Puerto Rico declared that he was willing to sign the new legislation. However, the measure died in the Puerto Rican House of Representatives when it failed to gather enough votes in June 2008. At least for this legislative term, there is no amendment to the Puerto Rican Constitution.

Quinceañera: A Right of Passage

The tradition of celebrating a woman reaching fifteen years of age in Puerto Rico began centuries ago. The indigenous people commemorated a woman's transition from childhood toward independence by taking her from her family so she could learn the history and traditions of her local tribe. Originally, this event was a festive but simple gathering. Then, the arrival of the Europeans in the 1500s transformed the celebration into something more formal. By the 1800s, the *quinceañera* festivities looked like a ballroom event. Once most of the population became Roman Catholic, a special Mass was included as part of the religious traditions. Nowadays, most young women wear white or light pastel formal dresses to celebrate their coming of age.

Music is a crucial component of the festivities. The first dance is a waltz reserved for the girl's father. He then proceeds to present his daughter as a young woman to the invited guests. Then, the *quinceañera's* court of fourteen boys and girls join her on the dance floor before ushering in the rest of the guests. They usually dance to a more modern and upbeat song.

FOOD AND DRINK

Food is a fundamental ingredient of Puerto Rican culture. Local cuisine reflects the island's history and is the result of an ethnic fusion that has evolved over centuries. The dining room table is also used as an informal classroom to show children important aspects of social and cultural interactions. Food (like music) is also a crucial component of most festivals and carnivals around the island, which take place year-round. The unique Caribbean food that has been perfected in Puerto Rico is locally known as *cocina criolla* (Creole cooking). It blends the influences of Taíno, Spanish, African, and even American tastes and ingredients. Rice, beans, and plantains are the basic staple food items in Puerto Rico. While multiple spices are used to develop a distinctive taste, Puerto Rican food is not hot and spicy like its Mexican counterpart.

Two basic components of most Puerto Rican dishes are *sofrito* and plantains. *Sofrito* is a seasoning sauce made with cured bacon or ham, garlic, green peppers, coriander, chili, cilantro, and onions, all sautéed in cooking oil. The sauce is then poured on top of rice or meat. A truly Caribbean ingredient typically used in Puerto Rican food is *plátanos,* or plantains. They are cut while still green, and they are fried, boiled, roasted, and sometimes even baked. The famous *tostones* are slices of plantains that are fried and typically served as a side dish with rice, *sofrito,* and a meat dish. The leaves of these plantains are never wasted since they are also used to wrap food items that will later be baked or boiled.

There is an indispensable item in every Puerto Rican kitchen: the *caldero.* This is a cauldron or kettle made of either aluminum or iron, with a round bottom. Some of the main meat dishes, such as *arroz con pollo* (rice with chicken), require the use of this *caldero* to obtain their unique flavor. Other typical meat dishes also include *mondongo,* made with small pieces of tripe and cooked in *sofrito* sauce, and *asopao,* a popular gumbo stew made with chicken and rice. For a more festive occasion, such as Christmas, *lechón asado* (barbecued pig) is a favorite dish. It is roasted for a few hours and served with *aji-li-moli* sauce, made with vinegar, olive oil, and chili peppers.

While almost 70 percent of the food consumed is imported into the island, Puerto Rican desserts, coffee, and rum are based on truly local ingredients. Most desserts, such as bread pudding and *arroz con dulce,* include the use of locally grown coconuts. Since there is an abundant supply of tropical fruits in the island, they are always used as healthy and yet mouth-watering desserts. Puerto Ricans also enjoy both the aroma and flavor of strong coffee. Even though its production has diminished for export purposes, it is still locally grown to satisfy the needs of hearty coffee appetites on the island. The sugar industry virtually disappeared by the late 1800s, but the production of rum left in Puerto Rico a tangible connection to its sugar-producing past. It is commonly accepted that Juan Ponce de León first introduced rum to the island during the early 1500s. Today, rum is definitely the national drink, and it is used as the basic ingredient in myriad alcoholic drinks. The most recognizable brand of rum produced on the island is Bacardi, and it is still a very profitable enterprise in Puerto Rico. Actually, more than 70 percent of the rum consumed in the United States is supplied by several Puerto Rican rum companies and distilleries.

Snacks purchased from *friquitines* (street vendors) or casual shops are extremely popular in Puerto Rico. Surrounded by water, the island produces a lot of fish, so *bacalaítos fritos* (deep-fried pieces of codfish) are almost as popular as *alcapurrias* (croquettes filled with pork or beef). The turnovers known as *pastelitos* are filled with deep-fried cheese and meat. However, nothing makes for a more refreshing snack on a hot day than *piraguas,* a cone of shaved ice topped with syrup of tropical flavors such as papaya, tamarind, coconut, and guava.

Nowadays, cooks and chefs get numerous requests for vegetarian and vegan dishes. The *comida criolla* already has a few traditional meatless dishes such as *arroz con gandules* (rice with king peas), *arroz con habichelas* (rice with beans), and fresh tropical fruit for dessert. These dishes are widely available everywhere on the island. However, while chefs in upscale resorts know that a dish without meat is not necessarily vegan, this may not be the case in small local restaurants, especially in rural areas. These apparently vegetarian dishes are often prepared with butter and pork lard.

Since the majority of food is imported onto the island, eating habits and culinary traditions have also been influenced by outside flavors and methods of cooking. Perhaps the most noticeable foreign influence are the American chains of fast food that have flooded all cities and towns in Puerto Rico in the past two decades. Fast-food restaurants are now favorite places not only for teenagers but also for busy adults, and even entire families. Thus the *comida criolla* is slowly being relegated to home cooking, and going out to eat now also includes options like pizza, hamburgers, hot dogs, and fried chicken. In addition, the fast pace of life in the cities sometimes leaves little time for cooking at home, and even staples like *sofrito* sauce are now sold in a can. On the other hand, there is a recent interest in promoting healthy seafood cooked using fresh and flavorful ingredients and preparing it grilled, rather than fried. With the rich variety of culinary choices on the island, it is a wonder that Puerto Rican cuisine is not yet internationally well known.

HOLIDAYS AND FESTIVALS

Puerto Rico's history is reflected in its holidays. The festivities celebrate a mixture of regional heroes, African roots, Hispanic heritage, religious fervor, nationalistic aspirations, and the official U.S. federal holidays. The celebrations specifically related to Puerto Rico's historical events include the

Monument to the abolition of slavery in 1873, Ponce. Photo courtesy of the author.

Abolition of Slavery Day on March 22, Luis Muñoz Rivera's Day on the third Monday in July, Constitution Day on July 25, José Celso Barbosa's Day on July 27, the Discovery of the New World on October 8, and the Discovery of Puerto Rico on November 19. The religious holidays are mostly related to the island's Roman Catholic heritage such as Christmas, Good Friday, and Easter. However, Puerto Ricans also celebrate the *Día de los Tres Reyes Magos* (Day of the Three Wise Men) on January 6. This is a festive event designated for children to receive toys.

Holidays based on Puerto Rico's relationship to the United States include Martin Luther King Day in January, President's Day in February, Memorial Day in May, U.S. Independence Day on July 4, Labor Day in September, and both Veteran's Day and Thanksgiving in November.

Festivals and Carnivals

In the early 1500s, the Spanish Crown gave a mandate to the conquistadores and settlers: impose the Spanish language and the Roman Catholic religion in all new colonies, and so the Spanish Catholic influence left a strong imprint in Puerto Rican traditions. To this day, every town celebrates its patron saint with a festival. These *fiestas patronales* (patron saint festivities) are usually held in a central location like the main plaza or near the relevant church or cathedral. They have a family ambiance with a carnival-like arrangement that includes food, music, dance, and children's games.

The Fiesta de Santiago, or the Loíza *fiesta patronal*, is perhaps the best-attended cultural event on the entire island, but mostly by local families and not necessarily by tourists. Currently the area of Loíza (about twenty-five miles southeast of San Juan) has one of the largest concentrations of blacks in Puerto Rico. This area is a relatively poor agricultural municipality, where the African heritage is very visible. The celebration is spread over nine days, starting at the end of July and concluding in early August. It is a festival dedicated to the patron saint of the town: St. James the Moor Slayer. He became the saint selected by the Yoruba slaves in Loíza after the Spanish friars forced them to convert to Christianity. At that time, slaves were forbidden from worshipping their Yoruba African *orishas,* or gods. The image of St. James as a mighty warrior reminded the slaves of their powerful god Changó. By adopting this patron, the slaves pretended to worship St. James, but they were really paying homage to Changó, right in front of the Spaniards. The colorful festivities include drummers, singers, parades, brightly designed costumes, the traditional *plena* music, and masks carved out of coconut husks with devil-type designs. A similar type of mask is also produced in Ponce but is created out of papier-mâché, using the same scary designs with multiple horns, big eyes, and bright colors.

The concept of cultural tourism has grown into a full industry in Puerto Rico. A tangible example is the Le Lo Lai Festival. The choreographed program offers folkloric dances that reflect the mix of indigenous, African, and Spanish heritages of the island. It also includes traditional musical performances that include *plena, bomba,* and salsa. Overall, this commercial show is designed to make cultural events easily available to both the tourist industry and the local population. The shows are offered a few times a week. The large numbers of foreign tourists who either begin or end cruise ship vacations in San Juan have responded well to this colorful display of Puerto Rican culture.

Barranquitas (Little Mud Slides) is a picturesque mountain town in the center of Puerto Rico. It is lush with vegetation and artistic talent. It is precisely here that the annual Feria Nacional de Artesanías (National Arts and Crafts Fair) takes place, which is perhaps the most important artisans' fair on the island. It attracts over two hundred artists to display a range of arts and crafts ranging from paintings, pottery, and carvings to textiles. Like most other

Traditional mask from Ponce. Photo courtesy of the author.

festivals in Puerto Rico, food and music cannot be missing from the scene. The festival offers a lively family atmosphere that attracts both *boricuas* and tourists. Once here, people discover that this was the birth place of Luis Muñoz Rivera and his son Luis Muñoz Marín, two of the most important historical figures in the political structure of Puerto Rico. Rivera is well known for working on the commonwealth arrangement that Puerto Rico now has with the United States. His son Marín was the first elected governor in the history of Puerto Rico. They both left a political legacy that is still acknowledged today.

HEALTH

Health conditions in Puerto Rico have improved dramatically since the United States took over the island in 1898. Before that time, Spain had not invested in a comprehensive medical package for the majority of the population. The United States encountered an island with a few rich families, but the majority of the population was poor and did not have adequate nutritional levels. In fact, after Puerto Ricans received U.S. citizenship in 1917, they often opted to sign up for military service to escape the island's chronic lack of opportunity; however, almost 80 percent of Puerto Ricans failed to pass the basic medical exam to join the military. After the 1930s and 1940s, the Puerto Rican diet included more balanced meals and began to improve the overall health of the population, particularly among children and the elderly.

Nowadays, most of the health care offered to the population of Puerto Rico is covered by medical insurance offered by employers or the government. For low-income families, Puerto Rico offers Medical to subsidize medical bills. In the 1990s, the government explored more ways to address the health needs of the island's almost 2 million people (half the island's population) who did not have health insurance. These people typically relied on publicly funded hospitals, but they often had to wait weeks for an appointment, and even months for actual treatment.

In 2004, the government of Puerto Rico developed legislation to adopt the controversial Puerto Rico Health Reform, simply known as La Reforma. This proposal advocated selling the government-run hospitals to private investors and implementing a low-cost insurance plan for needy individuals. It also requested that a patient's bill of rights be approved. The plan was implemented in 2005, and it provided health coverage to most Puerto Ricans who could not afford it previously. It also included a special feature in which doctors cannot legally be restricted from discussing all the treatment options available to their patients. The health insurance companies usually attempt to institute this so-called gag order on doctors, but the Puerto Rican legislature made specific provisions to avoid it. However, further detailed analysis revealed that the program quickly incurred extraordinary costs that were not predicted in advance. These expenses contributed to an unforeseen deficit in government spending that forced the government to shut down for two weeks in 2006 because it was unable to meet its basic payments and payroll obligations. Ever since then, there have been more requests by local legislators to impose closer scrutiny of the health expenses incurred by the health reform and stricter controls over the quality of care offered to the population intended to benefit from such services.

EDUCATION

Puerto Rico has one of the highest levels of literacy in the Caribbean since 94 percent of the population knows at least how to read and write. While this is certainly an accomplishment, only 60 percent of students obtain a high school diploma. This means that the dropout rate is extremely high, at 40 percent. In comparison, the average completion rate for high school for the fifty states of the U.S. mainland is 80.4 percent. This comparative view places

Puerto Rico as the fourth or fifth worst in educational achievement in the United States.

Since 1948, public education in Puerto Rico is administered by a regional commissioner of education, appointed by the governor. The overall responsibility for providing free and nonreligious education rests on the Departamento de Educación de Puerto Rico, which employs over forty-seven thousand teachers. Education is mandatory from elementary grades all the way through high school. In addition, there are private schools in Puerto Rico that are almost completely managed by religious groups, especially the Catholic Church. Both private and public schools must be accredited by the same body that regulates educational standards on the island.

One crucial difference with the United States is that all instruction in public schools is done in Spanish, but English as a second language is required at all levels from kindergarten through the twelfth grade. This was not always the acceptable practice. When the United States took over Puerto Rico in 1898, English was established as the language of instruction. However, in 1915, Spanish was added as one of the two official languages of Puerto Rico. Ever since then, Spanish has been the standard medium of delivery. The exceptions are a handful of private schools that conduct all their curricula in English and teach Spanish as a foreign language.

Recently, public schools on the island have begun to experience an interesting trend. There are families of Puerto Ricans who are returning to the island to settle down or retire after having lived in the United States for a long time. These families are coming back with children who do not speak Spanish, so the school district finds itself in the position of teaching Spanish to *boricua* children who never learned it at home while living on the mainland.

The large teachers' union staged powerful protests in January 2008, requesting better salaries, smaller classes, and repairs of neglected facilities. Currently teachers make an average of 19,200 dollars a year at all levels from kindergarten through high school. This salary is much lower than in the United States, and the problem is compounded because the cost of living in Puerto Rico is actually higher than in most places in the United States. The threat of an island-wide strike is not taken lightly since Puerto Rican law explicitly prohibits the disruption of the public education system, so teachers who go on strike could actually be legally fired. Since their needs and concerns have not been resolved, the teachers' union staged another massive march in July 2008 right in front of La Fortaleza, the governor's mansion. Their contractual details have yet to be resolved.

Puerto Rico has over fifty institutions of higher learning, including universities and community colleges. The largest public institution is the University of Puerto Rico, with a multicampus system that covers most of the main cities on the island. Its main campus is located in Río Piedras, a suburb of San Juan. The Inter-American University is a private college system with eleven campuses in the principal cities of Puerto Rico. In addition, there are specialized universities that focus on careers such as the Escuela de Medicina de San Juan Bautista, the Ponce School of Medicine, and the Music Conservatory of Puerto Rico. There are also two community colleges with specialized majors: the Instituto de Banca y Comercio (Institute of Banking and Commerce) and the Ponce Paramedical College. Despite the large numbers of universities and educational opportunities, the reality is that many recent college graduates cannot find professional jobs on the island. Consequently, Puerto Rico suffers from terrible emigration of educated youth, who leave for the U.S. mainland in search of a better future.

References

Associated Press. "Puerto Rico Governor Allows Referendum against Gay Marriage." *USA Today,* January 24, 2008.

Díaz de Villegas, José Luis. *Puerto Rico: Grand Cuisine of the Caribbean.* San Juan: University of Puerto Rico Press, 2004.

Fontañez, Edwin. *The Vejigante and the Folk Festivals of Puerto Rico.* Arlington, VA: Exit Studios, 1994.

Thompson, Donald, and Annie Thompson. *Music and Dance in Puerto Rico from the Age of Columbus to Modern Times.* Lanham, MD: Scarecrow Press, 1991.

Van Hyning, Thomas E. *The Santurce Crabbers: Sixty Seasons of Puerto Rican Winter League Baseball.* Jefferson, NC: McFarland, 1999.

Web Sites

Music of Puerto Rico, http://www.musicofpuertorico.com/. Web site with detailed explanations of the development of all kinds of Puerto Rican music.

Puerto Rican Food, http://www.gotopuertorico.com/puerto-rico-gastronomy.php. Web site with a useful history of the food and drink of Puerto Rico plus useful recipes.

Salsa Roots, http://www.salsaroots.org/. Web site with helpful articles on the history and development of salsa music and dance.

5

Broadcasting and Print Media

Puerto Rico has a long tradition of disseminating information in all media formats, including printed materials, radio broadcasting, and television programming. While English films, music, and news are important options for *boricuas,* most of the programs offered by radio and television stations on the island are actually done in Spanish. There is a rich history of how printed media developed during the Spanish colonial period (1493–1898), a process that included both advantages and perils. Then, the arrival of the United States after the Spanish-American War in 1898 opened the doors to dozens of new newspapers on the island. It was also during the early 1900s that Puerto Rico experienced the introduction of radio, telegraph, and television. It has certainly been a long journey of hard work and innovation. Currently the Constitution of Puerto Rico, adopted in 1952, protects freedom of expression and the press. More specifically, article II, section 4, clearly states that "no law should be made abridging the freedom of speech or the press." In addition, most of Puerto Rico's media are privately owned; hence the government has little control over content and possible censorship.

Recent technological advances are improving all communication media, and are also offering new challenges and opportunities. Several newspapers and magazines now offer online versions of their products. Television stations also release expanded video and information service via their Web sites. This option provides news updates with an incredible speed not widely available until the last decade. Furthermore, there are now academic and literary journals that exist exclusively in electronic format.

PRINT MEDIA

Newspapers and the Spanish Colonial Period (1493–1898)

The first newspaper published on the island appeared on December 31, 1806. It was called *La Gaceta de Puerto Rico,* and it was printed exclusively in Spanish. Initially, it was only four pages in length, and it was available twice a week, on Wednesdays and Saturdays. The Spanish governor at the time, Toribio Montes, was aware that Puerto Rico was way behind neighboring Cuba in publishing materials, especially since Havana had already been producing newspapers since the 1760s. So, he took to the task of importing the first printing press into the island just a few months before the first publication of *La Gaceta* appeared to the public in 1806. He purchased the printing press from a Frenchman named Delarue, and it is recorded that it came from the United States. Soon after the arrival of the press, the task of publishing *La Gaceta* became the priority for the Spanish government in Puerto Rico. While the Archive of the Indies in Sevilla has many samples of *La Gaceta* in its early printing days, the original version of December 31, 1806, cannot be found anywhere—either in Spain or Puerto Rico. The earliest original copy of this paper currently available dates back to Thursday, August 3, 1809. It is labeled as volume 4, number 29. By counting backward, it can be corroborated that the original publication date was in December 1806.

While publishing newspapers is an important cultural asset, the Spanish colonial government also quickly realized the potential danger of the printed media. The beginning of the nineteenth century was historically a period of social upheaval for Spain. For example, Napoléon Bonaparte took over the Iberian Peninsula and installed his brother José Napoleon as king of Spain. The American colonies were unsure what these events meant for them since they owed allegiance to the Spanish monarchy. Soon after, most of the territories in the Americas declared their independence from Spain in the decade of 1810. What followed were fifteen years of bloody battles, which resulted in the independence of most of the current countries from Mexico all the way south to Chile and Argentina. By 1825, the Spanish Crown only had two remaining colonies in the Western Hemisphere: Cuba and Puerto Rico. At the time, Puerto Rico remained a loyal colony to Spain. It was a period of economic prosperity because the Spanish overseas markets were now almost exclusively open to these two islands. It was a tremendously profitable decade at the height of the sugar industry in the 1840s and 1850s. So, Spain developed an ambivalent policy of trying to improve the social conditions of Puerto Rico, while simultaneously attempting to control its growth and development. The goal was to restrain the potential momentum of independence ideas. Given the chaos that the wars of independence created among the Spanish government structure, it is not surprising that many records were either displaced or destroyed, including the first publication of *La Gaceta de Puerto Rico* from 1806.

One of the basic social improvements that Spain established in Puerto Rico was the development of a literacy program. The first educational institution established for the purpose of improving reading and writing skills was founded in 1851. It was named the *Academia Real de Bellas Artes,* and it was intended to train teachers, organize writing competitions, and develop a comprehensive curriculum to improve literacy among the population.

Journalism of Resistance

Literacy is a basic requirement to be able to develop a wide readership of books and newspapers. However, it could also be a potential danger for an imperial power since printed materials make it easy to promulgate ideas to a wide segment of the population. For example, the Spanish Crown banned a book written by Eugenio M. de Hostos titled *The Pilgrimage of Bayoán* because it included a message of resistance against the colonial government. When messages of opposition were published in the local newspapers, the Spanish government also tried to suppress their publication and censure their content. For example, in August 1867, the local government of San Juan authorized a law that required newspaper owners to obtain a specific license and pay a substantial fee to serve as a deposit that they could lose if their newspaper continued to publish antigovernment materials. There was strong popular opposition to this measure, and it was somewhat overturned two years later.

In January 1869, the Spanish governor of Puerto Rico, Laureano Sanz, approved the policy that newspapers could openly question the government. The local rulers sensed an air of potential rebellion, and they decided to offer small concessions disguised as benevolent social gestures. The only requirement was that if newspapers wanted to exercise the option of criticizing the government, they had to pay a small fee for that privilege.

It turns out that Spain did have something to worry about after all. Puerto Rico's plan to obtain independence in 1868 erupted as the Grito de Lares (Shout of Lares), an unsuccessful rebellion organized by Manuel Rojas that took place in the central town of Lares but only lasted a few days. Spain quickly squashed that movement and sent Rojas into exile. Following that uprising, the new governor, Gabriel Baldrich, overturned all the liberal policies offered to the printed media. The journalists started to organize themselves, and the result was the Puerto Rican Press Association, formed in 1891 in the capital city of San Juan. For the remainder of the Spanish colonial period until 1898, numerous newspapers continued to advocate for the independence of Puerto

Rico—it just never came. Instead, another foreign power took over in 1898: the United States.

Bilingual Print Media

The arrival of the United States sparked the creation of dozens of new magazines and newspapers. Some of the most successful newspapers in English, founded in 1901, included the *Puerto Rico Herald* and *El Tiempo*. They took a specific position with regard to the political status of the island: the first advocated a model of self-government for Puerto Rico, and the second was an active supporter of converting the island into another state. Without the restrictions of the Spanish colonial government, the growth of local writers and editors presaged a wealth of opportunities for newspapers in both Spanish and English. While dozens of new ventures failed and disappeared quickly, three respectable newspapers dominated most of the twentieth century: *El Mundo, El Nuevo Día,* and the *San Juan Star. El Mundo* newspaper ran in circulation from 1919 until 1990. It offered a conservative point of view, and it was widely recognized as the best source of news at the time. *El Nuevo Día* came into the Puerto Rican scene shortly after *El Mundo* disappeared. It is still today one of the papers with the largest membership available on the island. Its marketing efforts make it very profitable since it draws about 20 percent of its income from its public circulation; the remaining 80 percent comes from advertising.

In 1959, the *San Juan Star* was created by William Dorvellier, a highly respected journalist and editor. His initial aim was to target an English-speaking audience that was economically active on the island. In addition, Dorvellier won the Pulitzer Prize for Journalism in 1960 for his coverage of how the Catholic Church intervened in the political elections of that year. The *San Juan Star* remains the only daily newspaper published in English, and the only one that can claim to be a Pulitzer Prize–winning paper in Puerto Rico. Seeking to expand on their respectability and business model, the paper started a Spanish version in 1997. The goal was to develop a network of regional papers outside of San Juan. The *Star* brand now includes *El Ponce Star, El Mayagüez Star, El Arecibo Star, El Star Extra,* and the *San Juan Weekend.* The paper has increased its revenue by offering the motto "Seis por uno" (six for the price of one), meaning that customers pay to post one announcement in the classified ads, and it will appear printed in all six papers in the network. This approach had proven extremely popular with the business community because it could reach regional markets outside of the capital city of San Juan by using a newspaper of proven quality. However, after operating uninterrupted for more than fifty years, the *San Juan Star* closed its doors in August 2008 citing unreasonable labor disputes with the worker's union. Apparently, the newspaper had been losing money for a few months, and the union leaders refused to concede to benefit cuts and layoffs. Rather than face complete bankruptcy, the paper was shut down, leaving a void in the English-language news print in Puerto Rico.

The business community is also well informed in Puerto Rico. The island has a dynamic economy, and San Juan is considered one of the best cities in which to carry out business ventures in Latin America. Actually, a recent article in the *San Juan Star* reported that the city of San Juan ranked as the city with the lowest overall tax burden for corporations and multinational businesses in the United States and another nine Latin American countries (Alvarado Vega 2008). Since many U.S. firms have large investments in Puerto Rico, especially pharmaceutical and textile companies, it is imperative for publications to provide updated and specific information. Due to the island's special relationship with the United States, most of the business and economic publications appear in English. One of the leading sources of information for the business sector is the *Caribbean Business Weekly.* It published its first issue in 1975 and has an approximate circulation of fifty thousand per week, distributed throughout countries in the Caribbean. It provides detailed and updated analyses on financial data, commercial ventures, real estate opportunities, and industrial trends. Another extremely useful publication covering the business world is the *Puerto Rico Business Review.* This magazine is published only four times a year, and it includes detailed articles that address the economic development possibilities on the island. In such capacity, it offers information for business executives on tax incentives, infrastructure updates, plans for job creation, and updated tourism statistics.

In addition to the daily papers, Puerto Rico currently offers twenty-one weekly newspapers and another eight papers published on a monthly basis. As a general practice, most Spanish newspapers on the island employ a large number of translators, who work immediately on stories as soon as they are sent to them by the Associated Press.

Cultural Magazines and Academic Journals

There seems to be a magazine dedicated to every human interest. Puerto Rico offers a large variety of cultural publications that cover contemporary topics like music, arts, sports, food, festivals, outdoor activities, entertainment, and travel. While there are an endless number of magazines available, the main cultural publications can be separated into three categories: (1) publications used as references for upcoming cultural events, (2) academic journals dedicated to cultural commentary and analysis, and (3) magazines specifically designed to promote local tourism activities. The first type includes *PulsoRock* and *Vea,* which distribute entertainment news. *El Cuarto de*

Quenepón is a publication in Spanish devoted to the latest cultural festivities in Puerto Rico. *El Boricua* is also an extremely popular bilingual monthly magazine with regional events available throughout the island. For food aficionados, *Tables* is a magazine dedicated to reviews of various restaurants in Puerto Rico, edited by Brabara Tasch. It features traditional *comida criolla* (local Puerto Rican food) and international cuisine.

The second category includes the academic journals published in Puerto Rico. They tend to cater to a more sophisticated level of cultural analysis, literary critique, and scientific emphasis. They are usually published by local universities and professional organizations and include articles based on research materials, in-depth articles, literary theory, and artistic discourse. Some of the literary journals include *Revista a Propósito* and *Añil*. Two popular choices for poetry aficionados are *Guajana* and *Letras Salvajes*. For more specific literary connoisseurs, the journal *Desde el Límite* offers a specific focus on the famous literature produced by the "Generation of 1980" in Puerto Rico. Another three journals that cater to specific professions are the law review titled *Revista del Colegio de Abogados,* the journal with a focus on computer and information science called *Simbiosis,* and the psychology journal *La Catársis de Quirón*. The magazine *Homines* offers a social science approach and articles on the Caribbean, but with emphasis on Puerto Rico. *Puerto Rico en Breve* is a popular choice for readers who want a journal with an emphasis on short articles related to history and culture.

Puerto Rico was the host of a recent conference on academic and literary journals throughout Latin America. The meeting took place in February 2005, and it attracted a large number of writers, editors, and graphic artists from Puerto Rico and abroad to discuss the future of these journals. One of the general goals for the organizing committee in the town of Humacao was to unify all the regional cultural journals under the umbrella of the Asociación de Revistas Culturales Puertorriqueñas. This group would include both popular cultural magazines and academic journals. The next step would be to ask to be affiliated to the larger organization of Federación Iberoamericana de Revistas Culturales (FIRC), or the Iberoamerican Federation of Cultural Magazines. Currently FIRC is managed by the Asociación de Revistas Culturales de España (ARCE)—the Association of Spanish Cultural Magazines. The goal of both ARCE and FIRC is to offer access to all the cultural magazines from the Spanish-speaking world, using its Web site as a portal to manage a central location for information. The current member magazines explore cultural and intellectual expression through a variety of themes, including literature, politics, music, photography, art, architecture, and social sciences. The use of electronic magazines and journals offers tremendous advantages for Puerto Ricans interested in learning and contributing to the knowledge of cultural topics that unify Iberian and Latin American cultures.

Main office of the Puerto Rico Tourism Company in San Juan, in a renovated colonial building that used to be the San Juan Penitentiary. Photo courtesy of the author.

The tourism industry is a strong and crucial arm of the Puerto Rican economy. It offers jobs relating to hotels, management, restaurants, cultural events, and outdoor adventures. The Puerto Rico Tourism Company (PRTC) is certainly aware that many travelers are only on the island for a few days. This prospect makes the publication of tourism-related magazines a key factor in the local economy. The PRTC publishes; *Qué Pasa!* as a bimonthly magazine highlighting the travel options and cultural activities available in San Juan and the nearby areas. Other consistent magazines are *Bienvenidos*, *El Boricua*, *Puerto Rico Magazine*, and *Recondito*.

RADIO

"Esta es WKAQ, en San Juan, capital de Puerto Rico, la Isla del Encanto y donde se produce el major café" (This is WKAQ, in San Juan, capital of Puerto Rico, the Enchanted Island and where the best coffee is produced).

These were the first words transmitted on December 3, 1922, at the launching of the very first radio station in Puerto Rico, WKAQ. At that time, it was the fifth radio station in the world. When Joaquín Agusty Ramirez de Arellano spoke these words, he became the pioneer of radio in Puerto Rico. WKAQ was heard on 580 AM, and it became known as Radio el Mundo (the World). This communication medium became extremely popular, and new radio stations proliferated rapidly throughout the island. Many of them disappeared quickly in less than two years when they proved unsuccessful or were financially bankrupt. An important radio station was also operated by the U.S. Coast Guard for almost fifty years (1939–1988). It was not limited to military information; it offered valuable local information, such as regional news and weather reports, which was crucial during hurricane season, from late July to October. Currently, there is an English radio station in San Juan, WOSO, 1030 AM, which offers hurricane advisories for the entire Caribbean region, but with an emphasis on Puerto Rico.

In an attempt to preserve the heritage of the radio pioneers, Puerto Rico established the Museo de la Radio (Museum of Radio) in 1990. The goal was to preserve the information, equipment, technological advances, and relevant biographies related to the development of radio transmission in Puerto Rico. It is currently located within the Universidad of Sagrado Corazón (USC) in Santurce, a suburb of San Juan. USC is a private, Roman Catholic, nonprofit university with a general liberal arts approach to education. During the twentieth century, its modern campus evolved into an important center for broadcasting and media. For example, it also developed a comprehensive television production program to train students. In addition, USC has created partnerships with local cable companies to broadcast its own television station, Telesagrado (Sacred TV), the general goal of which is to offer educational programs.

The creative energy of Puerto Rican musicians has always been an important staple of radio programming. Music is an intrinsic part of everyday life on the island. It reflects the African, Spanish, and indigenous past combined with the new and exciting blends recently created by young musicians. While Cubans and Puerto Ricans debate who actually invented salsa music, there are a large number of radio stations that specialize in that genre. The network Radio Rumba promotes itself as "la emisora para los que saben de salsa" (the station for those who know about salsa). Its main transmission is offered as 1520 AM in San Juan, but it actually has five affiliate stations in Mayagüez, Ponce, and Barranquitas. Salsasoul is another network playing salsa, merengue, and other Latin rhythms using its three stations in the San Juan metropolitan area (98.5), the western part of Puerto Rico (100.3), and the southern part of the island (101.1). Some of the most popular artists on salsa stations include Tito

Puente, El Gan Combo de Puerto Rico, and Marc Anthony. The traditional dance music of *bomba* and *plena* trace their roots to West Africa and utilize drums as their basic instruments. These two rhythms are also widely played on radio stations since they have influenced the development of new melodies and dance patterns. In addition, stations also offer pop music with outstanding *boricua* artists like Cheyenne, José Feliciano, and Ricky Martin.

The latest musical creation to come out of Puerto Rico is *reggaeton*. It came to the world stage in 2005 with an incredible popular appeal and force. It blends reggae, dance hall, Spanish rap, and digital sound together with fiery lyrics that expose the poverty and hardships on the island. It is a new, underground sound created by Puerto Rican youth who grew up in poor slums like La Perla in San Juan. Initially, all *reggaeton* music was banned on Puerto Rican radio stations, and police would confiscate *reggaeton* CDs. Its lyrics were viewed as vulgar and insulting to women. When some of the creators of this genre finally decided to adapt their lyrics to be less aggressive—but still include social commentary—radio stations on the island started to provide airtime for their music. In 2005, the song that launched *reggaeton* into the acceptable mainstream music world was "La Gasolina" by singer Daddy Yankee. It spread like wildfire, and it became a popular tune in nightclubs in the Caribbean, the United States, and Europe. The racy dance style that came with it became also a new trend in dance music. Nowadays, there are several radio stations that play *reggaeton* exclusively. More artists like Tego Calderón, Daddy Yankee, and Ivy Queen have continued to produce material that elevates their level of musicianship and also validates their struggle.

The *reggaeton* movement also has a financial aspect to it. In May 2006, Reggaeton 94, a relatively new station with fewer than two years on the air, became Puerto Rico's top radio station, according to Arbirton +12, which publishes the listener ratings on the island. The station filled a void by targeting a specific demographic of young listeners, which then translated into advertising dollars coming from a variety of clients such as banks, restaurants, beer companies, and nightclubs.

According to the Central Intelligence Agency (CIA) World Factbook (https://www.cia.gov/library/publications/the-world-factbook/geos/rq. html), currently Puerto Rico has seventy-four AM radio stations and fifty-three FM stations. Radio programming enjoys the largest rate of media penetration on the island, with a rate of 98 percent; these figures are higher than television programming and newspaper distribution. This means that roughly 3.5 million people listen to radio stations on a regular basis. These numbers make radio a powerful medium for entertainment, information, and advertising.

TELEVISION

Since Puerto Rico is part of the United States, it has to follow the guidelines of the Federal Communications Commission (FCC). Since its beginning stages in the 1940s, Puerto Rico's television industry has been under the control of the FCC, and continues to be today. As of 2008, there were thirty-two regional television stations on the island. This number includes at least three religious stations that transmit evangelical programming and another three stations managed by U.S. military forces. In addition, Puerto Rico has four main cable companies: Digital TV One, Centennial de Puerto Rico, Adelphia, and Liberty Cablevisión de Puerto Rico. Despite the large number of stations available, three major stations began to dominate the television audience on the island in the 1950s: Telemundo (channel 2), Univisión (channel 11), and Televicentro or WAPA-TV (channel 4). These three stations have a rich history of being pioneers since they participated in the technological advances of broadcasting media in Puerto Rico.

The FCC issued a permit for the construction of the very first commercial television station in Puerto Rico in 1952 to El Mundo-TV. However, El Mundo-TV officially received its license from the FCC to broadcast information on channel 2 on February 12, 1954. After all the requirements were completed, it actually started offering regular programming on March 28, 1954. The first television show in Puerto Rico was called *Telenoticias,* a news show that has remained the staple of this station until today. This new television station was owned by Ángel Ramos, who also owned Radio El Mundo (WKAQ) and the *El Mundo* newspaper. To maintain a consistent brand name for all these products, El Mundo-TV became known as Telemundo, a name that is still used today. During the 1970s and 1980s, Telemundo became very successful by producing its own *telenovelas* (Spanish soap operas), comedy shows like *Telecómicas*, and entertainment reviews like *Noche de Gala*. It also adopted the advertising slogan "*Tu canal*" (Your Channel), which has proved successful with the audience. Currently Telemundo is part of a larger conglomerate of affiliated stations in Latin America and the United States, with an estimated reach of over 10 million viewers. Since 2005, its formula for *telenovelas* continues with successful ventures that include *Pasión de gavilanes, Tierra de pasiones,* and *Victoria*. To satisfy the wide range of Spanish speakers, its *telenovelas* now blend actors and actresses from a variety of countries such as Mexico, Colombia, Cuba, and Argentina.

In 1952, the FCC also granted a permit for a second television station to Ramón Quiñonez, the owner of another radio station (WAPA). The second TV station, named WAPA-TV, started transmitting programs on May 1, 1954. Its name is partly derived from the acronym of its original owners' organization: Asociación de Productores de Azúcar (APA), or the Association of Sugar Producers. The original agenda for WAPA-TV included programs on comedy, cooking, drama, Mexican films, and up-to-date news. It transmitted using channel 4, and that is still how most people in Puerto Rico still know the station: *el canal 4.* The station also produced family entertainment but became successful by including American shows translated into Spanish. In addition, its comedy shows, such as *Barrio Cuatro Calles,* were very successful.

El Mundo and WAPA have competed fiercely for the largest viewer audience since the 1950s, but this competition also prompted innovations that benefited the television industry such as (1) the development of video technology in 1966, (2) the implementation of color television in 1968, and (3) broadcasting via satellite in 1968. A media monopoly between these two owners started to develop on the island rather quickly. Nevertheless, WAPA still seemed to remain behind Telemundo as far as number of viewers was concerned.

In 1955, a television station was founded in San Antonio, Texas, that would eventually become Univisión, one of the largest Spanish stations in the United States and Puerto Rico. Created by Raúl Cortez, it had a hard time achieving financial success, so it was quickly sold to investors, who turned it around. The new owners moved the station to Los Angeles in 1962 as KMEX-TV. This company would eventually become the Spanish International Network, the first official Spanish-language network in the United States. The 1980s were crucial for the direction of Univisión. The new CEO, Joaquín Blaya, developed two shows that charted the course for the station. He signed Cristina Saralegui as a talk show host to conduct *El Show de Cristina,* which became an instant hit. He also brought Mario Kreutzberger from Chile to duplicate his popular show *Sábado Gigante* (Giant Saturday) for American Spanish-speaking audiences. This show also became an overnight sensation, and Kreutzberger became an iconic figure simply known as Don Francisco. By the 1990s, Univisión was ready to expand throughout the United States in an effort to reach the Hispanic population in areas where it was heavily concentrated. The network signed affiliation agreements with stations in Atlanta, Georgia; Cleveland, Ohio; Raleigh, North Carolina; and Philadelphia, Pennsylvania.

In 1992, Univisión also signed a local marketing agreement with two stations in Puerto Rico. The two stations involved (WSUR in Ponce and WLII in Caguas) were eventually sold to Univisión three years later. This purchase allowed Univisión to penetrate not only the market in Puerto Rico, but also the areas in the United States with large numbers of Puerto Ricans such as New York City. Through these business partnerships, Univisión has continued to grow and to attract viewers in both the United States and Latin America.

Univisión has proven to be a visionary leader in the industry and has obtained a very respectable position in the field of television. It has certainly highlighted the potential market that Hispanics represent in the United States, and advertisers have become aware of the benefits of marketing products in the Spanish media. Univisión has also increased its influence in U.S. media circles. For example, its leaders argued that the 45 million Hispanics in the United States would compose an important constituency for the presidential elections of 2008, so Univisión partnered with the University of Miami to host both the Democrat and Republican debates for the U.S. presidency. On September 9, 2007, Univisión organized the very first Spanish-language presidential Democratic debate in the United States, hosted by the University of Miami. Then, in December 2007, it hosted the Republican presidential debate. The questions were asked in Spanish with simultaneous English translations. All the candidates answered in English, and the answers were also translated simultaneously for the Spanish-speaking audience. The presidential candidates agreed to these historic debates mostly because they were aware that Hispanics make up the largest-growing group of the voting electorate. Univisión transmitted both of the debates in prime time using a nationwide platform of delivery. The event highlighted how important Hispanic voters in the United States have become. It also served the purpose of showing to a national audience that Hispanics are not necessarily a unified political group and that they need to be addressed by both political parties.

Despite all the pioneer work of these commercial TV stations, they all came up for sale beginning in the 1980s. Starting in 1986, Telemundo went through a series of sales to different owners and corporations. Eventually, in 1987, Telemundo Puerto Rico was sold to an entertainment subsidiary of General Electric called the Spanish Network in the United States, where it continues to operate. Telemundo often links programming and trades personnel with NBC, one of the main networks in the United States, which is also owned by the industrial giant General Electric. WAPA-TV was also sold through a series of transfers and takeovers. Eventually, in 1980, it was purchased by Pegasus, another a subsidiary of General Electric. The other Spanish television station, Univisión, was also up for sale in 2006. In March 2007, the sale of the station was approved by federal regulators in the United States. The new owners were private equity investors, but their purchase was challenged in court by Univisión shareholders. In the meantime, as the legal dispute is finalized, Univisión has continued to expand its programming with stations in Nashville, Tennessee; Minneapolis, Minnesota; Seattle, Washington; and Detroit, Michigan.

Today, most Puerto Ricans receive television programming from TV channels from both the island and the U.S. mainland. In addition, cable companies offer packages that include programming in both English and Spanish, plus specific channels for sports, comedy, movies, and newscasts.

Cable Television

Cable service offered better reception than average TV signals in the 1970s. Cablevisión de Puerto Rico provided the first cable broadcast, but it was limited to the resort areas around San Juan. Its offerings were eventually expanded to include residential service in the late 1970s. By the 1990s, there were over ten cable companies covering the entire island. All cable systems now offer packages with movie channels, sports, science programs, the main networks from the United States (ABC, NBC, CBS, etc.), cartoons, weather, and so on. However, most of the broadcasting is heavily concentrated on English-language programming and a few limited Spanish channels. Currently there are four main cable providers in Puerto Rico that dominate most of the subscriptions on the island: Adelphia, Digital TV One, Cablevisión de Puerto Rico, and Centennial de Puerto Rico.

Independent Broadcasting

Broadcasting religious content over television stations has become quite popular in Puerto Rico since the 1990s. The Roman Catholic Church has a TV station called Telesagrado, based at the Universidad del Sagrado Corazón. It offers social and cultural programs but also films with religious themes. In addition, at least three Protestant churches also own TV stations, mostly to transmit televised formats of their religious services. They also offer both local and international news within a religious context. The most popular stations are Teleadoración de Puerto Rico (Teleworshipping) and Iglesia de Dios TV (God's Church TV). These both belong to a coalition of Christian television stations throughout Latin America called Sabor Cristiano Internacional (Christian Flavor International). This broadcasting group links Christian stations from countries such as Colombia, El Salvador, Honduras, Peru, Argentina, and the United States. Most of them offer music videos, Christian-themed films, televised religious services, and the ability to purchase Christian books via their respective Web sites. This is certainly a growing movement that is likely to continue.

PUBLIC RADIO AND PUBLIC TELEVISION

During the 1950s, soon after the initial television transmissions took place, the legislature of Puerto Rico approved Joint Resolution 94 to establish and finance the island's first public radio and television service. In June 1954, the public television service, based in San Juan, was assigned transmission on channel 6. It became the very first educational television station in Latin America when it started offering educational programming on January 6, 1958, on the *Día de Los Reyes Magos* (Day of the Three Wise Men), knowing this holiday would attract lots of children viewers. Seven years later, it expanded its offerings by opening another station in the city of Mayagüez, on the west coast of the island. These two stations then joined the Public Broadcasting Service in 1971, which resulted in increased offerings from the U.S. mainland, but now in English. Due to the joint offerings, the public television and radio stations in Puerto Rico became bilingual in nature.

ELECTRONIC MEDIA

According to the CIA World Factbook, as of 2005, there were seventy-six Internet service providers (ISPs) and 413 Internet hosts in Puerto Rico. This allows roughly 915,000 users to access the Internet as a major tool of communication. To achieve this level of Internet access, Puerto Rico has a modern system of submarine cables that connect the island with the United States, Central America, and South American nations. These underwater cables offer capabilities for high-speed Internet access. With this level of connectivity, it is not surprising that most print and broadcast media also offer expanded information via their respective Web sites. Electronic media offer the possibility of reading information online, and not necessarily by using real and palpable books, periodicals, or journals. Moreover, the island has an ambitious but successful program through which the public can access all the main libraries of Puerto Rico via virtual libraries online. For example, the University of Puerto Rico system offers access to its catalogs, including a large selection of electronic journals, legislative documents, research statistics, and data from the school of medicine. Another similar portal program is offered by the Universidad Interamericana de Puerto Rico from its main location in Arecibo. It offers a virtual library called *Infotrac*. Its online portal allows researchers to obtain complete articles (not just summaries or partial printouts) from over 8,700 electronic journals. This data bank is updated daily to include almost 1,400 legal review publications, biographical information on over 130,000 literary writers, over 250 titles covering the link between religion and society, a searchable bank on company profiles for businesses operating on the island, journals with the latest innovations on computer science, and an enormous set of journals addressing the humanities and social sciences.

The wide choice of materials available on the Internet, however, has both advantages and perils. The positive aspects include quick access to information and without the cost of buying so many books and reference materials. It is also easier to access data from the home or office and not have to set foot in a library. Moreover, information can be easily updated. One negative factor of relying too much on Internet information is that some Web sites contain questionable data without revealing specific sources for their content. Many librarians also decry the reduced number of people who want to read actual books, especially among the younger population. Publishing companies find it difficult to compete with online materials. Book publishers offer excerpts of books online, but they try not to give it all away. Libraries have turned toward the purchase of electronic academic journals when they are offered in such format. This practice reduces the need to keep all published journals on the shelves.

Another sector deeply affected by the availability of material online is the small specialty bookstores and regional newspapers. These small businesses cannot compete with large chain stores that offer deep discounts on books, but also, they continue to see a declining interest in the purchase of tangible reading materials. For example, the Christian bookstores have called the Internet development a crisis for their profit margin. Even while Puerto Rico is considered to be an excellent target for Evangelical books, sales have seen steep declines in the last twenty years. Another dilemma is faced by newspapers: it is a financial challenge to sell newspapers for just a few cents when so many other sources of news are available for free on the Internet. So, newspapers have had to adapt to the new realities of the business and offer their daily news in electronic format—for free—in the hope that they can attract enough advertisers to their Web sites to make up the cost of diminished paper sales. In addition, nowadays, almost every Puerto Rican radio station can be heard on the Internet, and television stations actually offer enhanced content on their Web sites. For better or for worse, this is a new world for both print and broadcasting media.

REFERENCES

Alvarado Vega, José. "KPMG: San Juan Has Lowest Corporate Tax Burden." *San Juan Star*, July 29, 2008.

Flores-Caraballo, Eliut Daniel. "The Politics of Culture in Puerto Rican Television: A Macro/Micro Study of English vs. Spanish Television Usage." Ph.D. diss., University of Texas at Austin, 1991.

Márquez, Miguel B. "Sobre los comienzos del periodismo en Puerto Rico." *Revista Latina de Comunicación Social* 33 (2000). http://www.ull.es/publicaciones/latina/aa2000kjl/x33se/55marquez.htm.

Mohr, Eugene V. *Language, Literature and Journalism in the American Presence in Puerto Rico,* ed. Lynn-Darrell Bender. Hato Rey, Puerto Rico: Publicaciones Puertorriqueñas, 1998.

Newcomb, Horace, ed. *Encyclopedia of Television.* 2nd ed. Chicago: Museum of Broadcast Communications, 2004.

Romeu, José A. *Panorama del periodismo puertorriqueño.* Río Piedras: University of Puerto Rico Press, 1985.

Sterling, Christopher, and Michael Keith, eds. *Encyclopedia of Radio.* Chicago: Museum of Broadcast Communications. 2003.

Thompson, Donald, ed. *Music of Puerto Rico: A Reader's Anthology.* Lanham, MD: Scarecrow Press, 2002.

Thompson, Donald, and Annie Thompson. *Music and Dance in Puerto Rico from the Age of Columbus to Modern Times.* Lanham, MD: Scarecrow Press, 1991.

Torregrosa, José Luis. *La Historia de la Radio en Puerto Rico.* San Juan: Esmacos, 1991.

Torre Revello, José. *El libro, la imprenta, y el periodismo en America durante la dominación española.* Buenos Aires: Instituto de Investigaciones Históricas, 1940.

Web Sites

CIA World Factbook, https://www.cia.gov/library/publications/the-world-factbook/geos/rq.html.

Instituto de Arte y Cultura de Puerto Rico, http://iprac.aspira.org/.

Instituto de Cultura Puertorriqueña, http://www.icp.gobierno.pr/.

Museum of Broadcasting Communications, http://www.museum.tv/.

Universidad Interamericana de Puerto Rico, http://www.arecibo.inter.edu/biblioteca/bases.htm. Infotrac virtual library.

6

Cinema

THE DEVELOPMENT OF the Puerto Rican film industry has corresponded with important historical and political events. In the past one hundred years, Puerto Rico's imaginative and creative talent has participated in the creation of documentaries, comedies, thrillers, dramas, and even animated films. While there is a wealth of artistic creativity on the island, filmmaking projects have gone through stages that include high levels of production followed by steep declines in interest. At the end of the twentieth century, Americans discovered a handful of talented Puerto Rican musicians, such as Ricky Martin, Marc Anthony, Cheyenne, and Jennifer Lopez, since they are all part of the Latin pop explosion that happened in 1999. While these contemporary artists have earned their icon status recently, Puerto Rico has a rich artistic history, with hundreds of actors and musicians who made Puerto Rican popular culture appealing to the masses. They were the pioneers of television and film on the island. Since the beginning, one of the most significant challenges for filmmakers has been the complicated process of achieving appropriate film distribution. The growth of Puerto Rican cinema is discussed in this chapter over five specific periods.

THE BEGINNING STAGES (1898–1945)

The United States invaded Guánica Bay, Puerto Rico, in 1898 as part of the Spanish-American War. The American soldiers brought with them heavy military machinery but also film cameras to record the events. This was the first experience Puerto Rico had with cinema. What followed was a series of documentaries filmed on the island. Then, in 1912, Rafael Colorado D'Assoy recorded *Un drama en Puerto Rico*—the first film produced in Puerto Rico that was not a documentary. He was a Spanish military officer who came to Puerto Rico during the Spanish-American War. Colorado started out by importing films from New York in 1910 and distributing them to the movie house Tres Banderas in San Juan. When he decided to produce his own film in 1912, he became one of the pioneers of Puerto Rican cinematography. Roughly at about the same time, another film pioneer, Juan Emilio Viguié Cajas, was beginning to experiment with cinema in the southern city of Ponce.

The success of his early venture encouraged Colorado to partner with Antonio Capella Martínez to create a new cinema company called the Sociedad Industrial del Cine de Puerto Rico (The Industrial Society of Puerto Rican Film). They quickly started production in 1916 with films like *La hembra y el gallo*. The response of the artistic community fueled the creation of other film undertakings such as the Tropical Film Company in 1917. This company focused on *costumbrista* cinematography, which portrays themes of how the local population thinks, feels, suffers, and celebrates life. One of their first productions was *Paloma del monte* (Mountain Dove). This film was produced and directed by the famous poet Luis Llorens Torres. Then, the film company Porto Rico Photoplays was founded in 1919 and started its business agenda with the production of *Amor tropical* in 1920, with two American actors: Ruth Clifford and Reginald Denny. This film was intended for the American audience, but it did not succeed in that market. The beginning stages of these two companies were seriously hampered by world events beyond their control. This is the period when the United States joined World War I. Since both companies depended on supplies coming from the United States, they could not even purchase film to record their movies, so they both failed and disappeared from the industry.

Up until the 1920s, all productions were silent films. The first step toward providing sound in entertainment was the opening of the first radio station in 1922 (WKAQ El Mundo of San Juan). Then, Mexico produced the first movie with sound (in Spanish), titled *Santa*. Producer Juan Viguié Cajas was impressed with this film and aimed to do something similar in Puerto Rico. In 1934, Cajas produced *Romance tropical*, the very first film with sound produced in Puerto Rico. The acclaimed poet Luis Palés Matos wrote the script about a young musician who ventures onto the ocean in search of his fortune. The film was widely promoted, but it was a financial failure. The company went bankrupt after the first film and disappeared.

All the movies recorded at the beginning of the twentieth century set the foundation for an industry of producing motion pictures on the island. Despite the historic value of these films, there is not a single copy of them available. The Archivo General de Puerto Rico has not been able to locate a sample of these films to preserve for future generations. Their existence is only known and corroborated because the names and personnel involved are mentioned in journals of the time. Overall, the creation of motion pictures in Puerto Rico languished until the end of World War II.

A PROLIFIC PERIOD (1946–1960)

In 1946, U.S. President Harry Truman designated the first native-born Puerto Rican governor, Jesús T. Piñero. During the same year, the Comisión de Parques y Recreos Públicos de Puerto Rico founded a special cinema division with the purpose of creating education films. This historic project produced five documentaries covering informative social topics and explaining how the government functioned at the time. This venture proved to be the spark for multiple creative and artistic ventures.

Three years later, Puerto Rico created the División de Educación de la Comunidad, in 1949. The governor at the time, Luis Muñoz Marín, strongly supported Law 372, which created an economic fund and provided the vision to use film as a medium to deliver material of artistic and social value to the Puerto Rican community. The goal was to disseminate basic education, local history, artistic pride, and health information. The education fund used various communication forms, such as films, posters, fliers, and small community gatherings, to deliver their message. The process was designed to reach both rural and urban populations, and it had a pedagogical approach to it. The project was extremely successful since it recruited popular actors, writers, musicians, and technicians in the production of 117 films. While the themes varied widely, the focus was always on providing a basic level of education to the communities of Puerto Rico and to portray popular culture in a positive light. Most films used local inhabitants as extras in their movies, and they used local buildings and landscapes as backdrops for their stories. For example, *El yugo* was a film released in 1959 that shows how a fishing community pooled its resources to take control of their destiny by getting rid of the middlemen who took most of their profits. The documentary *Las manos del hombre* (A Man's Hands), produced in 1952, reinforced the pride involved in working in manual labor jobs. *Ignacio* was another popular documentary that depicts a shy man from the countryside who eventually gets ahead in life when he develops the courage to speak up and stand up for what he believes. The topic of physical abuse endured by women in the countryside was portrayed in the film *Modesta* in 1956. The movie features a woman who decides that she will no longer tolerate her husband's abuse. The clear message is that women can be empowered to exercise their legal rights in Puerto Rico. In addition, the quality of these films and documentaries was competitive at international levels. For example, the film *Una voz en la montaña* (A Voice in the Mountain), produced by Amilcar Tirado in 1952, was recognized as one of the best films at the Edinburgh Film Festival.

The 1950s were a period of innovation. The first two television stations opened in Puerto Rico in 1954 (Telemundo and WAPA-TV). The emergence of television provided an impetus for cinematographers interested in developing a comprehensive film industry on the island. The División de Educación de la Comunidad had already established a reputation of quality filmmaking. Now, during the 1950s, the División de Educación took to the task of actually training an entire generation of new filmmakers. Within this context, there were five outstanding films produced during the 1950s in Puerto Rico. First, an inspirational film from 1951 titled *Los peloteros* (The Ball Players) was based on a true story about the coach of a children's baseball team. The director, Jack Delano, selected poor local children who were not actors to play the roles of the children's team. Ramón Rivero was a comedian who played the main actor in his first dramatic role. This film is often considered to be the best example of cinematography produced by the División de Educación de la Comunidad because it offers a reflection of local experiences. Another company, Probo Films, also produced three major classic films during the 1950s. The musical *El otro camino* (The Other Road), from 1955, was well done, but it did not receive wide distribution. The second film, *Maruja* (1959), became a runaway commercial success. The story line portrayed the eventful life of a sensual woman who becomes involved with several men, ending with tragic results. It was set in the rural areas of Bayamón, and it also highlighted daily life struggles in Puerto Rico. The main actors—Marta Romero, Roberto Rivera Negrón, Mario Pabón, and Helena Montalbán—later became household names in Puerto Rican television. In addition, the film's appeal included extraordinary musical scores at a time when Puerto Rican music was becoming solidified on the national scene. *Maruja* was picked up by the Hispanic Division of Columbia Pictures for distribution in the United States and Latin America, and it enjoyed even wider distribution. Another important film of the decade was *Palmer ha muerto* (Palmer Has Died), a coproduction between Puerto Rico and Spain. This film became successful in Spain, but it was not well promoted on the island. Another partnership was created with the United States for the production of *Man with My Face* in 1951. This was a film that explored the lives of Americans living in Puerto Rico at the time. This was a crime-thriller motion picture based on the novel by the same title written by Samuel W. Taylor. It was more successful in the United States than in Puerto Rico, where it only had limited exposure and distribution.

Multiple factors came together to make the 1950s one of the most prolific decades in the Puerto Rican film industry. The Division of Community

Education fund was already well established and had developed a reputation for high-quality productions. Viguié Films Productions provided an advanced laboratory for postproduction editing. Highly talented technicians were educated locally, and others came from abroad to work in the developing film industry on the island. The association with Columbia Pictures provided the seed to search for wider distribution options and the financial backing for future films.

Overall, the decade of the 1950s was very productive for the film industry, and it is often referred to as the golden age of Puerto Rican cinema. It even prompted successful Puerto Rican artists working abroad to return to the island to participate in innovative projects. This was the case of singer and actress Mapy Cortés, who was considered a success in the Mexican cinema industry during the 1940s. She returned to Puerto Rico in the 1950s to collaborate in new projects, propelling the national cinema and television of Puerto Rico to new heights.

A Period of Decline (1960–1980)

The period from 1960 to 1980 can be viewed as both good and bad simultaneously. The 1960s offered an increasing interest in creating films in Puerto Rico. The attention of the world brought foreign investment, and numerous films were coproduced with Mexican companies. However, most of these joint ventures were actually Mexican films with Mexican actors, Mexican directors, and Mexican cinematic formulas but shot using Puerto Rico as a background. One of the films created in this pattern was titled *Romance en Puerto Rico.* It was released in 1961, and it was the very first Puerto Rican film to be produced in color. Due to so much exposure, the Mexican style of directing and creating films in Puerto Rico became an influential factor in the industry. At the same time, film companies from Spain, Argentina, Germany, France, Venezuela, and the United States were actively working on their own film developments on the island. The explosion of new motion pictures did not necessarily give birth to highly acclaimed films. For example, *Last Woman on Earth* was an American film shot in 1960. The plot evolves around three Americans who happen to be on vacation on the island, and they become the only survivors of a world apocalypse. Another unpopular American movie was *Frankenstein Meets the Space Monster*, released in 1965. The story line describes Martians who actually land in Puerto Rico because that is where they can kidnap lively and vivacious go-go dancers.

There were three notable exceptions that revealed the possibility that high-quality films could still be produced on the island during the 1960s. One of those exceptions was the movie titled *La chica del lunes* (Monday's Girl), for which director Leopoldo Torre Nilsson received a nomination at the Cannes Film Festival. In 1968, the United States had a somewhat successful film with Bob Hope as the main actor: *The Private Navy of Sergeant O'Farrell*. Perhaps the most outstanding film of the 1960s was the production of the comedy *La criada malcriada* (The Misbehaving Maid) in Puerto Rico. The wit of the main character, Azucena, portrayed both innocence and comedic genius. This film quickly became a classic of Puerto Rican film. It was shot in 1965 with a cast of talented and established television actors and actresses. Actors such as Velda González, José Miguel Agrelot, and Jacobo Morales made this motion picture a source of true comedic pride that enhanced the appreciation of popular culture. The film was sporadically played on local television, but then disappeared. It was until the Archivo Nacional de Cine y Teatro del Ateneo Puertorriqueño found it that it became available in DVD format to the general public.

While these projects, carried out in the 1960s, brought some jobs for local musicians and secondary actors, the main acting and technical crews were usually foreign. The trend for the film industry was beginning to set; creating production agreements with foreign companies could secure wider distribution plans and a better chance for commercial success. This pattern, however, was detrimental for the production of national cinema. New films lost their focus to project the lives and social topics relevant to Puerto Rico. In addition, the foreign cinema ventures provided limited opportunities for *boricua* writers, talented actors, local technicians, and regional musicians.

During the 1970s, there was a period of deep decline both in film production and in the quality of movies that were actually made. For example, regional film companies produced movies based on the lives of notorious Puerto Rican criminals, which were not well received by the public. At the time, Anthony Felton was a Puerto Rican producer who lived in New York. He focused on low-budget films that were notorious for their foul language to depict the lives of the island's delinquents such as *La venganza de Correa Coto* (1969), *La palomilla* (1969), and *Luisa* (1970). That was not what *boricuas* had in mind when they requested a return to national themes. Mexico was in a similar or worse position than Puerto Rico since its golden era of filmmaking had certainly faded by the late 1970s. The production of significant motion pictures gave way to small companies producing low-budget films (called *churros* in Mexico) that mostly portrayed the life in brothels and the adventures of small-time delinquents. As a result, foreign distributors in Latin America were now even less interested in promoting Mexican films. As a result of the collapse of Mexico's film industry, Puerto Rico also suffered because Mexico had to dramatically curtail its investments on the island. In the meantime, the United States kept up its filmmaking in Puerto Rico. However, most of the films were also void of interesting plots and story lines. Such films include *The Man from O.R.G.Y.*, produced by Sydney W. Pink.

Not everything in the 1970s was completely negative. Two films became examples of classic Puerto Rican cinematography and story lines; one was American and the other one was Puerto Rican. Woody Allen directed the film *Bananas* in 1971, in which the Puerto Rican actor Jacobo Morales played a supporting role. He had a comprehensive résumé spanning almost twenty years as a television actor and screen writer. His work in *Bananas* later helped him to land an important role opposite Barbra Streisand in the film *Up the Sandbox.* In 1979, Jacobo Morales made the leap from television to the big screen to play the leading role in the film *Dios los cría* (God Makes Them). It was produced by masterfully stringing together a collection of five short stories. The movie quickly received notable international awards. This outstanding Puerto Rican film sparked Morales's career as a writer and director, a talent that would deliver outstanding results in the next two decades.

Ironically, while the production of feature-length films declined in the 1970s, the development of documentaries actually increased. This is a period with two main social concerns in Puerto Rico: the independence movement and the struggles of *boricuas* who migrated to the northeastern part of the United States. The political debate in Puerto Rico was addressed by Puerto Rican filmmakers and directors who lived in New York and Boston. The documentary *Puerto Rico: Paraíso invadido* (Puerto Rico: Paradise Invaded) was directed by Alfonso Beato in 1977. The film highlights the reality of the island from a point of view that supports political independence from the United States. The trials and tribulations of the Puerto Rican migrants are addressed in the films *The Oxcart* (1970) and its Spanish version, *La carreta* (1972), directed by José García Torres. The films narrate the notion that leaving Puerto Rico is sometimes an economic necessity, but Puerto Ricans are not always accepted in other U.S. communities, even though they are American citizens.

NEW HOPE FOR NATIONAL FILMS (1980–2000)

The opening of *Dios los cría* (God Makes Them) in 1980 created tremendous optimism among the Puerto Rican film industry. The writer and director, Jacobo Morales, was able to return to true *boricua* topics, story lines, and characters and a reflection of life on the island. It meant the resurgence of national themes reflected in art. Morales would later direct crucial films such as *Nicolás y los demás* (Nicholas and the Others) in 1986. He also wrote and directed *Lo que le pasó a Santiago* (What Happened to Santiago) in 1989. Both movies were highly acclaimed both in Puerto Rico and in international circles. *Lo que le pasó a Santiago* is a melodrama that reveals qualities of its characters a little bit at a time, keeping the audience always interested. Toward the end, Morales incorporates a hint of magical realism, a genre that is popular in Latin American films and literature. This is the stage of the film in which fantasy and reality are blended together and offer viewers the possibility to develop their own interpretations of the scenes. This box office hit was selected to represent Puerto Rico in the category of Best Foreign Film at the Academy Awards in the United States. However, it did not win; the film *Cinema Paradiso* from Italy took the Oscar that year. Nevertheless, the work of Jacobo Morales became prominent in Puerto Rican cinematography. His influence became palpable in the production of *La gran fiesta* (The Big Feast) in 1986. This was the very first release by a new company called Zaga Films. *La gran fiesta* was produced by Roberto Gándara and directed by Marcos Zurinaga. The film portrays wealthy Puerto Ricans and their last celebration at the Casino de Puerto Rico in 1942, when it had to be turned over to the U.S. military. This is a social theme that was deeply felt in Puerto Rico since the 1940s was a historical period when the island was beginning to obtain self-government status. The quality of Puerto Rican films was recognized in international competitions once again. In fact, Puerto Rico has been submitting films to the Foreign Film category of the Academy Awards since 1985.

The 1980s also offered a continuation of documentaries, but now with larger budgets and more experienced crews. This is the decade when independent filmmakers in Puerto Rico produced the so-called films with a social purpose. Most of the reels produced addressed controversial topics in Puerto Rico such as the political future of the island, economic development programs, and poverty linked to migration. Films like *El arresto* (The Arrest) in 1982 and *Puerto Rico: A Colony the American Way* (1982) dealt with the complicated political and economic relationship between Puerto Rico and the United States. Another controversial film of the period was *Manos a la obra: The Story of Operation Bootstrap* (1983), directed by Pedro Rivera and Susan Zeig. It offers a critical analysis of the economic incentive program implemented in the 1950s, and the social advantages and consequences that became visible thirty years later. The military control of the small island of Vieques became an increasingly political topic in the 1980s. The film *La batalla de Vieques* (The Battle for Vieques) depicts the social struggle and the dangers to the civilian population who lives on Vieques as a result of daily military exercises with live ammunition. The director Zydnia Nazario portrayed images and interviews that fueled the political discourse on the island. By the end of this decade, a powerful film emerged by directors Peter Piella and Frances Negrón-Muntaner, who explored the topic of AIDS in the Puerto Rican community living in Philadelphia. *AIDS in the Barrio: Eso no me pasa a mí* (AIDS in the Barrio: It Wouldn't Happen to Me) was released in 1989 and offered a social critique of homophobia, the use of drugs, and discrimination. All these films generated controversy and social dialogue, just as was expected. After all, these were all films with a social purpose.

During the 1990s, most film recording moved to a digital format. This arrived just in time for a resurgence of artistic creativity in Puerto Rico. The new focus on local themes inspired director Luis Molina Casanova to create *La guagua aérea* (The Air Bus) in 1993. The film returned to a *costumbrista* style by portraying the feelings and customs of the island's population. It was a commercial success. Actually, it holds the record as the Puerto Rican film that has earned the most money. In addition, it also holds a Guinness World Record for being the only film that was premiered on a flight from San Juan to New York City. However, this is a decade of outstanding independent films that are not necessarily blockbusters, but have elevated the quality of cinematography on the island. Such films include *Héroes de otra patria* (Heroes of Another Country) in 1998, *Callejón de los cuernos* (Horn's Alley) in 1998, and *Plaza vacante* (A Vacancy) in 2001.

Toward the end of the century, Puerto Rico was used extremely often as a shooting location, but the films were not necessarily set on the island. Instead, Puerto Rico has served as a substitute setting for other locations such as Vietnam, Hawaii, Cuba, and Africa. For example, foreign companies have used the island for important films like *Amistad,* directed by Steven Spielberg in 1997. Actors Morgan Freeman, Anthony Hopkins, and Djimon Hounsou received various nominations for international awards based on their respective roles in the film. This entire movie was also nominated for an Oscar. At the end of the story, a slave fort is destroyed, which is actually the El Morro Fortress that surrounds the city of San Juan in modern times. Another box-office hit partially filmed in Puerto Rico was *Golden Eye*—part of the James Bond film series. The British actors Pierce Brosnan and Sean Bean made this suspense and action film a commercial success. In *Golden Eye*, Puerto Rico is used for its alluring scenes, but they are supposed to be a substitute for several locations in Cuba. The use of Puerto Rico as a shooting location brings considerable income to the local economy, and it employs local people for the duration of these artistic ventures. However, the local government started to search for better ways for Puerto Ricans to become more active participants and collaborators in the filming process. Long government discussions with committees and subcommittees paved the way for a desire to develop a solid film industry on the island.

CREATING A NATIONAL FILM INDUSTRY (2000 TO PRESENT)

The new century brought encouraging news for Puerto Rican cinema. On August 17, 2001, the local government decided to create the Puerto Rico

Film Commission with the purpose of promoting the development of the film industry on the island. The legislature approved Law 121 to establish the Corporación para el Desarrollo de las Artes, Ciencias e Industria Cinematográfica de Puerto Rico. Moreover, it created the Local Puerto Rico Film Industry Fund to financially support and stimulate local film production. The fund offers a yearly competition and provides roughly 3 million dollars a year in seed money for independent films. This opportunity has been used by local filmmakers to carry out projects that also provide jobs for the local population. After implementing its initial projects, the film commission quickly realized that financial support of this nature was not enough. To develop a national film industry, the government had to think in bigger terms. Several legislators pointed out that the Puerto Rican government has previously taken a much more comprehensive approach when it wanted to develop other local industries. For example, the Puerto Rico Tourism Company received official support to develop the island into its current position as the most comprehensive cruise and airline hub in the Caribbean. Similarly, the use of special tax incentives helped to develop pharmaceutical companies into a flourishing industry that provides thousands of regional jobs and important sources of local revenue. If the government was serious about creating a competitive film industry in Puerto Rico, it needed to act in similar ways to encourage private investment from both individuals and corporations.

The result was that the government of Puerto Rico approved a series of tax benefits and incentives that promote quality filmmaking on the island. It addition, these proposals generate thousands of jobs for local talent. For example, Puerto Rico now offers one of the highest incentives for any film company to shoot, record, edit, or finalize its films using the island's talent and technical facilities. It actually offers a 40 percent tax credit on the production of motion pictures, television series, or original music sound track recordings done on the island. Besides offering attractive settings as film locations, the film fund has been used to provide studios with the latest technical equipment to do postproduction editing. The 40 percent exemption also applies to infrastructure projects that invest a minimum of 5 million dollars in the construction or remodeling of recording studios, laboratories, or editing facilities. One tangible result is that now foreign companies are employing local, highly trained technical crews, experienced musical directors, graphic artists and designers, accommodation coordinators, and logistics managers to facilitate the filming process. In 2003, the legislature also approved Act 272 to provide additional support to the film industry. Section 24F waives all the taxes on hotel rooms for all personnel working on filming projects authorized in Puerto Rico. Furthermore, real estate owned for the purpose of film production is exempt from 90 percent of municipal and state property taxes. To qualify for all or any of these tax breaks, companies must shoot at least 50 percent of their principal film photography in Puerto Rico.

The emergence of local talent is already showing tangible results. At least four films supported by government funds have won the praise of film critics: *Desandando la vida* (Walking through Life) in 2003, *Desamores* (Falling Out of Love) in 2004, *Revoluciones en el infierno* (Revolutions in Hell) in 2004, and *Pa' eso estamos* (That Is Why We Are Here) in 2005. According to Roberto Ramos-Perea, a respected theater and film critic on the island, these productions are evidence that government support can translate into excellence in the arts. The recent explosion in Puerto Rican visual arts is expected to flourish even more within the next ten to twenty years.

The creation of film industry incentives could easily end up benefiting only outsiders, if not managed properly. The Puerto Rico Film Commission is keenly aware that it needs a long-term vision that includes preparing and training the future generations of Puerto Ricans interested in the different components of filmmaking. The Fundación de Cine de Puerto Rico was specifically created for that purpose. It offers students a comprehensive curriculum that includes three crucial components: (1) writing film scripts, (2) using cameras to direct film production, and (3) editing. The campus for the Fundación de Cine de Puerto Rico is located in San Juan. It includes a comprehensive film library of Puerto Rican classic films, an expanded library for students, and a general film collection available to the surrounding community. In addition, the Fundación de Cine organizes the Festival Internacional de Cortometrajes de Puerto Rico. This festival of short films and documentaries is locally known simply as Cinefiesta.

The training for new filmmakers now requires not only artistic talent but also a crucial knowledge of the technical aspects of the industry. The evolution to digital media has added tremendous and profound changes to how a film is actually prepared from beginning to end. The increasing interest of the local artists led to a joint venture with the prestigious Digital Film Academy of New York City to open a film school on the island. This accredited school offers a practical mix of academic classes with hands-on practice in digital labs and opportunities for shooting projects on location. After years of preparation, the Digital Film Academy officially opened in San Juan in July 2006 to offer a graduate program in cinema. Now, Puerto Ricans do not have to travel abroad if they want to pursue their passion for film and convert it into serious academic and technical training.

Puerto Rico uses several film festivals to showcase the most recent projects in film, documentaries, and commercials. The Rincón International Film Festival is an annual event that takes place at the end of April. Since Rincón is considered to be the mecca for surfers in Puerto Rico, it is not surprising that this event has a casual atmosphere adjacent to beach locations. Its mission is to support culture and the arts through the medium of film. While the festival accepts entries in all languages, it has special award categories for Spanish-language films and specific awards for Puerto Rican filmmakers. Being a surfer's paradise, the film festival is always actively looking to screen films focused on the theme of surfing. In 2008, the special surfer film invited to be showcased there was *One California Day*, directed by Jason Baffa and Mark Jeremias. They have already developed a reputation for films that portray the surfing experience and culture.

Another important film festival is the Cinefiesta, which takes place every year in Caguas, a suburb of San Juan. Officially known as the Festival Internacional de Cortometrajes de Puerto Rico, it began in August 2003, and it now attracts an international crowd of filmmakers. In 2007, thirty-one countries submitted entries for the event. From the 485 films received for consideration, only 82 were selected for the competition. The event has hired international advisers and observers to transform it into a well-established film festival that has become well accepted at an international level. Despite the highlighted exposure during film festival weekends, several independent filmmakers from Puerto Rico are somewhat discouraged because their films do not receive much publicity on the island, and not too many movie theaters are willing to show them. They suggested that, instead of chasing the acceptance of foreign markets, the goal should be to achieve a national distribution pattern that appeals to more Puerto Ricans.

INTERNATIONAL RECOGNITION

Puerto Rico has a long tradition of actively contributing to the film industry. Motion pictures have been used not only to entertain but also as important education tools. Movies have played a crucial role in Puerto Rico's quest to preserve its culture—language, food, music, dance, and art—even when it faces the strong influence of the United States. *Boricuas* on the island already know that they have outstanding entertainers, musicians, and actors with a long trajectory of artistic pursuits. In addition, recent Puerto Rican films have captured the attention of sophisticated audiences when they competed for nominations and international awards. However, the most widely known Puerto Rican artists today have been catapulted to international fame especially after they have succeeded in the United States.

There is a long list of multitalented *boricuas* who have exceeded expectations on Broadway and in Hollywood. For example, Rita Moreno (1931–) is a dynamic actress, dancer, and singer who was born in Humacao. She became a film sensation when she appeared in the film version of *West Side Story* in

1961. The multifaceted actress was the first entertainer in history to win all the major awards in the United States: an Oscar, an Emmy, a Grammy, and a Tony. She continues to be very active in both television and film. Recently, she had a supporting role in the popular series *Cane,* opposite Jimmy Smits, another Puerto Rican actor. Raúl Juliá (1940–1994) was born in San Juan. He worked both in theater and on the big screen. He performed a memorable dramatic role in the film *Romero*, in which he played a priest who was assassinated in El Salvador. However, he became extremely popular for his lead role as the father in the Addams Family series of comedic films.

An increasing number of Puerto Ricans have also been nominated for Academy Awards in different categories. As of 2008, there have been only three Puerto Ricans who have won an Oscar for their performances. José Ferrer (1912–1992) was the first Puerto Rican to win Best Actor for the film *Cyrano de Bergerac* in 1950. Second, Rita Moreno won the Oscar in the Best Supporting Actress category for *West Side Story* in 1961. Almost forty years went by until another *boricua* would get an Academy Award: Benicio del Toro won in the Best Supporting Actor category for his role in *Traffic* in 2000. Other Puerto Ricans have also earned a nomination for an Oscar but did not win. These include José Ferrer in 1948 for *Joan of Arc*, and again in 1952 for his role in *Moulin Rouge.* The actress Rosie Pérez was nominated as Best Supporting Actress for her work in the film *Fearless* in 1993. Another talented Puerto Rican born in San Juan, Joaquin Phoenix, was nominated as Best Actor for *Walk the Line* in 2005, and as Best Supporting Actor for *Gladiator* in 2000. In the writing categories, José Rivera was the first Puerto Rican nominated, in 2005, for an Oscar in the Adapted Screenplay category for his adaptation of Che Guevara's journal into the film *Diarios de motocicleta* (Motorcycle Diaries). Another important production in which Puerto Rico participated was *Voces inocentes* (Innocent Voices), released in 2004. It portrays the harsh realities of war in El Salvador during the 1980s, but viewed through the lens of children. The film was coproduced by Mexico, Puerto Rico, and the United States. It won several international awards in 2004 such as the Glass Bear at the Berlin Festival, the Silver Ariel in Mexico City, and Best Film in the Seattle International Film Festival.

The collaboration of Puerto Rican filmmakers with their international counterparts is elevating recognition of the island as a producer of artistic talent. The dedication of gifted actors from Puerto Rico also continues to bring pride and joy to international audiences who follow their careers in film and television. Jimmy Smits is well known for his television roles as an attorney in *L. A. Law*, a police detective in *N.Y.P.D. Blue,* and most recently, as a rum baron in *Cane.* Actor Héctor Elizondo left memorable performances in films like *Pretty Woman* and *The Princess Diaries*, and on the television show *Cane.*

Benicio del Toro recently won an Oscar for his role in *Traffic* (2000), but he had other important roles in *Sin City* (2005), and *Things We Lost in the Fire* (2007). His talent has earned him roles not only as an actor but also as a writer, director, and producer.

The role of digital media has changed the ways in which films are written, directed, produced, and edited. Puerto Ricans working on independent films often wear multiple hats as writers, directors, producers, and actors. This is the case of Ricardo Méndez Matta, who wrote, directed, and produced the award-winning film *Ladrones y mentirosos* (Thieves and Liars) in 2006. The film exposes the role that Puerto Rico has in the illegal drug trade due to its key location in the Caribbean. The plot masterfully explores how violent crime, corruption, and drug trafficking have an impact on the lives of three separate families from different socioeconomic levels on the island. It was nominated for an Academy Award, but it was not selected. However, Ricardo Méndez Matta received the Copper Wing Award in the Phoenix Film Festival for Best Director in 2006. Another talented *boricua,* Benicio del Toro, participated in *Maldeamores* (Love Sickness) as both an actor and executive producer in 2007. The film is essentially a comedy with a dark sense of humor that skillfully weaves three love stories by portraying the advantages, perils, and ironies of being romantically involved. The codirectors, Carlitos Ruíz Ruíz and Mariem Pérez Riera, premiered the movie at the Tribeca Film Festival in New York. It also defeated four other competitors to be selected as the film to represent Puerto Rico for a possible Oscar in the Best Foreign Film category in 2008. These films are tangible testimony that the artistic efforts of Puerto Rican filmmakers are slowly being recognized in multiple international cinematic forums.

NUYORICANS: THE FILMS OF THE PUERTO RICAN DIASPORA

Puerto Ricans have now spent over three generations traveling back and forth between the island and the U.S. mainland, especially the New York area. They are such an established group in the northeastern area of the United States that the term *Nuyorican* is now used to refer to New Yorkers of Puerto Rican descent or Puerto Ricans who have moved to the area. The term is a blend of the terms *New York* and *Puerto Rican*. While there are almost 4 million Puerto Ricans living in the United States, it is estimated that over half a million of them live in the northeastern part of the United States. In New York, they have congregated in areas such as Spanish Harlem, the South Bronx, and Queens. Starting with the establishment of the Nuyorican Poets Café in 1975, a long list of artists and writers have related their experiences about migrating to New York and the struggles of adapting to life in the Big Apple. Film is not an exception.

Nuyorican filmmakers bring to the big screen plots dealing with reasons for leaving the island, how families are divided, the options graduate students seek on the mainland, reverse migration, musical and literary developments, and the use of language. These artists constantly try to evaluate what they lost— and what they gained—when they moved north. The evolution of Nuyorican art in film can be divided into three stages. First, during the decades of the 1950s and 1960s, Puerto Rican actors (and most Latinos) in films were often portrayed in the roles of criminals, drug addicts, prostitutes, Latin lovers, or lazy characters. The distorted images of *boricuas* in motion pictures could not change until they took some control over the creative process such as writing scripts, developing different characters, and directing and producing their own films.

Second, the 1970s and 1980s represent a clear attempt by Nuyoricans to develop an identity to be portrayed on the big screen. They became keenly aware that they were already a little different from their counterparts still living on the island, but they were also slightly different from the mainstream society that surrounded them but did not accept them as U.S. citizens. Films like *La carreta*, produced in 1970, offer a juxtaposition of binaries such as urban versus rural, old values versus new experiences, and migrating north versus staying on the island. This type of movie allows both filmmakers and audiences to look introspectively and become comfortable with the life they left behind in Puerto Rico. In the same period, *Los dos mundos de Angelita* (Angela's Two Worlds), which premiered in 1982, offered a plot in which traditional values clash with new ideas about social integration. Also, language is a crucial component that highlights the expression of traditional expectations. In the film, the two main protagonists are recent immigrants, and of course, they speak Spanish. English is used to present the more established Puerto Ricans in the United States. The use of bilingual dialogues would become a constant feature of Nuyorican films.

Films of the 1980s deal with the melancholy topic of reverse migration back to the island. Films from this period often explore the perennial need of some Puerto Ricans to abandon the big, crowded cities and return to a simple and pleasant life of retirement in Puerto Rico. The plots usually reveal that the images of San Juan, Ponce, or San Germán that these people had are no longer accurate. They were illusions based on the life they once knew in Puerto Rico, but in a distant past. Films such as *The House of Ramón Iglesias* (1982) highlight that returning to the island also divides families, in the same way the original migration to the United States had done in the previous generation.

Now, the parents want to go back to Puerto Rico, but their sons already have careers, friends, and marriages established in the United States, so it is natural that some members of the family refuse to go back to the island.

Third, the 1990s allowed Puerto Rican filmmakers in the United States to explore social topics from a critical perspective and analyze the impact they had on *boricua* communities both on the mainland and in Puerto Rico itself. The movie *La operación* (The Operation) is designed to make the world aware of how Puerto Rican women were victims of high levels of sterilization during the 1950s, leaving almost one-third of the female population unable to have children. This was a very controversial film when it was released for public viewing. In addition, films such as *Brincando el charco* (Crossing the Pond) from 1994 and *Go Fish* from 1996 are focused on topics of homosexuality, lesbianism, feminism, and the intolerance experienced by Puerto Rican urban enclaves in the United States. Frances Negrón-Muntaner is an accomplished writer who produced *Brincando el charco* and also *AIDS in the Barrio: Eso no me pasa a mí*, openly discussing the acculturation and discrimination experienced by several of the Puerto Rican gay communities. Then, during the first decade of the twenty-first century, U.S.-based Puerto Rican actors and cinematographers went back to explore the links between their beloved island and their new life in the United States. By doing so, they question the meaning of being *boricua* and what that entails in practical terms. In 2006, films such as *Yo soy boricua pa'que tú lo sepas* (I'm *Boricua*; Just So You Know) decided that it is all rooted in cultural pride. Being *boricua* means not losing your native language and maintaining the stories and traditions of the past, while adapting to a new reality of bilingualism and professional opportunities in the United States. This movie—directed by Rosie Pérez and narrated by Jimmy Smits—also allows average Puerto Ricans to express their opinion on relevant topics such as (1) the bombing of Vieques, (2) the political status of the island, (3) the advantages and perils of being connected to the United States, (4) the imprisonment of proponents of independence, and (5) the forced sterilization of women. One of the big challenges of films like these is still the main concept of distribution. To deliver the message intended in Puerto Rican films, it is required that people actually see the movies. If not, they are not financially profitable.

To improve the problem of distribution, Puerto Rico is taking yet another official government step. In 2007, it launched a project called Cinema Puerto Rico, based in the city of Santa Monica, California. This undertaking is actually part of the Film Corporation's attempt to revitalize the film industry on the island. Cinema Puerto Rico will serve as a centralized location in the United States to highlight movies recently released and the ones still in production. Within Puerto Rico, the organization will assist with the distribution of films to all the existing 260 movie theaters in Puerto Rico. Abroad, it will continue to promote the tax incentives available to investors in film production, the improvements in technical facilities, and the work done in the post-production stages of filmmaking. The artistic talent of Puerto Ricans is creatively reflected in their films. They are no longer only hired personnel in foreign ventures. Puerto Rican musicians, actors, technicians, and filmmakers have become active contributors to the world stage, and they are well on their way to establishing a vibrant film industry on the island.

References

Colo, Papo. *Films with a Purpose: A Puerto Rican Experiment in Social Films.* New York: Exit Art, 1987.

Espada, Frank. "The Puerto Rican Diaspora." *Hispanic* 20, no. 6 (2007): 48–53.

Flores Carrión, Marisel. *Cuarenta años de cine puertorriqueño.* San Juan: Archivo General de Puerto Rico. http://www.preb.com/devisita/marisel.htm.

García, Ana María, ed. *Puerto Rican Film and Video "Made in USA."* San Juan: University of Puerto Rico Press, 2000.

García, Kino. *Breve historia del cine puertorriqueño.* Bayamón, Puerto Rico: Taller de Cine La Red, 1984.

García, Kino. *Historia del cine puertorriqueño 1900–1999: Un siglo de cine en Puerto Rico.* San Juan: University of Puerto Rico Press, 2003.

Jiménez, Lillian. "From the Margin to the Center: Puerto Rican Cinema in the United States." *Centro de Estudios Puertorriqueños Bulletin* 2, no. 8 (1990): 28–43.

Kelly, Gary D. "The Emergence of U.S. Hispanic Films." *Bilingual Review* 18, no. 2/3 (1993): 192–231.

Ramos-Perea, Roberto. "Un nuevo cine puertorriqueño." *Intermedio*, October 17, 2007.

Safa, Helen Icken. *Urban Poor in Puerto Rico: A Study in Development and Inequality.* New York: Holt, Rinehart, and Winston, 1974.

Web Sites

Digital Film Academy of Puerto Rico, http://www.digitalfilmacademy.com/puertorico.php.

Puerto Rico Film Commission, http://www.puertoricofilm.com/.

7

Literature

COMPARED TO ITS Latin American neighbors, Puerto Rico was a latecomer to the literary scene. Since the island has been a colony for over five hundred years, the development of literature on the island is closely linked to historical and political events. Puerto Rico has produced notable novelists, poets, essayists, and playwrights, but a large percentage of its writers have been poets. In the early 1800s, many of them got their start as journalists for newspapers, where they started writing politically charged columns. For almost two hundred years of literary output, *boricuas* have used consistent themes such as poverty, nationalism, migration, and the loss of old values. However, topics and writing styles continue to evolve as social conditions in Puerto Rico change.

There are two main historical periods for the development of literature in Puerto Rico: the Spanish colonialism until 1898 and the period following the U.S. invasion in the same year. The former represents a strong sense of literary repression in the hands of the Spanish Crown, and the latter deals with twentieth-century contemporary themes such as political ambivalence, cultural identity, and emigration linked to poverty. In addition, contemporary Puerto Rican literature is now viewed as having two branches: the work produced on the island and the literary energy expressed by writers in the United States, initially called the Nuyorican movement. However, it does not necessarily mean that both sides readily acknowledge and validate each other's work. Points of tension between these two groups reflect the variety and complexity of modern *boricua* literature. These differences emerged from the need

to develop a national and cultural identity. The expression of literature simply highlights the inherent contradiction that Puerto Ricans are U.S. citizens,
but yet they are also culturally and linguistically different from those on the
mainland.

Spanish Control and Censorship (1493–1898)

For the first three hundred years after the arrival of the Spaniards in 1493,
there was virtually no trace of Puerto Rican literature written on the island.
The earliest writings related to Puerto Rico were produced by Spanish settlers
and soldiers who wrote letters to Spain to narrate and describe their experiences in the Caribbean. Writers like Fray Bartolomé de las Casas, Juan Ponce
de León, and Gonzalo Fernández de Oviedo y Valdés wrote such reports, but
their main purpose was to keep the Spanish Crown informed of the status of
the colonies. Their writings did not express the point of view of Puerto Ricans
at all.

Overall, Spain tried to repress the production and dissemination of local literature during the colonial period (1493–1898). Only government officials,
ecclesiastical figures, and rich landowners had access to reading materials from
abroad. People native to the island were specifically prohibited from reading
any kind of literature; violators faced punishments that ranged from prison
terms to even exile from the island. These restrictions became more intense
during the revolutionary period of Latin America (1810–1840), when most of
the viceroyalties were engaged in bloody battles for independence. The Spanish fear was that Puerto Ricans would also find a way of developing a cohesive
voice by reading dangerous materials about independence and freedom, the
way it had occurred in other Spanish colonies. The restriction of reading materials was further enhanced since Puerto Rico did not have a printing press
until 1806. In contrast to other Spanish colonies, the Spanish Crown did not
authorize the creation of an educational system in Puerto Rico or the founding
of prestigious universities. Consequently, the levels of illiteracy on the island,
even at the beginning of the 1800s, were extremely high, reaching almost 80
percent. The only people who were educated came from families who had the
financial means to send their sons to study in Europe.

There were two notable early books written by Spaniards about Puerto Rico.
First, Fray Iñigo Abad y Lasierra wrote in 1778 what was considered to be the
first complete history of Puerto Rico, with a rather lengthy title: *The Geo-
graphic, Civil, and Political History of the Island of Saint John the Baptist of
Puerto Rico.* This outstanding historian published his manuscript in Madrid,
and it included a detailed section on Puerto Rican folklore and customs. Overall, it offered a history of the island from 1493 to 1783. The first book to

actually be published in Puerto Rico was titled *Ocios de la juventud* (Youth's Leisure), and it appeared in 1806. It was written by Juan Rodríguez Calderón, a celebrated Spanish poet. However, there were still no Puerto Rican writers at this point.

Despite all the censorship and restrictions, literature still managed to develop on the island, usually by expressing the hardships of daily life in Puerto Rico. The initial topics took the form of folktales that could be spread orally. They were called *coplas* and *décimas*. The *décima puertorriqueña* (or *décima jíbara*) had a metric combination of ten verses. Oral storytelling became the earliest form of literature and expressed the concerns of the average population, and hence did not necessarily follow European literary standards or movements.

The year 1849 was crucial for the tangible beginnings of literature in Puerto Rico. Manuel Alonso Pacheco (1822–1889) wrote *El Jíbaro* (The Mountain Farmer), a book that is often considered to be the cornerstone of all literature produced on the island. It was written in a combination of poetry and prose. This was the very first time that the distinct local culture of Puerto Rico was presented in written form by a Puerto Rican writer. There were also a few Puerto Ricans who left the island and wrote about their homeland while abroad, such as Manuel A. Alonso, who also published a sociological study of Puerto Rico in 1849. He described the details of average events in the life of Puerto Ricans using both narrative essays and poetry. Two years later, the Spanish governor assigned to Puerto Rico, Juan Pezuela Ceballos, actively advocated for the opening of the Real Academia de Bellas Artes in San Juan in 1851. This certainly was a major step toward improving education, and hence literacy, in Puerto Rico. This new academy trained teachers, attempted to design an appropriate curriculum, and even organized literary contests. However, the main beneficiaries of the institution were people who were already educated and enjoyed a privileged position on the island.

Some of the Puerto Rican writers in the middle of the nineteenth century started out as journalists expressing their political points of view against Spanish oppression. These were times of extreme political unrest, even if there were no overt wars of independence in Puerto Rico. Their columns decried the injustices of slavery and the massive poverty experienced on the island. Spain responded by sending into exile dangerous writers like Francisco Gonzalo Marín. Many of these exiles were sent to Cuba, the Dominican Republic, and even the United States, where they continued promoting a revolutionary movement. The ideas expressed by these writers provided the spark for the only independence rebellion ever held in Puerto Rico in 1868, which became known as the Grito de Lares. This failed attempt at independence and the abolition of slavery was quickly dissipated by the Spanish military. Its main organizer, Manuel Rojas, was immediately sent into exile.

The failed insurrection of the Grito de Lares fueled even more literary output in the early 1870s. The need for a cultural and national identity became a primary concern for *boricua* writers, and nationalism had a sense of urgency in the literature of the period. José Gautier Benítez (1851–1880) produced poetry presaging the birth of a new nation. Another notable writer who was deeply moved by the Grito de Lares rebellion was Lola Rodríguez de Tío (1843–1924). She grew up surrounded by politicians and intellectuals, a dangerous combination that would eventually influence her writing, which caused her to be exiled from Puerto Rico not once, but several times. For example, she wrote the patriotic lyrics for "La borinqueña," which were considered to be too subversive by the Spanish authorities. The song became quite popular. Her subsequent books, such as *Mis cantares* in 1876 and *Mi libro de Cuba* in 1893, caused her and her family to be exiled first to Cuba, and then to New York, where she actually ended up working with the famous Cuban writer José Martí on revolutionary topics. She lived in Cuba for almost twenty-five years. She has been recognized for suggesting that Puerto Rico should use the Cuban flag—with the colors reversed—as the model for its own flag. The words to "La Borinqueña" were eventually changed, but it has remained as the official patriotic anthem of Puerto Rico.

It was not until the 1890s that Puerto Ricans actually started to write novels. Manuel Zeno Gandía (1855–1930) became the very first novelist when he published his seminal work *La charca* (The Stagnant Pond) in 1894. The general story attacks the social conditions of the average population on the island. It narrates the difficult situation of peasants living in the mountains used for coffee production. The plot argues that the Roman Catholic Church, combined with large landowners, played an important part in restricting the freedom and development of poor people in Puerto Rico. Zeno was a medical doctor by training but also had a strong interest in politics. Up until his death in 1930, he continued to be an outspoken supporter of Puerto Rican independence. His novel *La charca* is usually taught in most schools on the island. If Puerto Rico had achieved its complete independence, most likely, this novel would have been the impetus for a new literary movement aligned with a nation-building period.

Toward the end of the 1800s, two distinguished Puerto Rican writers worked arduously to promote freedom, equality, and human rights not only on their island but also at an international level. They possessed a unique blend of political knowledge, a quest for social justice, philosophical thought, and a willingness to fight for their ideals. They are true examples of how a pen is mightier than a sword. First, Román Baldorioty de Castro (1822–1889) was elected to represent Puerto Rico in the Spanish Cortes in 1870, where he openly expressed his antislavery ideals—not a popular position at the time. While in Spain, he founded and edited the journal *Asuntos de Puerto Rico* (Puerto Rican Affairs). He returned to the Caribbean in 1873 and settled in the southern town of Ponce, where he started the newspaper *El Derecho* (Basic Rights), which became increasingly critical of the Spanish government. He had to flee to Saint-Domingue (now the Dominican Republic), where he founded the College of the Antilles. He then returned to Puerto Rico five years later to start yet another publishing venture. This time, *La Crónica* (The Chronicles) was a political venue to express and support the independence of Puerto Rico. Even though he was in trouble with the authorities, he founded the Autonomist Political Party, which landed him in jail. He was imprisoned in the El Morro Fortress in Old San Juan. He was released rather quickly, but died in Ponce soon after, in 1889. Another acclaimed Puerto Rican writer who obtained international prominence was Eugenio María de Hostos y Bonilla (1839–1903). He was trained in Spain from elementary school all the way to his university studies in the legal profession. During the 1870s, he traveled throughout Latin America, advocating the abolition of slavery, equal civil rights, and greater collaboration among Hispanic countries. He was a prolific writer with a social agenda. For example, his writings and petitions in Chile helped women to obtain the right to enter professional schools. His report on the treatment and abuse of Chinese workers in Peru helped to change work conditions and public opinion about the railroad industry. He also worked on reforming the educational curriculum and instruction in the Dominican Republic. In the literary field, he produced a long list of essays, poems, and novels. Perhaps his most distinctive work was *La peregrinación de Bayoán* (The Pilgrimage of Bayoán), published in 1863. It was written as fiction, but it presented a disguised message regarding the oppressive colonial regime of authoritarian Spanish rulers. He was a writer until the end of his life. He even wrote his own epitaph: "Deseo que digan: En la isla de Puerto Rico nació un hombre que amó la verdad, deseaba justicia, y trabajó por el bienestar de todos los hombres" (When I die, I wish people will say: "There was a man born in Puerto Rico who loved the truth, fought for justice, and worked hard for the improvement of all mankind").

THE UNITED STATES TAKES CONTROL IN 1898

The Spanish-American War had a profound effect not only on the literature of Puerto Rico but also on the entire society. Local literature flourished after the United States took control of the island, especially poetry. At the beginning of the twentieth century, clusters of Puerto Rican writers grouped themselves around cohesive themes that reflected the reality of their daily lives and local struggles. These literary movements seem to form every two or three decades, and their writers became known as the "generation" of that decade. There are at least four specific movements.

Generation of 1898

When the United States took control of the island in 1898, it created a significant shift in local society. It sparked uncertainly about regional politics, the moribund economy, the question of potential independence, and the use of Spanish versus English as the official form of communication. Initially, most of the writers living on the island were optimistic about the potential opportunities that Puerto Rico could experience by being linked to the United States, both politically and economically. The hope was that Puerto Rico would be granted independence. However, the island was quickly defined as a territory of the United States and a military government took control of virtually all local affairs. Even worse, the new ruling country imposed English as the official language of instruction in all schools. The reaction by members of the literary class was to write poetry and novels using patriotic themes that opposed the Americanization of the island. Writers like Román Baldorioty, Ramón Emeterio Betances, Eugenio María de Hostos, and Lola Rodríguez de Tío had already established a reputation for advocating independence from Spain; they continued writing nationalistic works, but now the target of their resentment was the U.S. government.

Manuel Zeno Gandía was a writer who obtained even more literary prominence as part of the Generation of 1898. He had already written the classic novel *La charca* in 1894. After that success, he was a witness to the Spanish-American War, which deeply impacted his work. Zeno went on to produce a trilogy of novels under the collective title *Crónicas de un mundo enfermo* (Chronicles of a Sick World); the word *chronicles* implies a high level of truth. The three novels were published over a span of thirty-five years: *Garduña* in 1890, *El negocio* (The Business) in 1922, and *Redentores* (The Redeemers) in 1925. In his literary works, Zeno paints a picture of Puerto Rico in even further cultural and political decline after the United States became the new ruler of the island. The literary production of this recognized novelist offers a crucial bridge between the end of the Spanish colonial period and the beginning of the United States' new colonization pattern.

Another prominent writer from the *Generación del 98* was Luis Muñoz Rivera (1859–1916). He published a collection of poems titled *Tropicales*. However, his other interests in journalism and politics prevented him from being completely dedicated to pursuing life as a poet. As a politician, he denounced independence ideas and instead advocated a diplomatic solution to improve the conditions of Puerto Ricans living on the island. He was originally part of a commission representing the island when he visited Spain to request and negotiate an autonomous government for Puerto Rico in the early 1880s. As a writer, he also started as a journalist on important newspapers. However, to better channel crucial political ideas, he founded the newspaper *El Territorio* in 1899 to express the points of view of the landowners who were negatively affected by the arrival of the United States as a colonial power. In 1901, he moved to New York City and founded the *Puerto Rican Herald.* This bilingual publication also proved to be successful. Five years later, he returned to Puerto Rico with a new political idea: to establish a new political party based not on independence, but on cooperation with the United States. He avoided radical political positions and followed a more moderate approach to negotiations. The result of his efforts was that he founded the Unionist Party. His interest in political life at this point turned into a lifelong service to represent Puerto Rico, first in the House of Delegates on the island, then as the resident commissioner to the U.S. House of Representatives in 1910, and eventually, as the island's governor. One of his major accomplishments was to negotiate the details of the Jones Act in 1917, which granted U.S. citizenship to all Puerto Ricans born on the island. This prolific writer and poet is now frequently referred to as the grandfather of Puerto Rican politics.

Two additional poets took a clear anticolonial position against the United States. José de Diego (1866–1959) and Luis Lloréns Torres (1878–1944) embraced their Hispanic heritage and used cultural elements such as language and religion to express opposition to the Americanization of the island. However, it is also important to highlight the ironic position of these authors, who wrote hostile poetry against the United States but were also part of the elite social class who were economically benefiting from the American investments in Puerto Rico.

Generation of the 1920s

Literature in the 1920s took a pessimistic and dark turn. The *Generación del 20s* developed a consistent rhetorical style by writing about social injustice, a feature that was even more salient in the countryside. Authors in this movement include Emilio Belaval, Tomás Blanco, and Antonio Pedreira.

In addition, many Puerto Rican writers, especially poets, were influenced by the new literary movement started by the Nicaraguan poet Rubén Darío. His new school of literary thought was called modernism. This new model of writing was radically different than the ones offered by Spain, which had traditionally been copied and emulated by writers from the Americas. This was the first time that a former Spanish colony did not follow the European guidelines for literary standards. For example, modernist writers were no longer restricted to using imagery based only on Roman and Greek mythology; they now also evoked the beauty of Aztec, Taíno, and Inca ancestors. Also, their allegoric descriptions did not have to follow European metaphors of comparison. In addition, novels could now be placed in Brazilian jungles, Nicaraguan lakes, or Mexican mountains. During this period, it was common to find vivid descriptions of Puerto Rican landscapes and natural beauty.

Poets like Luis Palés Matos and Julia de Burgos are shining examples of this new literary movement. Luis Palés Matos (1898–1959) became particularly known for writing the so-called Negro poetry. His Afro-Antillean poems offered rhythms and metrics that had not been previously used in Puerto Rico. He believed that the *jíbaro* (a white mountain farmer) had been a traditional figure in Puerto Rican literature, but his prominence excluded the black population from taking its place in the island's cultural identity. Together with Nicolás Guillén (an Afro-Cuban writer), they infused Africanism into their respective national literatures. Matos published his initial poems in newspapers. Eventually he published a collection of his poems in 1937 in a book titled *Tum Tum de pasa y grifería.* His work was extremely successful and earned him national literary recognition in Puerto Rico. However, he faced harsh criticism by the black community, who sometimes felt offended by his poems—mostly because Matos himself was white. Toward the end of his life, he changed his style to write poems themed with a broader spectrum of the Antilles, and not necessarily with African themes. His contemporary, Julia de Burgos (1914–1953), is often considered to be the best poet of the twentieth century in Puerto Rico. At the level of Latin America, Burgos and Gabriela Mistral are referred to as the two best female poets. Burgos published three books with all her poetry. A large number of her poems express intimate romantic moments with a hint of eroticism. The first book, titled *Río Grande de Loíza,* reflects her inspiration based on nature and the section of Puerto Rico with a large African population. She noticed a lack of interest from marketing companies, so she actively promoted her first two books around the island. Her third book, *Yo misma fui mi ruta* (I Was My Own Route), was published posthumously after her death in 1953. Politically, Burgos was also a strong advocate for Puerto Rican independence, and she was an outspoken activist and defender of women's rights.

Generation of the 1930s and 1940s

The writers of the 1930s and 1940s focused more on a binary distinction of colonial status versus nationalistic pride. Their work reflected the collective search for a national consciousness, or at least cultural unity. In addition, writers began to incorporate realism, a new school of thought that aims to express events using real situations and characters. This new trend suggested the need to explore specific and tangible topics such as the consequences of World War II on the island's economy. The 1930s is also the decade when the great migration of Puerto Ricans to the promised land of the United States began. Authors like Pedro Soto and René Márquez actively explored the topic of migration in search of better opportunity. They linked the emigration off the island to the economic conditions and lack of employment opportunities on the island.

By the end of the 1930s, the nationalistic rhetoric turned more intense and radical in Puerto Rico. Small protests erupted, with people complaining about the economic depression prevalent in the southern and western parts of the island. The investments orchestrated by the United States were concentrated in San Juan and on the northern shores, while the rest of the island decayed into desperate conditions. Protesters claimed that—in an effort to bring foreign investment to the island—the United States froze wages on the island, which made working conditions sometimes intolerable. To bring these issues to light, there was a peaceful protest in the city of Ponce in 1937. When students and workers started singing the patriotic lyrics of "La Borinqueña," the American governor in charge of the island ordered that the protest be dissipated. The result was a harsh confrontation in which eighteen people were killed and over two hundred were injured. The event became known as the Ponce Massacre of 1937. The location of these tragic events (the corner of Aurora and Marina Streets) is now the site for the small but informative Museo de la Masacre de Ponce. René Márquez wrote the play *Palm Sunday* dealing with the protest and its dreadful conclusion. These actions also pushed Puerto Ricans to establish the Partido Popular Demócrata during the late 1930s to protest against and fight the new U.S. exploitation of Puerto Rican workers.

The 1940s offered a new literary movement in which authors focused on real historical events. Topics like migration, the Korean War, and nationalistic movements are described in detail. The stories are usually focused on the problems of specific characters and do not necessarily aim to represent an entire social entity like the church or the government. By focusing on real people, these writers could engage readers at a deeper and more relatable level. This is also an important literary period in which authors assign leading roles to women. They are shown as intelligent and complex individuals and not as the typical submissive characters they embodied traditionally.

Among this group of writers, René Márquez (1919–1990) was perhaps the best-known drama writer in the first half of the twentieth century. He published *La carreta* (The Oxcart) in 1940, a theater play about a family from the countryside moving to the poor slums of San Juan and eventually to New York City. In each location, Márquez narrated their struggle to adapt to a new life. At the end of the story, the family eventually returns to Puerto Rico to

a life that is now different from the one they had left. This theater production opened successfully in San Juan in 1951, much to the pleasure of the
boricua audience. Three years later, it opened in Manhattan, where the public
also gave it favorable reviews. Later, in 1965, the English version of *La carreta*
opened in a theater off Broadway, with Miriam Colón as the main actress.

At the end of 1930s and early 1940s, Puerto Rican writers started to analyze
Puerto Rican culture in a retrospective way after three decades of U.S. control.
They expressed strong concern for the struggle to retain their unique *boricua*
culture and resist the Americanization of the island. An author who actively
projected these topics was Enrique A. Laguerre Velez (1905–2005), who wrote
La llamarada (Flash of Fire) in 1935, which is often considered to be one of
the most important novels of the twentieth century; it vividly narrates the
exploitation of the working class. Other writers of the period also produced a
large quantity of novels, poems, and essays dealing with the perceived conflict
between preserving a unique Hispanic culture and the increasing American
influence in Puerto Rican society.

During the 1950s, the U.S. Congress passed important resolutions toward
defining the political future of Puerto Rico. First, in 1948, the United States
allowed Puerto Ricans to vote and select their own governor; the United States
would no longer appoint the ruling governor. The first one to serve as a locally
elected governor was the Puerto Rican journalist and poet Luis Muñoz Marín,
and he served in that post for seventeen years. Then, in 1952, the agreement
was to give the island a different status. The result of this agreement is known
by two different names, depending on the language being used: in Spanish,
it is called the Estado Libre Asociado, and it is known as the Commonwealth
of Puerto Rico in English. As a result of Law 600, Puerto Rico was able to
design its own regional constitution to manage local political and economic
affairs. However, the U.S. federal government would still provide a diplomatic
core, postal service, and the U.S. dollar as official currency. These political gestures initially made Puerto Ricans feel in control of their own destiny. While
these certainly are remarkable advances toward an autonomous status, in reality, the U.S. Congress still has complete control over Puerto Rico's political
future. Consequently, by the late 1970s, most writers and intellectuals on
the island pointed out that this agreement only perpetuated a new system of
neocolonialism.

The 1970s was a decade of dramatic social change in Latin America.
Most countries experienced the consequences of the Cuban Revolution as
the United States reshaped its foreign policy to the motto of "not another
Cuba" and to fight communism in the Western Hemisphere. The civil rights
movement in the United States was beginning to have an influence on the
minority populations in Latin America. There was also a sudden explosion of

additional publishing houses in Latin America that raised the quality of literature produced. Moreover, outstanding authors like Juan Rulfo (Mexico), Jorge
Luis Borges (Argentina), and Miguel Ángel Asturias (Guatemala) were taking
their place in the new literary landscape. All these social and literary events
affected the type of literature Puerto Rican writers were going to produce and
the stories they told during the following two decades.

One of the authors that best embodies the new breed of writers in the
1970s and 1980s is Rosario Ferré (1938–). She transformed the roles that
female characters had in *boricua* literature. Overall, Ferré addressed the issue
of inequality of women in the Hispanic culture. She offers female characters
who are not just objects of sexuality, but women who take control of their
own destiny in a very male-oriented society. In her book *Sitio a Eros* (Siege to
Eros), from 1989, she reveals characters who are strong, intelligent women,
but also sometimes lonely, which makes them relatable to the audience. This
collection of essays established her reputation as a contemporary writer.

Some of Ferré's other novels include *Papeles de Pandora* (Pandora's Papers),
published in 1979; *La mona que le pisaron la cola* (The Monkey Who Got Her
Tail Stepped On), released in 1981; *Fábulas de la garza desangrada* (Fables of
the Bleeding Heron), a collection of poetry from 1982; and *El vuelo del cisne*
(Flight of the Swan), a fictional book published in 2001. Among all the materials produced in her literary career, many literary critics consider "La muñeca
menor" (The Youngest Doll) her best short story ever published. It is included
within her first book *Sitio a Eros*. It is only six pages long, but it narrates over
three decades of *boricua* history, but told from the perspective of a woman.
However, Ferré's stories should not be viewed only as feminist stories. She has
a strong political background that initially supported independence, despite
the fact that her father—a former governor of Puerto Rico—advocated the
statehood position. Nevertheless, even though she includes social and political themes in her work, from a literary perspective, she was more influential
in changing the types of characters appearing in Puerto Rican literature. Her
work impacted a new group of writers who also incorporated the voices of
blacks and homosexuals as protagonists in their own stories. The difficulty for
the general audience was to decide how these underrepresented segments of
society would fit within the notion of national identity.

To further complicate the concept of cultural and national identity, a new
trend in Puerto Rican literature emerged in the 1970s. It is more like a new
literary branch, rather than just a temporary interest. It was in the 1960s and
1970s that Puerto Ricans living in the United States, especially New York,
became a cohesive unit and expressed their experiences via poetry and theater.
These writers, however, used different topics than their counterparts on the
island. They also had more linguistic choices available to narrate their journey

of integration into a new urban reality. They wrote in Spanish, English, or sometimes Spanglish.

PUERTO RICAN LITERATURE WRITTEN IN THE UNITED STATES

Puerto Rico has one of the highest levels of emigration in the world. According to the U.S. Census of 2005, there are now more Puerto Ricans living in the United States (almost 4 million) than there are living on the island (3.87 million). Since 1917, all Puerto Ricans are U.S. citizens, and this political relationship has facilitated the migration from the Caribbean island to the U.S. mainland, especially to the areas of New York and New Jersey. By the 1970s, at least three generations of *boricuas* had been traveling back and forth between the two locations. This migrating phenomenon is often known as the Puerto Rican diaspora. This political and economic relationship between the United States and Puerto Rico would inevitably be reflected in the arts, music, and literature.

The genesis of Puerto Rican literature produced in the United States can be traced back to the 1940s when Jesús Colón wrote *Puerto Rican Sketches and Other Stories,* which reflects the difficulties of assimilating to a new place. The development of a Puerto Rican subculture in the United States caused tension with other cultural groups in the northeastern part of the country. At the time, Puerto Ricans suffered discrimination and were often socially ostracized for trying to maintain their culture while living in a foreign land. *Boricuas* initially could not really understand why they were not accepted into the mainstream society when they were also U.S. citizens. For example, Pedro Juan Soto published *Spiks* (a negative term) in 1956. The book offers a collection of stories about Puerto Rican families and their experiences in the Big Apple.

The Nuyorican Poets Café

The need to channel their creative energy led intellectuals, writers, and poets to establish the Nuyorican Poets Café in New York City in 1973. Some of the founding members, such as Miguel Piñero, Nicholosa Mohr, and Pedro Pietri, aimed to develop and define their own identities via literature and artistic expression. The term *Nuyorican* is a combination of the terms *New York* and *Puerto Rican*. It is precisely during the 1960s and 1970s that Nuyorican literature becomes a unifying force for *boricuas* outside the island. Its popular themes reflect the concerns at the time for the economic conditions of recent Puerto Rican immigrants to New York and the identity crisis that is experienced by second-generation Puerto Ricans born on the U.S. mainland. After two generations of migrants, writers openly discussed the rejection *boricuas* faced in the big U.S. cities. Authors like Piri Thomas, who wrote *Down These Mean Streets* in 1967, highlighted the dilemma Puerto Ricans feel when they attempt to integrate into the mainstream culture in the U.S. urban centers. Nuyoricans are painfully aware that they are now a little different than their counterparts still living on the island, but they are not quite accepted by the main society that surrounds them in places like New York City, Philadelphia, and New Jersey. It is also important to highlight that even when Puerto Ricans are born on the mainland, they do not identify themselves as Puerto Rican-Americans; they are simply Puerto Ricans.

The main literary genres explored by Nuyorican writers in the 1970s were poetry and theater. In fact, their poetry has very unique features. It is essentially street poetry based on spoken language, but with a fusion of jazz and salsa rhythms. It is poetry meant to be performed and read to the audience. These poets were having poetry slams long before it was fashionable to do so. Another unique feature of Nuyorican literature is that it traditionally includes both Spanish and English for poetic expression. It is important to recognize that these writers are bicultural individuals who use images and sounds from both Spanish and English. As a result, they also play with the double meaning of words by using two languages.

During the 1970s, *boricua* playwrights from New York started to portray the urban experience of Puerto Ricans in the United States and adapted the stories to be performed in theater. Miguel Piñero is perhaps the most recognized playwright of this generation. He wrote *Short Eyes* while he was in prison. In 1974, it won the award for Best American Play offered by the New York Drama Critics. The play explores two main themes: how Puerto Ricans survive in American prisons and the relationships they have with other racial and ethnic groups. His work sparked other plays throughout the 1970s and 1980s that dealt with the harsh realities of living in the barrios of New York City and daily experiences with violence, drugs, racism, discrimination, and poverty.

In 2008, the Nuyorican Poets Café celebrated thirty-five years of providing an unrestricted forum for the expression of poetry, music, art, and theater. It offered a yearlong calendar of vibrant events that included weekly poetry slams, hip-hop performances, weekly Latin jazz nights, painting exhibitions, and theater plays. This important institution in New York has now surpassed its original goal of simply providing a stage for underrepresented artists. The creative energy of talented writers and performers has elevated this location to a cornerstone institution of *boricua* culture in the United States.

CONTEMPORARY AUTHORS

The literature of Puerto Rico is continuously evolving. A new breed of writers from the island emerged at the end of the twentieth century, and they are still incorporating into their work some of the social and political changes that have recently occurred. However, they are also posing important questions about the themes traditionally addressed in regional literature. For example, they are questioning whether the "*boricua* nationalism" so prevalent among previous generations of writers actually represented the opinion of all Puerto Ricans, or only a point of view shared by the elite social classes and not the masses. They make reference to the three plebiscites (or special votes) regarding statehood, independence, or the status quo as evidence that the island is deeply divided on the issue. Despite the fact that political parties have made their case to the voters, there is still no clear and collective point of view toward the political future of Puerto Rico. So, perhaps there was no single point of view on nationalism in the past few decades either. Simultaneously, Puerto Rican writers residing on the U.S. mainland have also changed the topics they address in their novels, plays, and poetry. The topic of migration is still a common theme in Puerto Rican literature, and the island has recently even been labeled as a "commuter nation." However, the issue of language is still a point of contention between the two groups of writers: the authors from the United States say that using English is only a reflection of an extended Puerto Rican experience, and writers from the island claim that the use of Spanish is the only option for true and original *boricua* literature. The differences and similarities reveal the richness and complexity of Puerto Rican literary expression.

Boricua Writers from the U.S. Mainland

Puerto Rican writers in the United States continue to write in English as their main medium of communication. By the end of the twentieth century, the literature produced took the predominant form of autobiographical novels. These authors are fiercely proud of their background as Puerto Ricans, but they have also come to terms with their new home on the mainland United States, where most of them were born. Some of the most recognizable writers of this period have found a large audience to which their books are marketed, such as Esmeralda Santiago with *When I Was Puerto Rican*, published in 1993; Abraham Rodríguez with *Tales of the South Bronx: The Boy without a Flag*, released in 1992; and Ernesto Quiñones with *Bodega Dreams*, printed in 2000. Writers such as Esmeralda Santiago have also expressed their points of view on the political options available to the island (independence versus statehood). In her essay "Island of Lost Causes," she states that these plebiscites are a distraction from the main problems of the island such as the high unemployment and crime rates. She further declares that the process only offers the illusion of self-determination. After all, the results of these special votes are nonbinding resolutions—not much more than a recommendation to the U.S. Congress. Her comments are on target, but they are not necessarily well received on the island.

Contemporary Writers from the Island

Many of the modern poets and novelists were trained at the University of Puerto Rico at Río Piedras during the 1980s. Consequently, they have become known as the *Generación de los 80s*. This is the first generation of *boricua* writers that is specifically educated and trained in the writing profession as literary critics, anthology editors, university professors, and of course, creative writers. Most of the previous authors in the twentieth century were lawyers, doctors, and journalists who enjoyed writing on the side, but never really made a lifelong commitment to being writers. Another important difference is that the *Generación de los 80s* includes a balanced number of both male and female writers; previous generations of Puerto Rican novelists and poets were traditionally dominated by men. The inclusion of the female voice is certainly a positive addition to the literary discourse on the island.

These new *boricua* writers from the *Generación de los 80s* started publishing their work in literary magazines like *Filo de Fuego* and *Tríptico* during their training years. They are also extremely prolific writers, poets, and literary critics. However, in contrast with the literature produced in the United States, these authors produce material only in Spanish. During the 1980s and 1990s, they participated in recitals, literary competitions, and cultural events that actively promoted a new style of contemporary poetry, novels, and essays. These writers are focusing on social themes and do not necessarily have political aspirations. However, political discussions are never completely absent from most conversations on the island, so they are also present in this modern literature. It just does not have the nationalistic sense of urgency expressed by previous generations. Their work is usually reviewed from the current theoretical perspectives that analyze categories such as gender, sexuality, race, and social class.

Some of the most recent and talented writers of the twenty-first century include Rafael Acevedo, who published his novels *Moneda de sal* (Salt Coin) in 2006 and *Cannibalia* in 2005; Moisés Agosto Rosario, with his work titled *Nocturno y otros desamparos* (Nighttime and Other Dangers) in 2007; Maribel Sánchez-Pagan, with her novel *Ese hombre* (That Man) in 2006; and Zoé Jiménez Corretjer, with multiple books released in 2007, including *Sala de espera* (Waiting Room) and *Cánticos del lago* (Songs of the Lake). This generation has also excelled in writing essays that contribute to the field of literary criticism in refereed journals like *Claridad, Revista Universidad de América,* and *La Revista del Ateneo de Puerto Rico.*

In addition, most contemporary writers recognize that the literature of the past must be preserved. With that goal in mind, many of the writers who form the *Generación de los 80s* are actively working as editors for literary anthologies of Puerto Rican writers. Such works include *Literatura puertorriqueña del*

El Ateneo Puertorriqueño: founded in 1876, it is the oldest cultural institution in Puerto Rico; it publishes academic journals, houses an enviable art gallery, and possesses a large film library. Photo courtesy of the author.

siglo XX: Antología (An Anthology of Twentieth-century Puerto Rican Literature), published by Mercedes López Baralt in 2004, and the ambitious work edited by Michele Dávila Goncalves and others titled *Poetas sin tregua: Compilación de poetas puertorriqueñas de la generación del 80* (Poets without Rest: A Collection of Female Puerto Rican Poets from the Generation of 1980), published in 2006.

Enrique A. Laguerre Velez: Nobel Prize Nominee

Many literary critics and literature lovers consider Enrique A. Laguerre Velez (1905–2005) to be the best Puerto Rican novelist of the twentieth century. He was a prolific writer who penned thirty-one novels; in fact, he is the only writer from the island ever to be nominated for the Nobel Prize for Literature. Chris Hawley published an article in the newspaper *Puerto Rican Herald* (March 3, 1999) in which he narrated how the nomination became a process that involved an entire community proud of its Puerto Rican son. A relatively unknown magazine, *The Reliquary,* started writing letters to the Nobel Prize organization so they could become acquainted with the work of Laguerre. Soon, university professors from the island started writing letters to Sweden for his nomination. Then the Puerto Rican Senate, the House of Representatives, and even Governor Rossello formed a unified front to urge the nomination of Laguerre for the prestigious award. It was remarkable that the literary work of Laguerre would inspire such a momentous letter-writing campaign that grew into a request for popular support over the radio airwaves and evolved into political agreements to ensure his nomination. The Federation of Teachers of Puerto Rico and even trade unions participated in writing letters of support so he might be considered for the Swedish literary award. He was finally nominated in 1999, but he did not get the Nobel Prize for Literature. The island was disappointed, but Laguerre was certainly moved by all the well-intended support he received.

Perhaps Laguerre's most famous novel, *La llamarada* (Flash of Fire), published in 1935, is considered to be a classic of Puerto Rican literature. The story takes place in the sugarcane fields, and it highlights the difficulties of the average Puerto Rican working-class person. This novel, together with *La resaca* (The Undertow), narrates how poor workers are exploited. These two literary gems are always taught in Puerto Rican schools. Some of his other popular published works include *Los amos benévolos* (Benevolent Masters) in 1976, *Solar Montoya* (Montoya's Plot) in 1949, and *Los gemelos* (The Twins) in 1992. Despite the fact that many of his novels are well known in Latin America, hardly any of his works have been translated into other languages. Laguerre did not express sorrow when he did not get the Nobel Prize for Literature. Instead, he simply said, "To know that my people have listened to me, that is the greatest prize I could ever get." Enrique A. Laguerre Velez died on June 16, 2005, just a month before reaching one hundred years of age. He left a rich legacy of literary tradition that explored the complexity of Puerto Rican culture and identity. His long literary trajectory also serves as a reminder that the literature of any country is inherently incomplete because it is always in constant flux.

REFERENCES

Alonso, Manuel Antonio. *El jíbaro.* San Juan: Publicaciones Puertorriqueñas, 1996.

Antush, John V., ed. *Nuestro New York: An Anthology of Puerto Rican Plays.* New York: Mentor, 1994.

Centeno, Jesse. *Modernidad y resistencia: Literatura obrera de Puerto Rico (1898–1910).* San Juan: Centro de Estudios Avanzados de Puerto Rico, 2005.

Dávila Gonçalves, Michele C., Madeleine Millan Vega, Marisol Pereira Varela, Maribel Sánchez-Pagán, Belia E. Segarra Ramos y Johanny Vázquez Paz. *Poetas sin tregua: Compilación de poetas puertorriqueñas de la generación del 80.* Madrid, Spain: Ráfagas, 2006.

Davis, Lucille. *Puerto Rico.* New York: Grolier, 2000.

González, José Luis. *El país de los cuatro pisos.* Río Piedras, Puerto Rico: Huracán, 1980.

Hawley, Chris. "Rosello, Hernández Colón, Ferré Urge Nobel Prize Literature for Enrique Laguerre." *Puerto Rico Herald,* March 3, 1999.

Hermandad de Artistas Gráficos de Puerto Rico. *Puerto Rico arte e identidad.* San Juan: University of Puerto Rico Press, 2004.

Levy, Patricia. *Puerto Rico—Cultures of the World.* 2nd ed. Tarrytown, NY: Marshall Cavendish International, 2005.

López Baralt, Mercedes. *Literatura puertorriqueña del siglo XX: Antología.* San Juan: University of Puerto Rico Press, 2004.

Reyes, Israel. *Humor and the Eccentric Text in Puerto Rican Literature.* Gainesville: University of Florida Press, 2005.

Rivera de Álvarez, Josefina. *Literatura puertorriqueña: Su proceso en el tiempo.* Madrid: Partenon, 1983.

Sánchez González, Lisa. *Boricua Literature: A Literary History of the Puerto Rican Diaspora.* New York: New York University Press, 2001.

Santiago, Esmeralda. "Island of Lost Causes." In *Boricuas: Influential Puerto Rican Writings—An Anthology,* ed. Roberto Santiago, 22–24. New York: Random House, 1995.

———. *When I Was Puerto Rican.* New York: Vintage Books, 1994.

Santiago, Roberto, ed. *Boricuas: Influential Puerto Rican Writings—An Anthology.* New York: Random House, 1995.

Thomas, Piri. *Down These Mean Streets.* New York: Vintage, 1997.

Torrez-Padilla, José, and Carmen Haydee Rivera, eds. *Writing Off the Hyphen: New Perspectives on the Literature of Puerto Rican Diaspora.* Seattle: University of Washington Press, 2008.

8

Performing Arts: Music, Dance, and Theater

PUERTO RICANS CERTAINLY know how to have fun. Music and dance are two crucial components of the abundant creativity on the island. The musical genres practiced there range from sublime classical music to upbeat folk music, romantic *boleros*, the captivating rhythms of salsa, sensual pop, and the aggressive lyrics of *reggaeton*. The local government considers the preservation and promotion of culture an important aspect of social development and community cohesion, Following this philosophy, it financially supports an aggressive cultural program that includes the Conservatory of Music, a carefully designed music curriculum for elementary schools, and a national theater company that continuously tours the island. Nurturing the artistic and creative talent of Puerto Ricans involves not only formal training, but also participation in local festivals and community events. For organizational purposes, this chapter is separated into three sections of music, dance, and theater. However, these three elements of performing arts are inextricably connected in Puerto Rico, especially when dealing with popular music in public places. For example, it is actually difficult to separate music from dancing when attending cultural festivities and community celebrations—and the island has a long list of them.

MUSIC

Musical Instruments

The musical heritage of Puerto Rico is a fusion of African traditions, Spanish influence, and Taíno rhythms. Each group created and contributed to the vast array of musical instruments currently used on the island to perform all the musical genres. Some instruments were brought to Puerto Rico by outsiders, some were adapted to the unique Caribbean sounds, and others were invented right on the island. For example, the Taíno Arawak Indians used mostly percussion instruments like maracas and the guiro (*güiro* in Spanish). They developed maracas by filling hollow gourds with beans or pebbles. Now, modern versions are simply made of synthetic materials. Maracas are still used as a crucial percussion instrument for salsa music. They also created the guiro, which is a long gourd (about ten to twelve inches) carved on the outside with lines; it is played by moving a stick up against it. This instrument is widely used in folk music, and it is now often made of metal, wood, or fiberglass. The *güiro* is sometimes known by other names in Latin America, including *guayo*, *rascadera*, and *calabazo*.

Most of the other percussion instruments, especially the ones in the drum family, came from Africa. The bongos, congas, timbales, and *palitos* are all used in several Puerto Rican musical genres today. The bongos are two small drums joined together. The larger of the two is often referred to as the female drum, and the smaller one is known as the male drum. They are usually played sitting down and placed between the knees. The players alternate sounds by using different fingers and the palm of their hands. The congas are two bigger drums that are played standing up. They used to be made of a hollowed out tree trunk with skin nailed to the top. There are actually four different kinds of conga drums: the smallest is known as the *niño* (the child) and the largest is called the *tumba*. The congas are definitely a crucial instrument in most musical compositions from Puerto Rico. A different set of drums called timbales are extremely popular in salsa and mambo music. These are metal drums mounted on a metal stand, and they are played standing up using two drum sticks. Sometimes, they also have a cowbell and other accessories attached to the stand. The timbales have a stretchable skin that can be tuned by the musicians. Perhaps the most famous Puerto Rican timbales player was Tito Puente. Another basic instrument of African origin is the *palitos* (sticks). These primitive sticks are simply banged together to produce rhythm. They are about ten inches long and one inch thick. Most musical genres—including salsa, *plena*, *bomba*, and rumba—use the *palitos* as a basic percussion instrument.

The Spanish colonizers also brought with them their musical instruments, especially guitars. Over time, in Puerto Rico, the guitar with six strings evolved into at least four different instruments: (a) the *bordonua*, (b) the *requinto*, (c) the *tiple*, and (d) the *cuatro*. The *tiple* is derived from smaller Spanish guitars and is used in orchestras to play music like waltzes. The *requinto* is also smaller than a guitar, and it has a higher pitch. The *requinto* has been used in many Latin American countries to be part of *bolero*, *trio*, and other ballads. Out of all these string instruments, the *cuatro* is completely unique to Puerto Rico. Its name, which means "four," comes from the fact that it originally had only four strings. However, it is estimated that around the 1870s, it was changed to include five sets of double strings, for a total of ten strings. The *cuatro* is smaller than the guitar, and it is usually made from laurel wood. Its unique sound has made it identifiable as the national instrument of Puerto Rico. It is used to play the *aguinaldos*, or Christmas songs performed from house to house, but it is inherently important in most musical genres played on the island. It is also often used in cultural events, religious festivals, and community celebrations. The *cuatro* is definitely a central part of *boricua* cultural identity.

Folk Music: *Décima, Seis, Aguinaldos, Bomba,* and *Plena*

During the colonial period in the eighteenth and nineteenth centuries, the Spaniards from southern Spain brought with them their romantic ballads, and these musical traditions blended with local approaches in Puerto Rico. The result was a mix of dances, instruments, and lyrical traditions that gave way to distinct genres of folk music on the island such as *décima, seis, bomba, plena*, and *aguinaldos.*

The *décima* is the foundation of what is nowadays known as *jíbaro,* or country music, in Puerto Rico. The mix that emerged in the eighteenth century was based on native musical rhythms, but applying the lyrics of Spanish music. The songs are always sung in an improvised manner. However, they follow ten couplets, each consisting of eight syllables. Musical groups like Mapeyé are extremely popular for the preservation of *jíbaro* music. Andrés Jiménez is also an influential solo singer—known as "El Jíbarito"—who focuses on rustic songs and traditional rhythms without too many adaptations to modern music.

The *seis* (literally translated as "six") has origins that can be traced to the Andalusia region of southern Spain during the 1600s. The lyrics are also improvised, and the singer is typically accompanied by a guitar, a guiro, a *requinto,* or the Puerto Rican *cuatro.* The name *seis* was based on the music's traditional choreographic arrangement involving six couples, but it was not unusual for the *seis* to be danced by a higher number of paired dancers. Traditionally, women and men form separate lines, and they face each other. The two groups then pass each other several times throughout the song, looking intensely at each other, and the dance finishes with a waltz section. The name of the specific song was often named after the town where it was created, such as "El seis de Ponce," "El seis de El Dorado," and so on.

The *aguinaldos* are Christmas songs performed in Puerto Rico, and they are similar to the Christmas carols from Spain. On the island, the tradition is to follow a *parranda,* a group of friends who walk from house to house to sing these carols. The singers are usually treated to food and drinks at the houses they visit. They used to be songs with traditional lyrics, but they have morphed into melodies or improvisations of *décimas*.

The *plena* has its origins in African dances and makeshift musical instruments. Since African slaves practiced this dance, it is now more prevalent in the coastal areas of the island, such as in the southern city of Ponce. The *plena* became popular in the early 1900s, and it attracted followers among farmers and former slaves, mostly because the lyrics reflected their daily lives and struggles. According to Evan Baylin, this genre is often called *el periódico cantado* (the sung newspaper), and it serves a similar purpose as the *corrido* of Mexico, the *porro* from Colombia, and the calypso from Trinidad. The lyrics of these genres routinely narrate events such as political scandals, satirical views on poverty, impossible love, and natural disasters. This genre offers the average community an important vehicle for expression.

From an organizational point of view, *plena* usually has a solo singer and a group of chorus backups. The main focus of the music is the singing part, and the dancing portion is not so crucial. The most common musical instruments of the *plena* are the *panderos*, or *panderetas* (tambourines). The group needs at least three *panderetas* to have a complete ensemble. In addition, there is a need for two drums (the lead drum and the *seguidora*), a guitar, a *cuatro*, and the inescapable guiro to play fixed rhythms. Occasionally, *plena* groups also include brass instruments such as a clarinet or a trumpet. The solo singer usually plays either the guiro or a single *maraca*.

As more farmers moved to the urban areas of the island, they took their musical tastes with them. Now the genre of *plena* has been revitalized, and many modern artists continue to compose music and sometimes incorporate *plena* into other musical fields like salsa. Writers such as Manuel Jiménez and Ismael Rivera have composed important pieces of *plena* music. However, the sales of this genre declined in the 1970s and 1980s. In an attempt to reenergize this genre, other artists, such as Willie Colón—a recognized salsa composer and performer—have incorporated it into their work. By doing so, Colón reintroduced *plena* to younger music enthusiasts who were not familiar with it.

The *bomba* is another musical genre developed in Puerto Rico, and it is meant to be enjoyed by dancing. Its roots are traced to West Africa, and it is very popular in the area of Loíza, an area of Puerto Rico with a significant African heritage. The *bomba* is mostly danced as a community event that involves both singers and dancers. Most *bomba* songs begin with a female soloist called a *laina*. Then the tempo is increased by the use of drums as percussion instruments. After that, the dancers start to perform moves, challenging the drum players to match them with sound. A drummer then does the reverse:

he or she plays a few rhythms that the dancers have to adapt to their dancing style. What is in fact created is a call-and-response type of environment between musicians and dancers. The lyrics are usually not predetermined, and they are improvised on the spot. Since African slaves could not worship their gods during the Spanish colonial period, they adopted Saint James as their patron saint. Nowadays, the celebrations in the Loíza area around the St. James Day festivities include dance, music, food, and artistic representations of these *bomba* traditions. While the musical genres of *bomba* and *plena* are based on African rhythms, the talented musician Rafael Cortijo was responsible for bringing them into the mainstream of Puerto Rican music.

Danza

The Spanish immigrants performed many songs to the *danza* style, which is similar in form to ballroom dancing. This is the Latin American musical genre that is closest in form to European classical music from the colonial period. The instruments for *danza* music include both string (guitars and violins) and wind (flutes and clarinets) instruments. The most popular *danza* song on the island is the national anthem, "La borinqueña." It is a song composed by Felix Astol, and it evokes a feeling of melancholy. *Danzas* can be either incredibly romantic or extremely festive, but they do not necessarily sound like one another. Puerto Rican *danza* music is often described as a fusion of waltz, African sounds, and Caribbean rhythms. Another famous *danza* song is titled "Violeta," composed by Rafael Alers. It has remained a favorite *danza* in the hearts of Puerto Ricans.

Classical Music

During the Spanish colonial period (1493–1898), the Spaniards imported formal and religious music, which was considered to be high class. So as Puerto Ricans improved their financial standing in society, they attempted to assimilate this musical genre, including by sending their children to be musically trained in Europe. Puerto Rican composers such as Manuel Talavares and Juan Morel Campos were accomplished musicians in the middle of the 1800s who participated in adapting the scores of classical music into new forms that resulted in the birth of *danza* music on the island. The Conservatorio de Música de Puerto Rico has had a crucial role in training talented local musicians, and the popularity of classical music is evident in the multiple music festivals and recitals held on the island. In the tradition of classical music and opera, the Puerto Rican Opera Company currently creates an artistic program every winter. Some of the most famous Puerto Rican opera singers have been Antonio Paoli (1872–1846), Jesús María Sanroma (1902–1984), and Justino Díaz (1940–).

The most recognized classical musician in Puerto Rico has been Pablo Casals (1876–1973). He was a Spanish cellist who moved to Puerto Rico in the 1930s and was mainly responsible for resuscitating and establishing a tradition of modern classical music on the island. His father was from Spain and his mother was from Mayagüez, Puerto Rico. He created the Puerto Rico Symphony Orchestra, which is currently considered to be the best in the Caribbean. In addition, he established the Puerto Rican Conservatory of Music. Pablo Casals died in 1973 in Puerto Rico, leaving a legacy of artistic productivity that has never been matched on the island. When he died at almost ninety-seven years of age, he—and his fellow *boricuas*—considered himself to be Puerto Rican.

The government created the famous Conservatorio de Música de Puerto Rico based on Law 35 on June 12, 1959. It is a public institution that offers both bachelor's and graduate degrees. However, it also provides general studies aimed at the local community. There were three general goals established from the beginning. The first objective is to offer a university program for the formation of professional musicians. The second goal is to train musicians for the Puerto Rico Symphonic Orchestra. Third, the aim is to offer training for the formation of composers and music teachers to support the musical heritage of the island. The first leader and director of the conservatory was Pablo Casals.

Since 2001, the Conservatorio de Música has developed a comprehensive educational curriculum for preschool and elementary schoolchildren called Despertar Musical (Musical Awakening). The program includes CDs of thirty-three songs and rhymes with specific lesson plans and activities to be used in the classroom. The overall goal is to nurture the creative energy of children and to promote the cultural heritage of Puerto Rico.

Salsa

Perhaps salsa is currently the most recognizable musical genre from Puerto Rico. Its origins are not completely *boricua*; instead, a mix of musical genres merged to produce a unique musical sound. Salsa is the fusion—and evolution—of musical instruments, cultural adaptations, and multiple musical genres. The combination includes influences from the Puerto Rican *plena*, Yoruba-Cuban Santeria rituals, Dominican merengue, Cuban *son*, Afro-American jazz, and a hint of rhythm and blues. Initially, there was no unanimous agreement on the name "salsa," which many musicians viewed as a commercial title for specific music such as *el son*, cha-cha, and mambo. Eventually, the term became acceptable, mostly because it helped with the sales of records.

Puerto Ricans and Cubans can argue forever about which country actually invented salsa, where they did it, and who exactly was responsible for its genesis. Of course, they both claim the right to it. While there is no agreement as to who first used the term *salsa*, the name for this genre started to circulate in the 1960s in New York City. The city functioned as the central location where talented musicians from around the world came to participate in this new genre being developed. In particular, many Cuban and Puerto Rican singers and composers moved to the city. The result was a fast-paced danceable music with sophisticated choreography and feisty lyrics.

What the world knows as salsa today actually started in the nightclubs of New York City in the 1940s, following the Second World War. The most recognizable salsa artist at the time was Tito Puente. He was a Puerto Rican born in Harlem, New York. He served in the U.S. Navy, and on his return, he enrolled in the Julliard School of Music. Right after graduation, he formed a group called the Puente's Latin Jazz Ensemble, which blended Caribbean sounds with the popular big-band style. At the same time, another musical branch was developing, which created a danceable fusion of merengue, Cuban *son*, mambo, and cha-cha. In addition, the *bata* drums used in Santeria ritualistic music were also incorporated as important elements in salsa. Moreover, the adaptation of Puerto Rican *plena* and *bomba* music was used as a foundation for the new musical style being developed. All these parallel developments eventually fused to provide the basic rhythms for what is now known as salsa music.

Currently, salsa bands have a complex instrumentation. They include a lead singer and a chorus to back up the singer. They also have a horn section (especially trumpets), a group of percussion instruments (congas, bongos, maracas, and even a cowbell), a piano, guitars, a *cuatro*, and bass. In addition, it is widely recognized that nowadays, the center of salsa has moved from New York City to Puerto Rico.

While the musicians were the creative force behind the new musical genre, the role of the Fania Record Company was crucial in converting salsa into a commercial success. The company was created in 1964 in New York City by the Italian Jerry Masucci and the Puerto Rican Johnny Pacheco. They formed the salsa band called Fania All Stars, which included some of the top musicians who participated in developing salsa music: Ray Barreto, Héctor Lavoe, Johnny Pacheco, Larry Harlow, and Willie Colón. These were the salsa pioneers of the time. Fania Records went on to include some of the greatest salsa performers such as Celia Cruz, Rubén Blades, Tito Puente, and Bobby Valentine. It must be noted, however, that to participate in the creation of a new musical style, musicians must be well versed and trained in some of the

Salsa dancers at the International Salsa Congress and Competition in San Juan, July 2008. Photo courtesy of the author.

fundamental elements that provided the origins for salsa music. These musicians made salsa extremely popular during the 1970s. Then, as expected, they eventually became successful in their solo careers. The popularity of salsa declined in the 1980s when other musical genres became more popular.

By the late 1990s, Puerto Rico again become famous for its salsa music on an international level. It took another Nuyorican, Marc Anthony, to bring salsa back from an abandoned position. In addition to singing in Spanish, this time, he adapted salsa music to English lyrics, creating another population to whom he could market his product. As a result, the world rediscovered the intoxicating rhythm that incites people to get up and dance. Some of the most recognized Puerto Rican salsa musicians today include Willie Colón, Gilberto Santa Rosa, El Gran Combo de Puerto Rico, La India, and Marc Anthony. Salsa is not a musical genre of the past; it continues to involve both young and mature generations of music lovers. In an effort to recognize the amazing contribution of salsa's previous talent, the movie *El cantante* (The Singer), portraying the life of Héctor Lavoe, was taken to the big screen in 2007. The main acting roles were performed by Marc Anthony and Jennifer López, but the film never achieved wide distribution or financial success. There is another film in the works to portray the life of Héctor Lavoe, and it is expected to be produced by La India, who is perhaps the best female salsa singer since Celia Cruz.

Pop Music

Puerto Rico has a long list of pop singers who have been popular in Latin America for decades as well as some recent talent. However, most of them sing only in Spanish. The English-speaking world has only recently discovered the talent of *boricua* performers as they have succeeded in their musical crossovers to the markets in the United States.

José Feliciano is one of the most traditional and famous Puerto Rican pop musicians. He was one of the bilingual pioneers capable of achieving musical hits both in Puerto Rico and on the U.S. mainland. He was blind from birth, but he taught himself to play guitar, the trumpet, and the harmonica. His fame arrived with the release of his song "Light My Fire" in 1968. Later, most radio stations played his popular song "Feliz Navidad" (Merry Christmas). He has earned six Grammy Awards and remains creatively active with multiple projects.

The public is also recently fixated on the emergence of young *boricua* entertainers. In the 1990s, Ricky Martin caught the attention of the United States when he performed "Livin' La Vida Loca" at the Grammy Awards of 1999. His fast-paced, modern rhythms infused with salsa steps and a heart-pounding trumpet ensemble certainly got the attention of his fellow artists and the television audience. He had arrived at the world's stage. However, Ricky Martin has a long artistic trajectory that started ever since he was a child. His popularity in the Spanish-speaking world was originally created as part of the teenage pop group Menudo, with which he toured the world in a series of concerts. He has also had a long career as a solo artist in the Latin American market, which knows him for his romantic ballads. His English CDs, with hits like "Livin' La Vida Loca" (1999) and "She Bangs" (2000), catapulted him to fame at an international level. His latest releases from *MTV Unplugged* in 2006 brought Ricky Martin back to his Latin roots, including a duo with La Mari for the main song "Tu recuerdo" (Your Memory), and a live album titled *Black and White Tour*, released in 2007. They were both astounding commercial successes.

There are, of course, other *boricua* artists who have decided to focus their energy on the Spanish-speaking markets and not pursue the crossover into the English-speaking market. Such is the case of ballad singers Cheyenne and Luis Fonsi. The Puerto Rican music industry also capitalized on the popularity of merengue from its Caribbean neighbor the Dominican Republic.

Nowadays, some of the most popular merengue singers are actually from Puerto Rico, including Melina León, Gisselle, Olga Tañon, and Elvis Crespo. They are extremely successful in promoting this fast-paced, danceable genre.

Reggaeton

The latest musical creation to come out of Puerto Rico is *reggaeton*. It came to the world stage in 2005 with an incredible popular appeal and force. It blends reggae, dance hall, Spanish rap, and digital sounds together with fiery lyrics that expose the poverty and hardships on the island. This was originally an underground sound created by Puerto Rican youth who grew up in poor slums like La Perla in the suburbs of San Juan. The new musical genre also created a new dance style known as *perreo* (doggie style), which makes reference to an overtly sensual dance move that resembles that specific sexual position. While most *boricua* teenagers grew up listening to salsa, *reggaeton* quickly became the sound of a new generation.

Initially, the government of Puerto Rico stepped in to request that all *reggaeton* music be banned from Puerto Rican radio stations. Its critics used derogatory adjectives to label it as immoral, monotonous, misogynist, and musically empty. The threat was that *reggaeton* featured topics of interest to youth (sex, racism, crime, etc.), but not to the establishment. Its lyrics were also viewed as vulgar and insulting to women. Puerto Rican police even took steps to confiscate *reggaeton* CDs. Music purists also criticized the new genre for not being original, but rather, a hybrid composition that relies too much on technology, rather than the intrinsic value of musical instruments. As expected, the attempts to regulate *reggaeton* only created free publicity and even more curiosity among the island's youth.

Moreover, the government strategy urging *reggaeton* artists to clean up their image and lyrics actually backfired. By the late 1990s, some of the creators of this genre finally decided to adapt their lyrics to be less aggressive—but still include social commentary. As a result, radio stations on the island started to provide airtime for their music. *Reggaeton* artists pointed out the hypocrisy of government officials who claimed moral superiority and a sense of community righteousness. Artists such as Eddie Dee created lyrics that specifically mentioned corruption cases filed against political leaders. For example, singer Eddie Dee cited Victor Fajardo (the secretary of education), who was convicted in 2002 for misappropriating federal funds, and the case of Edison Misla Aldarondo (a member of the House of Representatives), who was also jailed for extortion and money laundering.

In 2005, the song that launched *reggaeton* into the acceptable mainstream music world was "La gasolina" by singer Daddy Yankee. It spread like wildfire, and it became a popular tune in nightclubs in the Caribbean, the United States, and Europe. The racy dance style that came with it also became a new trend in dance music. As *reggaeton* quickly became the staple of club music, its main themes focused on partying and sex. However, its lyrics also continue to expose sensitive topics like police brutality, government corruption, and the overall discontent of Puerto Ricans regarding their political leaders. Nowadays, there are radio stations that play *reggaeton* exclusively. More artists, such as Don Chezina, Tego Calderón, Don Omar, Daddy Yankee, Luny Tunes, and Ivy Queen, have continued to produce material that elevates their level of musicianship and also validates their initial struggle.

The *reggaeton* movement also has a financial aspect to it. Artists like Daddy Yankee and Luny Tunes have reached platinum status, with sales of millions of CDs. Ironically, it was the government's actions that forced *reggaeton* artists to form their own recording labels and distribution patterns, a factor that allowed them to remain more in control of their product. The government unintentionally created musical entrepreneurs out of the *reggaeton* artists. Record labels like WY Records (owned by Wisín and Yandel) and El Cartel Records (owned by Daddy Yankee) have become extremely successful from a financial perspective. They have also allowed their artists to be more active participants in the control of their music and their finances. This business pattern is something that previous generations of Puerto Rican musicians have never experienced. The radio waves have also now embraced this new genre, which is no longer underground. In May 2006, Reggaeton 94 became Puerto Rico's top radio station, according to Arbitron +12, which publishes the listener ratings on the island. The station Reggaeton 94 filled a void by targeting a specific demographic of young listeners, which then translated into advertising dollars. As the music and lyrics of *reggaeton* appeal to a wider audience and achieve commercial power, there is now speculation that this genre might eventually become more popular than salsa.

DANCE

Most of the musical genres of Puerto Rico have an inherent connection between music and dance. There are formally trained dancers, who participate in formal performances; dancers who are members of folk dance groups; and the average *boricuas,* who simply enjoy dancing for fun. The Puerto Rican government sponsors several cultural centers to promote dance instruction. Most small towns also have patron saint festivals and community celebrations that always include music and dancing.

Plena and *Bomba*

The traditional dance music of *plena* and *bomba* traces its roots to West Africa and utilizes drums as its basic instruments. In *plena* music, the lyrics are crucial because they offer communities an important vehicle to express their concerns. This music genre was born in working-class neighborhoods, and the topics of the lyrics represent the daily struggle of the working class. *Plena* lyrics routinely narrate events such as political scandals, satirical views on poverty, impossible love, and natural disasters. In the *bomba* genre, the words, if used at all, are not so important. The main ingredient of *bomba* music must be the choreography and the dialogue between musicians and dancers.

The *bomba* is a musical genre that was developed in Puerto Rico specifically for dancing. The *bomba* had its genesis in West Africa, and it was locally revealed in the town of Loíza, where a strong population of African descent still thrives today. The original slave communities on the island developed these dance rituals as a source of spiritual strength. However, *bomba* is more than just a song or a melody; it is more like an entire event with specific stages and patterns. It has at least three separate but equally important components: dancing, music, and singing. As a result, these traditional dances are performed at special events and celebrations. The *bomba* usually starts with a female singer doing a solo; then, a chorus responds to her call. What follows is the response by the percussion musicians using multiple drums. In the meantime, the dancers slowly prepare their positions and get ready for a more intense rhythmical performance. The choreography to follow involves the dancers challenging the drums, creating a dialogue in the process. The drums respond with sounds that are then emulated by the dancers. The dialogue when the dancers and the drums correspond with one another is locally known as *controversia*. The different *bomba* styles are customarily named after the African region where they started, such as Belén, Yubá, and so on. Currently *plena* and *bomba* are widely played on radio stations since they have influenced the development of new melodies and dance patterns.

Danza

The *danza* genre of music was designed for social and ballroom dancing. This formal and elegant musical style was very popular during the nineteenth century. During the 1840s, there was always a *bastonero*, a director who decided how many couples could enter the dance floor and even coordinated the positions that dancers would take. By the late 1850s, the formality of the *danza* atmosphere started to change. The arrivals of Cuban immigrants brought faster and more flowing dancing patterns. The new *danza* became known as *habanera* because these new arrivals came from La Habana. Apparently, the youth of the time took to the new style, but it rattled the feathers of the social elite, who considered it scandalous that couples could stand so close to one another. By the end of the 1800s, pianists such as Manuel G. Tavarez, and later Juan Morel Campos, wrote hundreds of *danza* masterpieces that are still considered classics today.

Puerto Rican Ballet Company

The original Ballet Concierto de Puerto Rico was founded in 1978 by a former dancer named Lolita San Miguel. It was successful on the island and abroad for almost two decades. However, a labor strike froze all its presentations in 2004. All the dancers went on strike to protest the lack of job security due to, what they claimed, was inappropriate management of public funding. The strike, in fact, was never resolved. Instead, some of the former dancers of the Ballet Concierto founded the new Balleteatro Nacional de Puerto Rico (National Ballet Theater of Puerto Rico) in 2005. They performed for the very first time in April 2005 at a location called the Francisco Arriví Theater in San Juan. The artistic director selected to run the new ballet troupe was Miguel Campaneira, an accomplished former dancer with the Cuban National Ballet. The Balleteatro currently has its own ballet academy in the city of Guayanabo, Puerto Rico, where its future dancers are trained. This ballet group has three seasons of performances on the island, and they are also active in international presentations in the United States and Japan and at a few international dance festivals. They perform classical ballet as well as contemporary choreography.

FESTIVALS

It seems that Puerto Rico has festivals every month of the year. The festivities calendar published by the Puerto Rico Tourism Company confirms that this is true. There are celebrations based on religious holidays, the harvest season, patron saint days, and a long list of cultural events. Most of these festivals and carnivals involve music, singing, and dancing. These three components are almost unavoidable on the island.

Three main musical events stand out for their celebration of music, for their recognition of local talent, and as great examples of community participation. The Puerto Rican Jazz Festival held in early June brings the most notable jazz artists from the Caribbean. Tito Puente was a regular at this San Juan festival. The Fiesta de Santiago in Loíza Aldea is celebrated at the end of July. This is a location of the island where a strong African heritage is sustained via music, dance, food, and lively parades. The use of costumes with colorful colors and

Vejigantes in Ponce's carnival, celebrated in February. Photo courtesy of the author.

vejigantes, scary masks, is a tradition that dates back to the Spanish colonial period. There is a similar event held in Ponce during February that also uses the same masks and colorful costumes as part of its festivities.

Perhaps the most salient musical event on the island is the Festival Casals, founded by the notable cellist Pablo Casals, who once served as the director of the Puerto Rican Conservatory of Music. This classical music extravaganza draws classical musicians from all over the world for a period of two weeks to accompany the Puerto Rico Symphony Orchestra in a series of extremely popular presentations of chamber music on the island. It takes place in San Juan at the Luis A. Ferré Center for the Performing Arts.

Boricuas living in the United States are also passionate about participating in public celebrations that highlight their cultural heritage. For example, the famous Puerto Rican Day Parade in New York City has morphed into a cultural event that has lasted decades already and receives participating delegations from almost all the states in the union. The Puerto Rican Cultural Parade in Tampa, Florida, was established in 1988. In its twenty years, this one-day event in April continues to gain momentum and treat visitors to a display of *boricua* folklore, music, and dance. In California, the Festival del

Cuatro celebrates the recognition of the *cuatro* as the national instrument that reflects Puerto Rican pride. It was founded in 2006 with the goal of celebrating and promoting Puerto Rican culture. This festival attracts some of the most recognized *cuatro* master musicians such as Edwin Colón Zayas, Yomo Toro, and Alvin Medina.

THEATER

Theater did not arrive in Puerto Rico with the Europeans; it existed long before the Spanish came in 1493. In fact, theatrical representations were already used by the Taíno Indians before Columbus. According to Roberto Ramos-Perea (2005), the Taínos had *areítos dances*, with a narrator who discussed topics such as their gods, crops and fishing, invasions by other tribes, their local rulers or caciques, and so on. These topics are similar to the ones addressed in contemporary theater. While there are no written versions of these events, the Spanish chronicles make specific mention of the dances and events of the Taíno Indians in Puerto Rico. These indigenous theatrical events were immediately suppressed by the Catholic Church in Puerto Rico, mostly because their topical material worked against the goal of indoctrinating the local population and achieving their conversion to Christianity.

From the 1500s to the 1700s, the beginning form of theater could not be separated from the prevailing religious ideology on the island. The Roman Catholic Church used theatrical representations to teach the values of Christianity. During these three centuries, the ecclesiastical rulers and the Spanish Inquisition even prohibited the spread of literary pieces that were not "divine" in nature. When theater plays were performed, they usually had to address religious themes, and the churches served as theaters. The social control of the Church went as far as publishing the so-called *Sinodales Orders*, which prohibited many social aspects of daily life, including the possibility of doing theater without the Church's permission (Ramos-Perea 2005).

The 1800s were crucial for Puerto Rico in developing a theater that focused on a search for a national identity. The Roman Catholic Church could no longer regulate so many aspects of social life on the island. Individual entrepreneurs, and even local government agencies, started building formal theaters. For example, the Cabildo de San Juan owned and operated the Rancho de Comedias, a theater founded in 1797, and operated it until 1814. Then, the Teatro Los Amigos del País was built in 1822 in San Juan—a much larger venture that could accommodate almost two thousand people at a time.

Dramatic writers started to emerge in Puerto Rico during the nineteenth century. Perhaps the most recognizable playwright of the 1800s was Alejandro Tapia y Rivera (1926–1882). He wrote a long list of plays and also

Teatro La Perla in Ponce. Photo courtesy of the author.

founded La Filarmónica, a theater that was extremely popular in San Juan. Tapia wrote and produced the play titled *Roberto D'vreux*, which is often considered to be the very first verifiable play of Puerto Rican theater.

During the late 1800s, two crucial institutions served as the impetus for the development of the dramatic arts in Puerto Rico. One of the cultural accomplishments on the island was the founding of El Ateneo Puertorriqueño, a flagship cultural institution built in 1876 that is still functioning today in full force. The other one was the Teatro La Perla in Ponce, originally built in the 1860s. La Perla was a little smaller, with a seating capacity of only one thousand people but designed with great acoustics. Its architect, Juan Bartoli Calderoni, is often considered to be the main designer of the neoclassical style of architecture on the island. Its six-column facade makes Teatro La Perla a timeless masterpiece that has been renovated for aesthetic purposes and to improve the acoustics to enhance the theater experience for the public.

The 1900s brought to Puerto Rico different cultural patterns that also influenced the development of theater. When the United States took control of the island in 1898, it immediately imposed English as the official language, and theater plays in English were commonplace. New European ideals of social equality also had their effect on the island. For example, theater used to be considered an event for the middle and upper classes. However, in the 1900s, the rise of the *teatro obrero* (theater for the workers or trade people) became an important cultural trend. This movement started offering plays that addressed the themes and concerns of the working class.

In 1938, the Ateneo de Puerto Rico hosted a theater competition that produced incredible results. The three finalists ended up creating a movement that would drive an intensive exploration of national identity on the island. The winners were Manuel Méndez Ballester (*El clamor de los surcos*), Gonzalo Arocho del Toro (*El desmonte*), and Fernando Sierra Berdecía (*Esta noche juega el joker*). The main themes these playwrights explored were the rural to urban migration, the use of the land, and migration to the United States. These are topics that still resonate with the *boricua* public even after eighty years.

During the 1950s, the main theme explored by dramatic writers was the resistance to the Americanization of the island. The most famous play of the period was *La carreta* (The Oxcart), written by René Márquez. It narrates the story of a rural family and their migration to the big city in search of a better future. Instead, they find hunger and misery. They then migrate to New York, following the American dream. Their hopes are again dashed as they discover discrimination and alienation in a land where they are supposed to be U.S. citizens. Márquez's description of human emotions in this play is what makes this theatrical presentation one of the best of the twentieth century.

The Puerto Rican government also intervened to establish a strong tradition of theater on the island. The Productora de Teatro Nacional was founded in 1985 to carry out performances throughout the island, where most large- and medium-sized cities have active theaters. The company also includes two dance groups that offer performances as part of the same national company. This initiative also served to create the Archivo Nacional del Teatro (National Theater Archive), which was used to gather a sizable collection of plays, manuscripts, and performance announcements that reflect the rich heritage of Puerto Rican theater. The Archivo Nacional del Teatro is still housed at the Ateneo Puertorriqueño in San Juan. These initiatives provided the foundation for the formation of talented actors, writers, technicians, and theater managers. Another institution is intrinsically involved in the artistic development of Puerto Ricans: the Instituto de Cultura Puertorriqueña (ICPR) has a special program called Programa de Teatro y Danza (Program for Theater and Dance), which offers financial support to dance and theater companies when they participate in dance festivals and theater events throughout the island.

In 2008, the Teatro Nacional Puertorriqueño and the Instituto de Cultura Puertorriqueña had busy programs that included drama, classics, and modern plays that continue to explore the cultural richness of Puerto Rican society. For example, the ICPR organized the Forty-ninth Annual Festival of

Puerto Rican Theater in April 2008, an entire week of theatrical representations that included some classics, such as *Al final de la calle* (At the End of the Street), as well as new works like the play *Lágrimas negras: Tribulaciones de una negrita acompleja* (Black Tears: The Tribulations of a Black Woman with Low Self-Esteem), written by Eva Cristina Vázquez. The popularity of Puerto Rican theater is certainly not declining; it is actually thriving as a cultural phenomenon that helps to define the *boricua* national identity.

REFERENCES

Bailyn, Evan. "Music of Puerto Rico." http://www.musicofpuertorico.com.
Cobo, Leila. "El Gran Combo: Waving the Salsa Flag for 40 Years Strong." *Billboard* 114, no. 19 (2002): LM-10.
———. "The Sounds of Puerto Rico." *Billboard* 112, no. 41 (2007): 41.
Delgado Castro, Ileana. "Pioneros del jazz." *El Nuevo Día, Revista Domingo*, January 22, 2006.
Escalona, Saul. "La salsa, un fenómeno sociocultural en El Caribe hispano." Retrieved on March 27, 2008. http://www.salsafrance.com/.
Glasser, Ruth. *My Music Is My Flag: Puerto Rican Musicians and Their Communities, 1917–1940*. Berkeley: University of California Press, 1995.
Hernández-Candelas, Marta. "Policies for Early Childhood Music Education in Puerto Rico." *Arts Education Policy Review* 109, no. 2 (2007): 27–32.
Manuel, Peter, Kenneth Bilby, and Michael Largey. *Caribbean Currents: Caribbean Music from Rumba to Reggae*. 2nd ed. Philadelphia: Temple University Press, 2006.
Marshall, Wayne. "The Rise of Reggaeton." *Boston Phoenix*, January 19, 2006.
Negrón-Muntaner, Frances. *Boricua Pop: Puerto Ricans and the Latinization of American Culture*. New York: New York University Press, 2004.
———. "Reggaeton Nation." *NACLA Report on the Americas* 40, no. 6 (2007): 35–39.
Ramos-Perea, Roberto. "Panorama Histórico del Teatro Puertorriqueño," in *Teatro Puertorriqueño Contemporáneo*, ed. Roberto Ramos-Perea, 1–23. San Juan, Puerto Rico: Publicaciones Gaviota, 2003.
Rivera, Raquel Z. *New York Ricans from the Hip-Hop Zone*. New York: Palgrave Macmillan, 2003.
Serrano, Basilio. "Puerto Rican Musicians of the Harlem Renaissance." *Centro Journal* 19, no. 2 (2007): 94–119.

Web Sites

Fania Records, http://www.fania.com/.
Festival del Cuatro, http://www.festivaldelcuatro.org/.
Instituto de Cultura Puertorriqueña, http://www.icp.gobierno.pr.

9

Architecture and Visual Arts

ARCHITECTURE

MOST TOURISTS WHO plan visits to Puerto Rico have images of beautiful beaches and tropical forests. They also envision colonial towns with cobblestone streets, sixteenth-century mansions, impressive forts, and antique romantic street lighting. At least, these are the architectural images promoted by the Puerto Rico Tourism Company in travel pamphlets and cruise brochures. These features do exist in Puerto Rico, but they are concentrated mostly in the areas of Old San Juan and downtown Ponce. The architectural development of the island has actually evolved over five hundred years to make it what it is today. However, most of the visible transformation of public buildings has occurred in the last one hundred years.

The Spanish Colonial Period (1493–1898)

For almost four hundred years, Spaniards viewed San Juan as a military area to be protected. This city was the port of entry for most of the Spanish cargo ships coming to the Caribbean, and more important, it was the last safe location for ships carrying valuable treasures on their transatlantic voyages back to Europe. It is no coincidence that the city was raided by French ships, Dutch sailors, and British pirates in efforts to take control of the island. Consequently, the Spanish military government of the 1500s created the major architectural features that protected the area of Old San Juan, such as El Morro Fortress (the largest fortified structure anywhere in the Caribbean),

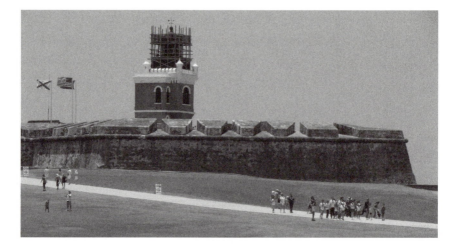

San Felipe del Morro Fortress in Old San Juan. Photo courtesy of the author.

the San Cristóbal Fortress, and La Fortaleza (the massive governor's house). From a cultural perspective, this architectural style reflected a centralized government backed by military force.

The early maps of San Juan reveal that it was designed as a military refuge but also as a spiritual center. Consequently, it is logical that heavily armed forts, austere government buildings, and multiple churches were the main staples of the city center. Some of the fortified and massive religious buildings include the San Juan Cathedral, built in 1540; the Dominican Convent, erected in 1523; and the San José Church, also from the sixteenth century. However, the architectural style of these structures can best be defined as neoclassical, with the simplicity of Roman and Greek architecture (basic arches, unadorned columns, straight lines, and sharp corners). However, in Puerto Rico, this style was used to evoke military control and avoid the creativity of ornate decoration. For four centuries, it was intended to represent colonial power, order, and discipline (Hertz 2002, 220). The cohesive architectural style was achieved because the San Fernando Royal Academy of Fine Arts in Madrid approved all the public buildings built in the Spanish colonies in the Americas. The academy selected the neoclassical style because it offered simplicity and elegance but also implied control and order. The highlight of this architectural style is represented in the Cuartel de Ballajá (the Barracks of Ballajá) in Old San Juan. They were built in 1854 to house the Spanish troops and their families and are the largest building constructed by the Spaniards in the Western Hemisphere. The barracks have been thoroughly renovated and currently house the Museum of the Americas.

The Spanish military barracks of Ballajá in Old San Juan. Photo courtesy of the author.

However, there was also a certain type of public building missing from the colonial landscape in Puerto Rico. Since Spain only had a limited view of the island as a mercantile and military stopover, it never really developed an educational system, a representative government tradition, or even cohesive urban planning. Consequently, there were no significant schools, universities, or government buildings of timeless beauty built during the first three hundred years of Spanish colonial domination.

It was not until the 1850s that the Spanish Crown finally invested in the architectural landscape of public buildings in Puerto Rico. Even then, these might have been token symbols to delay the inevitable cries for independence of its only remaining colonies in the Americas: Cuba and Puerto Rico. The monumental buildings of the period include the Real Intendencia (Treasury Building), from 1852; the Insane Asylum Hospital, from 1860; the Ballajá military barracks, from 1857; the Provincial Hospital, from 1876; and the Municipal Theater, from 1878 (Vivoni-Farage 2007). Once again, all these buildings followed the neoclassical style, with massive, austere exteriors and simple decoration.

1898: Here Comes the United States

After the Spanish-American War of 1898, Spain ceded Puerto Rico, Cuba, and the Philippines over to the United States. The United States found an island without infrastructure and lacking basic public services such as schools and community hospitals. The U.S. government quickly authorized the construction of a significant number of projects, including universities, roads, churches, schools, and government buildings. Initially, these ventures generated tremendous optimism on the island, and people generally supported the arrival of a new colonizer with the hope that the island would eventually be granted independence.

Architecture reflects cultural values, and Puerto Ricans quickly realized that these new projects would change their society in profound ways. For example, the United States introduced the separation of church and state—a huge difference from the previous Spanish government. This meant that the Roman Catholic Church would no longer have complete control over the educational system. Instead, there would be a new schooling program created and intended to educate the entire population—not only the wealthy elite. Moreover, Protestant churches were now being built, something never seen in the formerly Roman Catholic colony. Another crucial social change was that the previous legal system was replaced by the American legal code, which also needed the construction of specific new buildings for its court system. The United States sent scores of architects to help the Puerto Rican ones in the design of new public buildings, and the *boricua* architects were sent to the United States to study more architecture. As expected, the plans for most of these new buildings called for a variation of the neoclassical style popular in the United States at the time. The new structures reflected the cultural views of educational reform, changes in civil administration, the legal code, and an ambitious capitalist system. Given all these changes, Puerto Ricans started to resent the so-called Americanization of their island, and they protested in a vociferous manner.

The Spanish Revivals (Mission, Moorish, and Renaissance Styles)

The United States sensed the resistance to the architectural style proposed for the new buildings. In a conciliatory gesture, the United States decided that it should use more of a so-called Hispanic design for the new public buildings. As a result, American architects misappropriated the style of the California missions, thinking that the style was Spanish and that it would facilitate cultural coexistence with Puerto Ricans. This approach became known as the mission revival. However, this architectural fashion had never been used in Puerto Rico. Strangely enough, Puerto Ricans accepted this new style, but mostly because it evoked a feeling of nostalgia regarding their Spanish heritage.

From 1900 to 1920, the mission revival style was used in Puerto Rico to build new schools, private homes, Protestant churches, office headquarters for sugar companies, and regional city hall buildings. Specific examples include the Ponce Methodist Church, designed by Anthonin Nechodoma in 1907. Similarly, the schools created for the public education system imported from the mainland were all initially designed in 1908 in the mission revival style, including the famous José Julián Acosta School in San Juan, also known as Public School No. 1. The design for most of these schools was done by the firm Clarke, Howe, and Homes from Rhode Island. It is important to note that American architects associated the mission revival style with Spain, but Puerto Ricans never did; for *boricuas*, this was simply a Spanish-American design brought about by the new colonizers.

The 1920s was also the period when the first wave of Puerto Rican architects trained in the United States began to return home. These graduates were educated in the Spanish revival design, including a new Moorish revival style that was much more ornate in its decoration and intricate exteriors. According to Enrique Vivoni-Farage (2007), these new *boricua* architects were indoctrinated into believing that the adoption of Spanish revival approaches defined "Puerto-Ricanness," meaning that these were the appropriate designs for the island. However, this was not an architecture defined by the experiences of Puerto Rico, but rather by the image the United States had of what Hispanic architecture should be. The mission revival evolved into a more sophisticated architecture with ornate facades, and it was often adopted by designers of stately homes in Florida. This architectural fashion was eventually adopted in Puerto Rico, especially by the wealthy, those in politics, and the educated population. These new influences resulted in the creation of specific buildings erected for the University of Puerto Rico, the headquarters for the newspaper *El Mundo*, the Puerto Rican State Prison, and the current offices and theater for the Ateneo de Puerto Rico.

The 1910s and 1920s were also two crucial decades for another separate, yet related, period in architecture known as the Spanish renaissance revival. It was not developed in Spain, but rather in California and Florida. This new design was based on some of the greatest features of Spanish architectural design throughout Latin America and adapted to the needs of specific locations. It included stately public buildings with ornate decoration, elegance in style, and functionality of purpose (education, government, etc.). The United States had taken the highlights of Spain's heritage, appropriated it for itself, and then exported it to the world as an architectural renaissance. The specific venues to promote this new style were two professional conferences called the Panama-Pacific International Expositions, held in San Francisco in 1915 and San Diego in 1917. The name was intended to coincide with the opening of the Panama Canal, one of the greatest engineering challenges in history, of which the United States was the main developer. The U.S. organizers of the conferences—together with most of the architects, civil engineers, and

The capitol building of Puerto Rico, located in San Juan. Photo courtesy of the author.

government officials who attended the event—adopted the Spanish renaissance revival as an architectural element that would be exported all over Latin America.

In Puerto Rico, the Spanish renaissance techniques served as the foundation for some of the most important public buildings still currently used on the island. Some of the buildings done in the Spanish renaissance revival style include the Customs Building in San Juan, finished in 1929, and the School of Tropical Medicine, in 1924. Local Puerto Rican architects such as the prolific Francisco Roldán also used the Spanish renaissance style to design private homes for wealthy clients. He even used this style to develop apartment buildings in the city of Santurce. His last work on the island was the ambitious project of the Puerto Rican State Penitentiary (1926)—a prison, but done in great style. Another salient building from this period was the domed capitol building of Puerto Rico, located in San Juan. In 1920, the architect Adrian Finlayson designed the concrete-based structure for the capitol building. It was inaugurated in 1929, and it has been the home of the legislative assembly ever since. Currently the functions of the capitol of Puerto Rico have grown with adjacent buildings to house the Puerto Rican Senate, offices, archives, and a parking structure.

The decade of the 1930s brought about the Great Depression and the Spanish Civil War. Consequently, government funds were directed away from architectural development and toward other priorities. Private commissions were less frequent, and political turmoil did not guarantee the completion of massive projects. Puerto Rico was deeply affected by these world events. The investment in private and public projects slowed down significantly, which in turn increased poverty and unemployment rates on the island. Moreover, the threat of World War II provided an air of uneasiness regarding the viability of projects funded by the United States on the island.

The Modernist Movement

Architectural styles were substantially different during the 1940s. Puerto Rico was also going through significant political transformations: the first Puerto Rican governor was appointed in 1946, and two years later, elections were held for the first locally elected governor. The international scene after World War I and the threat of another world war pushed many academic disciplines into a modernist movement. In architecture, it effectively meant the death of all the previous Spanish revival movements.

Puerto Rico created the Committee for the Design of Public Works in 1943. The group included members who would later have a strong influence on tropical architecture such as Henry Klumb, Osvaldo Toro, and Miguel Ferrer. Once money from the United States started to trickle back to the island, the emphasis for public projects was on hospitals, public housing, and rural schools. However, the modernist ideals also highlighted the importance of moving away from an agricultural society toward an industrialized economy. For this purpose, the local government founded the Puerto Rico Development Company to make such a transition. It was at this point in the 1940s that tourism was targeted as a possible channel to bring about jobs, create an infrastructure, and move the island into a more modern condition. The modernism style rejected the idea of historical foundation as a determining factor in new designs. This new architectural movement for the tropics was viewed as a vehicle for progress.

Since tourism meant industrialism for Puerto Rico in the 1950s, the government needed to invest in developing the necessary infrastructure such as airports, roads, hotels, tourism services, and so on. The first two hotels built for this new venture were the Caribe Hilton and Hotel La Concha, both designed and built by the local firm of Osvaldo Toro and Miguel Ferrer. These buildings were acclaimed as architectural masterpieces by international building organizations. While several American architects participated in the competition for these projects, they lost mostly because they were still submitting proposals based on the Spanish revival styles that were no longer palatable in Puerto Rico. The goal was to show the world a modern and industrialized island that could become the main center of tourism in the Caribbean and capable of attracting foreign investment. The modernist movement was slowly being cemented on the island, especially after the influential German architect Henry Klumb arrived to work in Puerto Rico.

Henry Klumb (1905–1984) became perhaps one of the most prominent architects in Puerto Rico, especially during the 1950s to 1960s. He arrived in San Juan in 1944 and remained there until his death in 1984. Klumb developed his modernist approach when he was an apprentice under the tutelage of the renowned architect Frank Lloyd Wright. He worked on multiple public projects, including the master plan for the campus of the University of Puerto Rico, and some of its specific projects, such as the Museum of Anthropology, the General Library, and the Law School building. He also took individual commissions and worked on private homes, hotels, and churches. Toward the 1970s, he worked with pharmaceutical companies that were building important factories on the island such as Roche, Eli Lilly, and Baxter. He died in 1984 in Puerto Rico in a car accident, and he left a legacy of innovative design that was highly respected worldwide and brought Puerto Rico into the international architectural scene.

Massive Renovation Projects

The five-hundred-year anniversary of Columbus's arrival to the Americas in 1492 served as an impetus for massive restoration projects of Spanish colonial architecture in Puerto Rico. More specifically, the renovations were concentrated in the section of Old San Juan and the center of Ponce. Over four hundred buildings in Old San Juan are being restored to update the tile roofs, ornate balconies, and colonial features of tropical architecture. The projects include repairing cobblestone streets, updating the facades of pastel-colored fronts, and replacing some of the heavy wooden doors.

Whenever possible, original materials are being used, which means that they sometimes have to be salvaged from other abandoned buildings or imported from Europe. An important factor in the restoration projects of Old San Juan is that the original plans for most of the public buildings, and even private homes dating back to the sixteenth century, were archived in the Archivo de las Indias in Seville, Spain. In the process, El Morro Fortress is being repaired, the facade of the San Juan Cathedral is also being updated, and the Dominican Convent has been reconfigured to house the Instituto de Cultura. One of the main reasons for these projects is to increase the appeal of tourism to the island. In addition, a project called the Paseo de la Princesa (the Princess Promenade) is a waterfront plan with fountains and trees that ends in La Princesa, a renovated prison that now houses the Puerto Rico Tourism Company. These sections of the promenade date from the 1800s, and they

Restored colonial homes in Old San Juan. Photo courtesy of the author.

offer an air of public Spanish architectural revival style. It has actually turned out to be a crowd pleaser with both locals and thousands of tourists, who keep coming year-round.

The southern city of Ponce has always been considered a more relaxed, sophisticated, and cultural city than the busy metropolis of San Juan. During the early 1900s, Ponce was a thriving business port (mostly for rum and sugar) and a respected cultural center for the Antilles. The architectural renovation projects here are the most ambitious and extensive ever attempted in the Caribbean. The Commonwealth of Puerto Rico has selected a sixty-six-block area in downtown Ponce that includes almost 1,050 buildings scheduled for restoration. In Ponce, the funds for these projects came from the local administration, the government of Spain, the Institute of Puerto Rican Culture, and a long list of private donations.

The architecture in Ponce ranges from Spanish colonial to art deco, neoclassical, Spanish revival, and even British Victorian. The reconstruction of public spaces is a crucial component of the plan, especially the Plaza las Delicias (Plaza of Delights), one of the main squares in town. However, Ponce's renovation projects also include parks, plazas, public markets, museums, and old firehouses.

La Princesa Promenade, in Old San Juan, toward the ocean. Photo courtesy of the author.

Plaza las Delicias in Ponce. Photo courtesy of the author.

Ponce's cathedral. Photo courtesy of the author.

Since tourism is also a key factor, the Puerto Rico Tourism Company has instituted an official motto, "Explore Beyond the Shore," hoping that tourists venture inland beyond the comforts and conveniences of Old San Juan. It seems that the motto has worked, and tourism is booming in Ponce, only two hours away from San Juan using a fast highway. The local administration has now instituted a program that offers free horse-drawn carriage rides around Plaza las Delicias that evoke a feeling of nostalgia for the Spanish colonial period, with the beautifully renovated cathedral and Casa Alcaldía (the main administration offices). Then there is the practical side of these public works renovations: they have generated local jobs and brought investment dollars into tangible projects that enhance the island's beauty.

Sometimes architecture cannot be separated from art; they actually flow together. In Puerto Rico, this was certainly true during the 1800s. For example, the renovation of colonial churches often requires the reconstruction and restoration of important paintings and murals. Another public art program has recently received a lot of attention: the mayor of San Juan, Sila Marí Calderón, started a 3-million-dollar urban art project between 1996 and 2000. The city commissioned twenty-five pieces of sculpture to be included in the renovation of public venues such as parks, markets, schools,

Casa Alcaldía (mayor's offices) in Ponce. Photo courtesy of the author.

plazas, and waterfront promenades. This beautification project provided local artists like Annex Burgos, Carmen Inés Blondet, and Eric Tables with a platform to display their creative work (mostly sculptures) to wide audiences as part of everyday life—and not necessarily in a museum. When Sila Marí Calderón became the first female governor of Puerto Rico in 2000, she continued to support the arts, but this time beyond San Juan. In 2002, she announced her Puerto Rico Public Art Project, to fund over one hundred new artistic pieces to be displayed throughout the island. She included a budget of 15 million dollars to be used over the next three years. The projects will vary from ultramodern sculptures to abstract figures, lifeguard stations, artistic bus stops, and creative park entrances. Vitality and energy in artistic pursuits has a long history in Puerto Rico, and modern artists continue to search for meaningful forms of expression. This time, it certainly helps that the government is interested and engaged in supporting the artistic efforts of its population.

VISUAL ARTS (PAINTING AND SCULPTURE)

The Spanish Colonial Period (1493–1898)

The Spaniards placed little effort into developing the artistic talent in Puerto Rico. Unlike other Spanish colonies in the Americas, only a handful of local

Public art: Sculpture along Paseo La Princesa
in Old San Juan. Photo courtesy of the author.

painters emerged during the four hundred years of Spanish control. The two
salient painters from this period were José Campeche during the 1700s and
Francisco Oller in the 1800s. These artists had to search for artistic learning opportunities on their own because the Spanish Crown did not offer any
venues for formal training.

José Campeche (1751–1809) was born and died in San Juan; his father
was from the Canary Islands in Spain, and his mother was a free slave from
Puerto Rico. José learned to paint from two people: his own father and Luis
Paret y Alcaza, a Spaniard who had relocated to the island in 1776. This Spanish court painter taught Campeche the rococo style of overtly decorated art.
Campeche actually turned out to be a prolific painter, producing over four
hundred pieces of art, most of which can be placed into two categories: religious paintings and portraits of the social elite on the island. His religious
work followed a baroque style that evokes meditation, calmness, and prayer.
Some of his religious masterpieces, such as *Vision of San Francis of Assissi* and
The Birth of Christ, are displayed in churches around San Juan. Aside from ecclesiastical art, his commissions for private portraits were done in the rococo

style that highlighted elegance, wealth, and the image of high culture. Perhaps the most famous of his portraits was *Don Miguel Antonio de Ustariz*, the island's governor from 1789 to 1792. The Museo de Arte de Ponce, the best art repository on the island, proudly includes paintings from this Sanjuanero in its permanent collection.

Francisco Manuel Oller y Cestero (1833–1917) is often ranked as the best Puerto Rican painter of the 1800s. He had an entirely different background than his compatriot José Campeche. For example, Oller was born twenty-five years after Campeche's death, so there was no continuity of artistic themes or movements between these two famous Puerto Rican painters. Oller studied art in Europe, where he also met artists such as Camille Pissarro, Claude Monet, Pablo Picasso, and Pierre-Auguste Renoir. Their work certainly influenced Oller's art. However, even though many of the European artists were leading the way in the impressionist movement, Oller only adopted hints of it, and he remained essentially a realist painter. His work titled *El estudiante* (The Student) is considered a realist masterpiece, and it is actually the only painting by a Latin American artist displayed in the Louvre Museum in Paris, France.

Francisco Oller differs from José Campeche in two significant ways. For example, despite his privileged background and accessibility to the local elite, Oller declined to paint portraits of wealthy Puerto Ricans. In addition, Oller did not work on religious art. Instead, he focused on expressing Puerto Rican themes such as the tropical landscape and the celebration of routine traditions. His goals in paintings such as *El almuerzo del pobre* (The Luncheon of the Poor) and *Un mendigo* (A Beggar) were to create symbols of Puerto Rican life.

Oller truly stands out as an original artist with his masterpiece *El velorio* (The Wake). This 1893 painting reflects his attention to folk traditions. It narrates a former custom to celebrate the death of an infant or small child. Instead of representing the wake as a mourning experience, this painting serves a historical purpose to show how this tradition used to be a representation of a lively event that would celebrate the loss of such a young life.

Early-twentieth-century Art (1900–1940s)

The beginning of the 1900s was a turbulent period for Puerto Rico in the political and social sense. The departure of the Spaniards and the arrival of the Americans as the new colonizers did not necessarily lead to a new art movement. Instead, painters followed in the tradition of the Puerto Rican realist style created by Francisco Oller. The focus was on depicting tropical landscapes, country people, and local traditions. Two notable artists emerged in the first two decades of the 1900s: Ramón Frade and Miguel Pou. They were both witnesses to the Spanish-American War of 1898 and noticed the attempts to Americanize the island immediately afterward. At the time, the level of unemployment was extremely high, and the poverty rate was escalating. Therefore, it is not a coincidence that Frade's and Pou's paintings reflected the pride of the Puerto Rican people and displayed the resilience of the poor population.

Ramón Frade (1875–1907) aimed to portray the local farmers and country folk as proud and dignified, even if they were poor and socially despondent. The painting that best exemplifies his style is *El pan de cada día* (Our Daily Bread), which shows a barefoot *jíbaro* with an air of self-confidence and pride. This work became an icon to represent the defeated but determined country farmers of Puerto Rico. Other famous works by Frade include *Ensenada* and *El niño campesino* (The Peasant Child). Ramón Frade died rather young, at thirty-two years of age, but he left a legacy of artistic creativity that highlighted the Puerto Rican experience of the average population.

Miguel Pou (1880–1968) focused on painting the Puerto Rican landscape, both rural and urban. He tried to leave politics out of his work at a time when the island was deeply divided regarding the role of the United States in all local affairs. His realist style is evident in paintings like *La promesa* (The Promise), *La catedral de Ponce,* and *Los coches de ponce* (Ponce's Cars). Pou also had a didactic role on the island. He founded an art school in 1910, which he directed until 1950. As a result, his painting style influenced generations of Puerto Rican artists who would carry out his tradition until the end of the twentieth century.

Contemporary Art and Important Institutions

The 1950s was a crucial decade for the plastic arts due to the creation of three important cultural institutions: the Museo de la Universidad de Puerto Rico, founded in 1952; the Instituto de Cultura de Puerto Rico, created in 1955; and the Museo de Arte de Ponce, established in 1959. Even today, these cultural centers continue to receive both government and private funding to support the artistic development and education of Puerto Ricans of all ages.

The 1950s also marked a significant transition of artistic themes on the island. The art community in Puerto Rico responded to the political environment, which experienced rapid changes in this decade. For example, Puerto Rico was able elect its own governor in 1948 and to establish its own constitution in 1951. These events sparked enormous interest on the island, but they also fueled a sense of nationalism that was missing from the previous four decades. *Boricua* painters also incorporated scenes of national pride in their work and even ventured into using their paintings as a platform for social protest. A good example of such transition is Lorenzo Homar's painting called *Le-lo-lai*. The title makes reference to the island's tradition of the festival celebrated on January 6, signaling the arrival of the three wise men. This painting, however, also shows in the background scenes from La Perla, one of the poorest slums in San Juan. His work, along with the work of other artists such as Eduardo Vera and Rafael Tufiño, aimed to display the social conditions in parts of the island that had increasing violence, poverty, and crime rates.

The following decades of the 1960s and 1970s included outstanding artists like Myrna Baez, Tomás Batista, and Francisco Rodón. It was also a period of painters and sculptors who were influenced by their academic studies and training abroad, both in Europe and the United States. Their experiences led them to experiment with cubism, realism, and even expressionism. However, they all came back to Puerto Rico to adapt their knowledge and use it to create a vision of Puerto Rican culture, population, and landscape. During the 1960s, Myrna Baez (1931–) used special techniques in paintings such as *Noviembre* and *In the Bar* to display a feeling of isolation even in crowded places. Her work is still available for sale in several art galleries in San Juan. Francisco Rodón (1934–) has being painting in Puerto Rico for over three decades, and he remains one of the most influential painters on the island. He studied and worked in countries like Mexico, Guatemala, France, Spain, and the United States. He has produced portraits of famous Puerto Ricans but infuses techniques that blend realist and abstract styles. In his other paintings, Rodón uses bold colors with thick black lines that provide a balance of composition and movement.

Tomás Batista (1935–) is considered perhaps the best *boricua* sculptor of the 1900s. He was also trained abroad in both Mexico and the United States. He often works with wood to create three-dimensional art. However, he also produces massive stone public sculptures such as *Caracol, Indios de Borinquén,* and *El cacique Jayuya.* His masterpieces have been displayed in international forums such as Spain, Mexico, Puerto Rico, and the United States. His work is also likely to continue since he became the director of the School of Plastic Arts in Puerto Rico in 1966.

Since the 1980s, most Puerto Rican artists have lived and studied abroad. Painters such as Rafael Ferrer, Lorenzo Homar, Jorge Zeno, and Consuelo Gotay live abroad for long periods of time and then return to the island for inspiration and to carry out their work. The vitality of these contemporary artists keeps the creative energy alive on the island. Their work has now moved beyond the themes of regionalism in the 1940s and transitioned away from the nationalistic topics of the 1960s. It now addresses more universal social topics such as race, gender, poverty, violence, and social inequalities.

Popular Art

Folk artists are rarely recognized for their contributions to the plastic arts or local culture. Their work is often relegated to impromptu arts and crafts markets that are erected during a festival or regional celebration. However, these artisans and craftspeople have a long history in Puerto Rico, which includes the influence of Taíno Indians, Spanish religion, and African musical heritage. Their work dates back hundreds of years, and they continue to use the same rudimentary tools that have proven to be adequate for centuries. While there are many forms of popular art in Puerto Rico, there are two outstanding examples of local art produced on the island: carved religious figures and allegorical masks used for specific celebrations.

Santos

The Spanish Roman Catholic Church left a strong heritage throughout Latin America. Although the Spaniards officially left in 1898, their Christian heritage is still very much alive today in Puerto Rico. One salient local feature is the adoration of Catholic saints. During the colonial period, saint figures were brought from Spain, but they were extremely expensive for the average person, so local artisans began carving their own *santos* (carved, wooden saint figures) using local tropical wood and creating simpler designs. This tradition goes back to the 1500s, and *santos* are now one of the most impressive crafts produced on the island. However, these *santos* are not simply figures produced to sell to tourists; most local people actually have a saint figure at home to which they pray on a daily basis. Moreover, every town on the island has a patron saint who is also venerated with an annual celebration or festival.

Some *santos* are very popular, like the three wise men, the holy family (Mary, Joseph, and baby Jesus), and specific saints who serve a special purpose. For example, San Antonio de Padua is popular among single women who follow the tradition of standing him on his head until they find a husband. In addition, it seems that almost everyone has a special saint to whom he or she prays. There is a saint for travelers and drivers (San Cristóbal), a saint for doctors (San Lucas), a saint for teachers (San Juan Bautista de la Salle), a saint for desperate and difficult times (San Judas Tadeo), and even a saint for tax collectors (San Mateo). As a result, these saint figures of about ten to eighteen inches tall have come to represent very personal needs and customs. Traditionally, every home has a saint who brings special blessings to the family residing there, especially to those who actually pray.

Over the years, the quality of *santos* has improved, and the carved *santos* have become collector's items on the island. Figures dating back to the 1500s are certainly worth a great deal of money, if they are kept in good condition. Since many saints were burned and trashed during the period of the Catholic Reformation, the families who kept their *santos* from the 1600s consider them to be family heirlooms. The tradition of carving *santos* is kept alive by families who have specialized in this craft such as the famous *santeros* (saint carvers) Rafael Rivera, Zoilo Cajigas, and Norberto Cedeño.

Masks

One of the most traditional crafts in Puerto Rico is the creation of *caretas/máscaras*; these frightening masks are specifically created for carnivals in two locations: Ponce and Loíza Aldea. These scary masks have multiple horns, eyes popping out, and long teeth. They are intended to represent a blend between the devil and scary animals. In Ponce, the masks are mostly made of papier-mâché, and the ones created in Loíza Aldea are made of coconut husks. These colorful masks are usually worn by giants during a parade intended to scare people, especially children. These giant figures are called *vejigantes*, a word for which no English translation exists. The name originated with the

Masks for Ponce's carnival in February. Photo courtesy of the author.

word *vejiga* (cow's bladder) because the Spaniards originally used an inflated cow's bladder (painted in frightening colors such as red and black) during the 1600s to represent the devil. On the island, these processions take place in July at the Loíza Aldea and in February in Ponce. During these events, these giant figures wear colorful suits with wings, use scary masks, and carry a stick with a cow's bladder attached to it. They go around hitting people with the bladder in a harmless way. Originally, the tradition was that these devil-like figures would scare people into going to church and denouncing their sinful ways.

The tradition of the *vejigantes,* dating back to the seventeenth century, has actually created a new interest in these masks, but people now buy them as decorative pieces. The main centers where they are manufactured are in Ponce and the small town of Loíza Aldea, but they can now be purchased in craft stores throughout the island. Their colorful patterns have sparked another recent interest in the traditional Puerto Rican folk arts.

It is important to recognize the contributions of folk artists toward the general culture of Puerto Rico. Their work highlights the blend of old traditions with contemporary needs. Moreover, their creativity is slowly being recognized as their crafts are now displayed in local and international art galleries and museums.

Boricua artists have a long history of Spanish, Taíno, and African influence; their heritage is palpable in their artistic creations, but their work is also adapted to modern settings and displays the richness of Puerto Rican culture.

REFERENCES

Cullen, Deborah. *None of the Above: Contemporary Work by Puerto Rican Artists.* Hartford, CT: Cullen Real Art Waves, 2004.

Dávila, Arlene. *Sponsored Identities: Cultural Politics in Puerto Rico.* Philadelphia: Temple University Press, 1997.

Duany, Jorge. *The Puerto Rican Nation on the Move: Identities on the Island and in the United States.* Chapel Hill: University of North Carolina Press, 2002.

Hermandad de Artistas Gráficos de Puerto Rico. *Puerto Rico arte e identidad.* San Juan: University of Puerto Rico Press, 2004.

Hernández, Yasmín. "Painting Liberation: 1998 and Its Pivotal Role in the Formation of a New Boricua Political Art Movement." *Centro Journal* 17, no. 2 (2005): 113–133.

Hertz, John B. "Authenticity, Colonialism, and the Struggle with Modernity." *Journal of Architectural Education* 55, no. 4 (2002): 220–227.

Instituto de Cultura Puertorriqueña. *The Art of Puerto Rican Santeros.* San Juan: Instituto de Cultura Puertorriqueña, 1986.

Mignucci, Andrés. *Arquitectura contemporánea en Puerto Rico, 1976–1992.* San Juan: American Institute of Architects, 1992.

Ramírez, Yasmín. "Puerto Rican Visual Artists and the United States." *Centro Journal* 17, no. 2 (2005): 4–5.

Vivoni-Farage, Enrique. "The Architecture of Power: From the Neoclassical to Modernism in the Architecture of Puerto Rico." *Online Journal Aris,* vol. 3: Colonization and Architecture. Carnegie Mellon University, Department of Architecture, (2007). http://www.CMU.edu/Aris_3/vivoni/frameset_vivoni.html.

———, ed. *Hispanophilia: Architecture and Life in Puerto Rico 1900–1950.* San Juan: University of Puerto Rico Press, 1998.

Glossary

areytos Ceremonial dances and songs of the Taíno Indians.

asopao Popular gumbo stew made with chicken and rice.

Babalawo Male priest in the Santeria religion.

boricua Synonym of *Puerto Rican*.

Borinquén Original Taíno name for the island.

botánica Shops that sell candles, charms, incense, herbs, and other elements used in Santería.

cemíes Small, carved figures representing Taíno gods.

Changó African god of fire and war. Slaves worshipped him as the Roman Catholic saint Santa Barbara.

coquí Small frog from Puerto Rico. It is claimed that the *coquí* only survives on the island. Its name comes from its singing sound.

costumbrismo Literature based on expressing local customs and traditions.

criollo Originally, a person born in Puerto Rico of Spanish parents. Now, the term is used to describe something truly developed on the island such as *comida criolla* (Puerto Rican national cuisine).

cuatro A string instrument uniquely developed in Puerto Rico. It is smaller than a guitar, and it has five sets of double strings. It is considered to be the national instrument of Puerto Rico.

fiestas patronales A community celebration on the day of a town's patron saint. In Puerto Rico, each festival or carnival lasts ten days, with food, music, dance, crafts, and religious processions.

friquitines   Street vendors.

gallera   Cockfighting ring; cockfighting is legal in Puerto Rico.

jíbaro   A countryside and mountain farmer.

mundillo   Woven lace with intricate patterns made only in Puerto Rico and Spain.

Nuyorican   New Yorkers of Puerto Rican descent. The word is a combination of the terms *New York* and *Puerto Rican*.

orishas   Afro-American gods. Deities worshipped in Santeria and often having a parallel Roman Catholic saint.

piragua   A cone of shaved ice topped with a syrup of tropical flavors.

Ponceños   Residents of the southern city of Ponce.

Sanjuaneros   Residents of San Juan.

Santería   Afro-Caribbean religion that includes features of Catholicism and African Yoruba elements from Nigeria.

santero   A priest in the religion of Santería; also, the carver of saint figures.

sofrito   A sauce made with sautéed garlic, bell peppers, onion, chili, and sometimes cured bacon or ham; it is served over rice or meat.

Taínos   Original indigenous population of Puerto Rico.

vejigantes   Traditional carnival figures wearing frightening masks.

Yoruba   A tribe of people from West Africa who were brought to Puerto Rico as slaves.

Bibliography

Aliotta, Jerome J. *The Puerto Ricans.* Peoples of North America Series. New York: Chelsea House, 1991.

Alonso, Manuel Antonio. *El Jíbaro.* San Juan: Publicaciones Puertorriqueñas, 1996.

Antush, John V., ed. *Nuestro New York: An Anthology of Puerto Rican Plays.* New York: Mentor, 1994.

Associated Press. "Puerto Rico Governor Allows Referendum against Gay Marriage." *USA Today*, January 24, 2008.

Bailyn, Evan. "Music of Puerto Rico." http://www.musicofpuertorico.com/.

Bea, Keith. *Political Status of Puerto Rico: Background, Options, and Issues in the 109th Congress.* Washington, DC: Congressional Research Service, 2005.

Bernier-Grand, Carmen T. *In the Shade of the Nispero Tree.* New York: Orchard Books, 1999.

———. *Poet and Politician of Puerto Rico: Don Luis Muñoz Marín.* New York: Orchard Books, 1995.

Brandon, George. *Santería from Africa to the New World: The Dead Sell Memories.* Bloomington: Indiana University Press, 1993.

Camara-Fuentes, Luis Raúl, José Javier, Colón-Morera, and Héctor M. Martinez-Ramírez, "The Death Penalty in Puerto Rico." *Centro Journal* 18, no. 11 (2006): 146–165.

Centeno, Jesse. *Modernidad y resistencia: Literatura obrera de Puerto Rico (1898–1910).* San Juan: Centro de Estudios Avanzados de Puerto Rico, 2005.

"Church in Puerto Rico Looks to Future." *America* 196, no. 21 (2007): 6.

Cobo, Leila. "El Gran Combo: Waving the Salsa Flag for 40 Years Strong." *Billboard* 114, no. 19 (2002): LM-10.

————. "The Sounds of Puerto Rico." *Billboard* 112, no. 41 (2007): 41.

Colo, Papo. *Films with a Purpose: A Puerto Rican Experiment in Social Films.* New York: Exit Art, 1987.

Cullen, Deborah. *None of the Above: Contemporary Work by Puerto Rican Artists.* Hartford, CT: Cullen Real Art Waves, 2004.

Dávila, Arlene. *Sponsored Identities: Cultural Politics in Puerto Rico.* Philadelphia: Temple University Press, 1997.

Dávila, Gonçalves, Michele C., Madeleine Millan Vega, Marisol Pereira Varela, Maribel Sánchez-Pagán, Belia E. Segarra Ramos, and Johanny Vázquez Paz. *Poetas sin tregua: Compilación de poetas puertorriqueñas de la generación del 80.* Madrid, Spain: Ráfagas, 2006.

Dávila, Jesús. "U.S. Hardens Position on Puerto Rico." *El Diario Prensa,* December 22, 2007.

Davis, Lucille. *Puerto Rico.* New York: Grolier, 2000.

Delano, Jack. *Puerto Rico Mío: Four Decades of Change.* Washington, DC: Smithsonian Institution Press, 1990.

Delgado Castro, Ileana. "Pioneros del Jazz." *El Nuevo Día, Revista Domingo,* January 22, 2006.

Díaz de Villegas, José Luis. *Puerto Rico: Grand Cuisine of the Caribbean.* San Juan: University of Puerto Rico Press, 2004.

Duany, Jorge. *The Puerto Rican Nation on the Move: Identities on the Island and in the United States.* Chapel Hill: University of North Carolina Press, 2002.

Escalona, Saul. "La salsa, un fenómeno sociocultural en El Caribe hispano." http://www.salsafrance.com/.

Espada, Frank. "The Puerto Rican Diaspora." *Hispanic* 20, no. 6 (2007): 48–53.

Ezratty, Harry A. *500 Years in the Jewish Caribbean: The Spanish and Portuguese Jews in the West Indies.* Baltimore: Omni Arts, 2002.

Falcón, Angelo. "The Diaspora Factor: Stateside Boricuas and the Future of Puerto Rico." *NACLA Report on the Americas* 40, no. 6 (2007): 28–31.

Flores-Caraballo, Eliut Daniel. "The Politics of Culture in Puerto Rican Television: A Macro/Micro Study of English vs. Spanish Television Usage." Ph.D. diss., University of Texas at Austin, 1991.

Flores Carrión, Marisel. *Cuarenta años de cine puertorriqueño.* San Juan: Archivo General de Puerto Rico. http://www.preb.com/devisita/marisel.htm.

Fontañez, Edwin. *The Vejigantge and the Folk Festivals of Puerto Rico.* Arlington, VA: Exit Studios, 1994.

Fortuño, Luis. "People of Puerto Rico to Determine Their Own Status." *Puerto Rico Herald,* July 14, 2005.

Fradin, Dennis Brindell. *Puerto Rico.* Danbury, CT: Children's Press, 1995.

García, Ana María, ed. *Puerto Rican Film and Video "Made in USA."* San Juan: University of Puerto Rico Press, 2000.

García, Kino. *Breve historia del cine puertorriqueño.* Bayamón, Puerto Rico: Taller de Cine La Red, 1984.

————. *Historia del cine puertorriqueño 1900–1999: Un siglo de cine en Puerto Rico.* San Juan: University of Puerto Rico Press, 2003.

George, Linda, and Charles George. *Luis Muñoz Marín.* Danbury, CT: Children's Press, 1999.

Glasser, Ruth. *My Music Is My Flag: Puerto Rican Musicians and Their Communities, 1917–1940.* Berkeley: University of California Press, 1995.

González, David. "Heroes, Poets and Even a Dog, but No Puerto Ricans." *New York Times,* June 1, 2004.

Harlan, Judith. *Puerto Rico: Deciding Its Future.* New York: Twenty-first Century Book, 1996.

Harold, John M. Charles F. Westoff, Charles W. Warren, and Judith Seltzer. "Catholicism and Fertility in Puerto Rico." *American Journal of Public Health* 79, no. 9 (1989): 1258–1262.

Hauberg, Clifford A. *Puerto Rico and the Puerto Ricans.* Immigrant Heritage of America Series. New York: Twayne, 1974.

Hermandad de Artistas Gráficos de Puerto Rico. *Puerto Rico arte e identidad.* San Juan: University of Puerto Rico Press, 2004.

Hernández, Carmen Dolores. *Puerto Rican Voices in English: Interviews with Writers.* Westport, CT: Praeger, 1997.

Hernández, Yasmín. "Painting Liberation: 1998 and Its Pivotal Role in the Formation of a New Boricua Political Art Movement." *Centro Journal* 17, no. 2 (2005): 113–133.

Hernández-Candelas, Marta. "Policies for Early Childhood Music Education in Puerto Rico." *Arts Education Policy Review* 109, no. 2 (2007): 27–32.

Hernández Hiraldo, Samiri. *Black Puerto Rican Identity and Religious Experience.* Gainsville: University Press of Florida, 2006.

Hertz, John B. "Authenticity, Colonialism, and the Struggle with Modernity." *Journal of Architectural Education* 55, no. 4 (2002): 220–227.

Herzig Shannon, Nancy. *El iris de paz: El espiritismo y la mujer en Puerto Rico.* Río Piedras, Puerto Rico: Huracán, 2001.

Insight Guide: Puerto Rico. Hong Kong: APA, 1987.

Instituto de Cultura Puertorriqueña. *The Art of Puerto Rican Santeros.* San Juan: Instituto de Cultura Puertorriqueña, 1986.

Jacobs, David, and Jason Carmichael. "The Political Sociology of the Death Penalty." *American Sociological Review* 67, no. 1 (2002): 109–131.

Jiménez, Lillian. "From the Margin to the Center: Puerto Rican Cinema in the United States." *Centro de Estudios Puertorriqueños Bulletin* 2, no. 8 (1990): 28–43.

Jiménez de Wagenheim, Olga. *Puerto Rico's Revolt for Independence: El Grito de Lares.* Boulder, CO: Westview Press, 1985.

Johnston, Joyce. *Puerto Rico.* Minneapolis, MN: Lerner, 1994.

Kelly, Gary D. "The Emergence of U.S. Hispanic Films." *Bilingual Review* 18, no. 2/3 (1993): 192–231.

Kornblum, Janet. "More Hispanics Losing Their Religion." *Puerto Rico Herald,* January 4, 2003.

Lee, Edward R. "The Caribbean Connection." *Blackfax* 6, no. 21 (1990): 7–10.

———. "Talking Color with Spanish-Speaking Caribbean Brethren." *Blackfax* 11, no. 48 (2007): 27–30.

Levy, Patricia. *Puerto Rico—Cultures of the World.* 2nd ed. Tarrytown, NY: Marshall Cavendish International, 2005.

López Baralt, Mercedes. *Literatura puertorriqueña del siglo XX: Antología.* San Juan: Editorial de la Universidad de Puerto Rico, 2004.

Loveman, Mara, and Jerónimo Muñiz. "How Puerto Ricans Became White: An Analysis of Racial Statistics in the 1910 and 1920 Censuses." Paper presented at the Center for Demography and Ecology at the University of Wisconsin–Madison, February 2006.

Makavet, Pedro A. *America's Colony: The Political and Cultural Conflict between the United States and Puerto Rico.* New York: New York University Press, 2004.

Manuel, Peter, Kenneth Bilby, and Michael Largey. *Caribbean Currents: Caribbean Music from Rumba to Reggae.* 2nd ed. Philadelphia: Temple University Press, 2006.

Márquez, Miguel B. Sobre los comienzos del periodismo en Puerto Rico. *Revista Latina de Comunicación Social* 33 (2000). http://www.ull.es/publicaciones/latina/aa2000kjl/x33se/55marquez.htm.

Marshall, Wayne. "The Rise of Reggaeton." *Boston Phoenix,* January 19, 2006.

Mignucci, Andrés. *Arquitectura Contemporánea en Puerto Rico, 1976–1992.* San Juan: American Institute of Architects, 1992.

Mike, Jan M. *Juan Bobo and the Horse of Seven Colors: A Puerto Rican Legend.* Illustrated by Charles Reasoner. Mahwah, NJ: Troll, 1995.

Mohr, Eugene V. *Language, Literature and Journalism in the American Presence in Puerto Rico.* Edited by Lynn-Darrell Bender. Hato Rey, Puerto Rico: Publicaciones Puertorriqueñas, 1998.

Morales Carrión, Arturo. *Puerto Rico: A Political and Cultural History.* New York: W. W. Norton, 1983.

Muckley, Robert I., and Adela Martínez-Santiago. *Stories from Puerto Rico/Historias de Puerto Rico.* Side by Side Bilingual Books Series. Lincolnwood, IL: Passport Books, 1999.

Murillo, Mario. *Islands of Resistance: Puerto Rico, Vieques and U.S. Policy.* New York: Seven Stories Press, 2001.

Needham, Vicki. "Puerto Rico Status Bill Heading to Floor." *Congress Daily AM,* October 24, 2007.

Negrón-Muntaner, Frances. *Boricua Pop: Puerto Ricans and the Latinization of American Culture.* New York: New York University Press, 2004.

———. "Reggaeton Nation." *NACLA Report on the Americas* 40, no. 6 (2007): 35–39.

Newcomb, Horace, ed. *Encyclopedia of Television.* 2nd ed. Chicago: Museum of Broadcast Communications, 2004.

Ortiz, Yvonne. *A Taste of Puerto Rico: Traditional and New Dishes from the Puerto Rican Community.* New York: Plume, 1997.

Pariser, Harry S. *Adventure Guide to Puerto Rico.* Edison, NJ: Hunter, 1989.

Quintero Rivera, Ángel G., ed. *Vírgenes, magos y escapularios: imaginería, etnicidad y religiosidad popular en Puerto Rico.* San Juan: Centro de Investigaciones Académicas en la de Universidad de Sagrado Corazón, 2003.

Ramírez, Yasmín. "Puerto Rican Visual Artists and the United States." *Centro Journal* 17, no. 2 (2005): 4–5.

Ramírez de Ferrer, Miriam. "Only Residents of Puerto Rico Should Be Entitled to Vote in the 1998 Plebiscite." *Puerto Rico Herald*, July 31, 1997.

Ramos-Perea, Roberto. "Panorama Histórico del Teatro Puertorriqueño," in *Teatro Puertorriqueño Contemporáneo*, ed. by Roberto Ramos-Perea, 1–23. San Juan, Puerto Rico, Publicaciones Gaviota, 2003.

———. "Un nuevo cine puertorriqueño." *Intermedio*, October 17, 2007.

Rehrmann, Alexis. "A Better Life Here, Yes, but Not without Worries." *New York Times*, January 10, 2008.

Reyes, Israel. *Humor and the Eccentric Text in Puerto Rican Literature.* Gainesville: University of Florida Press, 2005.

Rezvani, David A. "The Basis of Puerto Rico's Constitutional Status: Colony, Compact, or Federacy?" *Political Science Quarterly* 122, no. 1 (2007): 115–140.

Rivera, Raquel Z. *New York Ricans from the Hip-Hop Zone.* New York: Palgrave Macmillan, 2003.

Rivera-Batiz, Francisco L. "Color in the Tropics: Race and Economic Outcomes in the Island of Puerto Rico." Paper presented at the conference Puerto Ricans on the Island and in the Mainland United States, New York, May 21, 2004.

Rivera de Álvarez, Josefina. *Literatura puertorriqueña: Su proceso en el tiempo.* Madrid, Spain: Partenon, 1983.

Rivero, Yeidi M. *Tuning Out Blackness: Race and Nation in the History of Puerto Rican Television.* Durham, NC: Duke University Press, 2005.

Rodríguez, Clara E. "Puerto Ricans: Black and White." In *Boricuas: Influential Puerto Rican Writings—An Anthology*, ed. Roberto Santiago, 81–90. New York: Random House, 1995.

Romeu, José A. *Panorama del periodismo puertoriqueño.* Río Piedras: University of Puerto Rico Press, 1985.

Safa, Helen Icken. *Urban Poor in Puerto Rico: A Study in Development and Inequality.* New York: Holt, Rinehart, and Winston, 1974.

Sánchez González, Lisa. *Boricua Literature: A Literary History of the Puerto Rican Diaspora.* New York: New York University Press, 2001.

Santiago, Esmeralda. "Island of Lost Causes." In *Boricuas: Influential Puerto Rican Writings—An Anthology*, ed. Roberto Santiago, 22–24. New York: Random House, 1995.

———. *When I Was Puerto Rican.* New York: Vintage Books, 1994.

Santiago, Roberto, ed. *Boricuas: Influential Puerto Rican Writings—An Anthology.* New York: Random House, 1995.

Serrano, Basilio. "Puerto Rican Musicians of the Harlem Renaissance." *Centro Journal* 19, no. 2 (2007): 94–119.

Shokooh Valle, Firuzeh. "Menos boricuas se consideran negros." *San Juan Primera Hora*, November 8, 2007.

————. "Sin conciencia racial sobre la negritud boricua." *San Juan Primera Hora*, November 7, 2007.

Silva Gotay, Samuel. *Catolicismo y política en Puerto Rico bajo España y Estados Unidos: Siglos XIX y XX.* Río Piedras, Puerto Rico: University of Puerto Rico Press, 2005.

————. *Protestantismo y política en Puerto Rico.* San Juan: University of Puerto Rico Press, 1997.

Sterling, Christopher, and Michael Keith, eds. *Encyclopedia of Radio.* Chicago: Museum of Broadcast Communications, 2003.

Stevens Arroyo, Anthony M. "Catholicism's Emerging Role in Puerto Rico." *America* 182, no. 13 (2000): 8–11.

————. "Taking Religion Seriously: New Perspectives on Religion in Puerto Rico." *Centro Journal* 18, no. 11 (2006): 214–223.

Suntree, Susan. *Rita Moreno.* Broomall, PA: Chelsea House, 1992.

Suter, Keith. "Puerto Rico: Beyond the 'West Side Story.'" *Contemporary Review* 289, no. 1687 (2007): 442–448.

Thomas, Piri. *Down These Mean Streets.* New York: Vintage, 1997.

Thompson, Donald, ed. *Music of Puerto Rico: A Reader's Anthology.* Lanham, MD: Scarecrow Press, 2002.

Thompson, Donald, and Annie Thompson. *Music and Dance in Puerto Rico from the Age of Columbus to Modern Times.* Lanham, MD: Scarecrow Press, 1991.

Thompson, Kathleen. *Puerto Rico.* Austin, TX: Raintree/Steck Vaughn, 1996.

Torregrosa, José Luis. *La Historia de la Radio en Puerto Rico.* San Juan: Esmacos, 1991.

Torre Revello, José. *El libro, la imprenta, y el periodismo en America durante la dominación española.* Buenos Aires: Instituto de Investigaciones Históricas, 1940.

Torrez-Padilla, José, and Carmen Haydee Rivera, eds. *Writing Off the Hyphen: New Perspectives on the Literature of Puerto Rican Diaspora.* Seattle: University of Washington Press, 2008.

Valdez-Rodríguez, Alisa. "When Taking the Easy Way Out in Racial Labeling, the Truth Suffers." *Los Angeles Times,* August 14, 2000.

Van Hyning, Thomas E. *The Santurce Crabbers: Sixty Seasons of Puerto Rican Winter League Baseball.* Jefferson, NC: McFarland, 1999.

Vazquez, Carlos M. "Puerto Ricans Have Shown They're Happy with Status Quo." *Puerto Rico Herald Newspaper,* July 13, 2005.

Vivoni-Farage, Enrique. "The Architecture of Power: From the Neoclassical to Modernism in the Architecture of Puerto Rico." *Online Journal Aris,* vol. 3: Colonization and Architecture. Carnegie Mellon University, Department of Architecture, 2007. http://www.CMU.edu/Aris_3/vivoni/frameset_vivoni.html.

————, ed. *Hispanophilia: Architecture and Life in Puerto Rico, 1900–1950.* San Juan: University of Puerto Rico Press, 1998.

Wagenheim, Kal. *Puerto Rico: A Profile.* New York: Praeger, 1970.

Walker, Paul Robert. *Pride of Puerto Rico: The Life of Roberto Clemente.* San Diego, CA: Harcourt Brace, 1998.

NEWSPAPERS

El Expresso de Puerto Rico, http://www.elexpresso.com/.
El Vocero de Puerto Rico, http://www.vocero.com/.
Puerto Rico Herald, http://www.puertorico-herald.org/.
San Juan Nuevo Día, http://www.elnuevodia.com/noticias.
San Juan Star, http://www.thesanjuanstar.com/.

WEB SITES

CIA World Factbook, https://www.cia.gov/library/publications/the-world-factbook/geos/rq.html.
Fania Records, http://www.fania.com/.
Festival del Cuatro, http://www.festivaldelcuatro.org/.
Gobierno del Estado Libre Asociado de Puerto Rico, http://www.gobierno.pr/. Web site with official data regarding government programs and directories for government services. All in Spanish, except a link to "Federal Government."
Instituto de Arte y Cultura de Puerto Rico, http://iprac.aspira.org/.
Instituto de Cultura Puertorriqueña, http://www.icp.gobierno.pr/.
Museum of Broadcasting Communications, http://www.museum.tv/.
Music of Puerto Rico, http://www.musicofpuertorico.com/. Web site with detailed explanations of the development of all kinds of Puerto Rican music.
National Astronomy and Ionosphere Center, Arecibo Observatory, http://www.naic.edu/public/the_telescope.htm.
Office of the Governor of Puerto Rico, http://fortaleza.govpr.org/. A bilingual Web site with information on the island's highest government official.
Pharmaceutical Industry Association of Puerto Rico, http://www.piapr.com/.
Puerto Rican Food, http://www.gotopuertorico.com/puerto-rico-gastronomy.php Web site with a useful history of the food and drink of Puerto Rico and useful recipes.
Puerto Rico Film Commission, http://www.puertoricofilm.com/.
Puerto Rico Industrial Development Company (PRIDCO), http://www.pridco.org/. For information on technology and engineering services offered in Puerto Rico, including local tax incentives and tax credits for corporations to promote the creation of employment opportunities in the island.
Puerto Rico's Culture and History, http://www.prborinken.com. A comprehensive Web site that includes information on cultural traditions, historical documents, and food as well as government updates and international trade information.
Puerto Rico Tourism Company, http://www.welcometopuertorico.org.
Salsa Roots, http://www.salsaroots.org/. Web site with helpful articles on the history and development of salsa music and dance.
Santeria Religion in Puerto Rico, http://www.boricua.com/santeria.html.

Universidad Interamericana de Puerto Rico, http://www.arecibo.inter.edu/biblioteca/
    bases.htm. Infotrac virtual library.
University of Puerto Rico, http://www.upr.edu/. For information on the common-
    wealth's largest university and the state university system, with its main campus
    in the city of Río Piedras.

Index

About the Author

JAVIER A. GALVÁN is Professor of Spanish and Latin American History at Santa Ana College.